Perception and Its Objects

Perception and Its Objects

Bill Brewer

OXFORD
UNIVERSITY PRESS

OXFORD
UNIVERSITY PRESS

Great Clarendon Street, Oxford, OX2 6DP,

Oxford University Press is a department of the University of Oxford.
It furthers the University's objective of excellence in research, scholarship,
and education by publishing worldwide. Oxford is a registered trade mark
of Oxford University Press in the UK and in certain other countries

First published 2011
First published in paperback 2013

British Library Cataloguing in Publication Data
Data available

Library of Congress Cataloging in Publication Data
Data available

ISBN 978-0-19-926025-6
ISBN 978-0-19-967469-5 (pbk)

To Anna

Acknowledgements

This book has been a long time in the writing and has gone through a number of very significant changes in both form and content over the course of its production. I am extremely grateful for patient and persistent critical feedback from a great many colleagues and students over this time in a wide variety of settings. I would like to thank the following for specific comments and suggestions that I recall and that I know have helped: Michael Ayers, Tom Baldwin, Harry Binswanger, Simon Blackburn, Justin Broackes, Nicolas Bullot, Steve Butterfill, Alex Byrne, John Campbell, Quassim Cassam, David Charles, Bill Child, James Conant, Tim Crane, Eddie Cushman, Imogen Dickie, John Divers, Naomi Eilan, Ciara Fairley, Allan Gotthelf, Anil Gupta, John Hawthorne, Jane Heal, Christoph Hoerl, Jen Hornsby, Hemdat Lerman, Guy Longworth, John McDowell, Rory Madden, Mike Martin, Adrian Moore, Jennifer Nagel, Christopher Peacocke, Ian Phillips, Johannes Roessler, Greg Salmieri, Nick Shea, Susanna Siegel, Alison Simmons, Peter Simons, David Smith, Paul Snowdon, Matt Soteriou, Helen Steward, Tom Stoneham, Peter Sullivan, Charles Travis, Ralph Wedgwood, Michael Williams, Robbie Williams, and Tim Williamson.

I would especially like to thank Quassim Cassam, Adam Pautz, Ian Phillips, and an anonymous reader for OUP, who all gave me extended written comments on the whole or most of the manuscript at some stage.

The book was finally written in its current form whilst I was on sabbatical from the Philosophy Department at the University of Warwick. I am very grateful to both university and department for that extended period of uninterrupted study leave.

Peter Momtchiloff of Oxford University Press has once again been a very supportive, patient, and flexible editor; and I am grateful also for the copy-editing skills of Sylvie Jaffrey and the production, editing, and typesetting of SPI Publisher Services, Pondicherry, India. Thanks too to Clifford Willis for his careful and speedy proofreading.

I would also like to thank: Blackwell Publishers Ltd. for permission to use material from my paper 'Perception and Content', *European Journal of Philosophy*, 14 (2006), especially in ch. 3; Springer Publishing Co. for permission to use material from my paper 'Perception and its Objects', *Philosophical Studies*, 132 (2007), especially in ch. 5; Oxford University Press for permission to use material from my papers 'How To Account for Illusion', in F. Macpherson and A. Haddock (eds.), *Disjunctivism: Perception, Action, Knowledge* (2008), and 'Realism and Explanation in Perception', forthcoming (2011) in J. Roessler, N. Eilan, and H. Lerman (eds.), *Perception, Causation and Objectivity*, especially in chs. 5 and 7 respectively.

The photograph on the front cover is 'Boat on Water' from the Folded Paper series by Tansy Spinks.[1] I would like to thank her for permission to use the image in this way. I argue in the book that our perception of the physical world consists most fundamentally in our standing in relations of conscious acquaintance from a given point of view with its persisting mind-independent constituent objects, like the paper boat pictured here. The cover of my previous book showed Tansy's photograph of an *unfolded* origami boat; and the book concerned our capacity to integrate different points of view over different circumstances of perception. In this book I give what I now regard as correct priority to our basic perceptual experiential relation with unified physical objects themselves. This is mirrored in the two front covers.

I sent my draft manuscript to Peter Momtchiloff at OUP in the week before I married Anna Wormleighton and the book is dedicated to Anna Brewer with love.

---

[1] Millennium Images Picture Gallery.

Contents

Introduction

The history of the philosophy of perception in my view brings out a serious tension between two absolutely compelling ideas. First, the physical objects that we perceive are the very objects that are presented to us in our conscious perceptual experience. Second, those same physical objects are also mind-independent in the sense of being in their nature entirely independent of any perceptual experience or appearance of them. Of course these ideas are extremely roughly formulated as they stand; but it is already possible to see two extreme reactions. First, Berkeley (1975a, 1975b) and subsequent anti-realists argue that proper respect for the first idea simply rules out the second, although many of the features of our commonsense world-view that we may take to be indicative of the mind-independence of its constituent physical objects are nevertheless perfectly compatible with the resultant position. Second, realistically oriented philosophers under the influence of Descartes (1986) and Locke (1975) insist that various constraints upon physical objects implicit in the second idea entail significant indirectness *at best* in the implementation of the first.

Current philosophical orthodoxy has it that the tension is to be resolved instead by a kind of assimilation of perception to thought: perception involves representational *contents* that make direct reference to mind-independent physical objects. I believe that this response as it stands is unsatisfactory. Just as certain early modern empiricists notoriously face problems as a result of the way in which their theory of ideas seeks to assimilate thought and belief to perception, I contend that the reverse assimilation of orthodox modern philosophy of perception faces serious difficulties in truly accommodating the datum that we are consciously presented in perceptual experience with the physical objects themselves that we perceive.

I propose, develop, and defend an account of perceptual experience that is far more in keeping with what I regard as the early modern empiricist insight that such experience consists most fundamentally in a relation of conscious acquaintance with particular direct objects but insists as against the early moderns that these direct objects are mind-independent physical objects themselves.

The discussion throughout is organized around the Inconsistent Triad of claims set out in ch. 1 that I think captures the core tension between the two compelling ideas about perception and its objects that I began with. I also outline towards the end of ch. 1 the main contents of subsequent chapters.

Taking a somewhat broader perspective in what remains of this introduction for the purposes of a more informal orientation, the book is an extended reflection upon the nature of our perceptual relation with the mind-independent physical world.

Intuitively this relation is the source of our knowledge and understanding of the nature of the physical world itself. It provides us with at least our provisional conception of what mind-independent physical objects are that makes thoughts about specific such things possible and contributes to our most basic knowledge about them. This is possible because physical objects themselves are *subjectively presented* in our perceptual experience of them: the subjective experiential condition of standing in a perceptual relation with various objects in the world around us is *evidently* dependent upon the nature of those very objects themselves. Their nature is in this way *displayed* in perception. Given their mind-independence, though, there is plenty of scope for error in perception too. Perceptions may be misleading in various ways, things may look to be ways that they are not, and even complete hallucination is at least in principle possible. This suggests the need for a significant degree of complexity in the nature of the perceptual relation itself that may appear to threaten its intuitive status as a subjective presentation of mind-independent physical objects that provides us directly with a genuine conception of their nature. The challenge that I set myself here is to accommodate the required complexity without in any way undermining the initial intuition.

The solution that I offer and elaborate in chs. 5–7 is really quite straightforward. Our basic perceptual relation with the physical world is *just that*. Perception is a matter of our standing in relations of conscious acquaintance from a given spatiotemporal point of view, in a particular sense modality, and in certain specific circumstances of perception, with particular mind-independent physical objects themselves. The ways that things look, for example, in such perceptual experiences are precisely the ways that those very *things* look from that point of view and in the circumstances in question. That is to say, very roughly, their looks are grounded in their visually relevant similarities from that point of view and in those circumstances with the paradigms of various kinds of physical objects that play a central role in our understanding of the terms in which such looks are to be characterized. Thus, the ways things are for the subject in perception are certain of the ways that the objects of perception are from the subject's point of view. Of course this thumbnail sketch raises far more questions than it answers at this stage. My task in what follows is to provide answers to at least the most pressing such questions in the context of providing a successful motivation for and defence of the view. The upshot, I contend, is a satisfying vindication of our initial intuitive *empirical realist* conviction.

1

The Inconsistent Triad

Suppose that we identify *physical objects*, in the first instance, by extension, as things like stones, tables, trees, and animals: the persisting macroscopic constituents of the world that we live in. Of course, there is a substantive question of what it is to be *like* such things in the way relevant to categorization as a physical object. So this can hardly be the final word on the matter. Still, it is equally clear that this gives us all a perfectly respectable initial conception of what we are talking about; and it is an entirely adequate starting point for what follows.

It is without doubt our commonsense starting point that

(I) Physical objects are mind-independent.

Explication of the mind-independence involved here is a substantive matter in its own right, and the subject of extended discussion in what follows.[1] Still, the core idea is that entities of a given kind are *mind-independent* if and only if they are constituents of the world '*as it is in itself*', rather than being in any way dependent in their nature upon the way things do or might appear to anyone in experience of or thought about the world: the nature of such things is entirely independent of their appearance.[2] Entities are *mind-dependent* if and only if they are not mind-independent. Thus, their nature is to some extent dependent upon their appearance. I mean by the *nature* of the entities of a given kind the most

---

[1] See especially chs. 3 and 7 where I offer and defend criteria for mind-dependence and mind-independence derived from reflection upon a familiar model of the distinction between the primary and secondary qualities.

[2] The formulation is awkward here. My own view is that the ways that mind-independent physical objects look and otherwise perceptually appear just are a matter of certain of the ways that those very things are. Still, their being those ways is not itself a matter of their appearing any way to anyone. This latter is the sense in which I claim that mind-independence is independence in nature from any appearance. See chs. 3, 5, and 7 below for further development of these issues.

fundamental answer to the question of what such things are. This is also of course a contentious notion. I take it for granted here without argument at this stage and without committing myself to any specific philosophical elaboration. The justification I offer for doing so rests on the merits of what follows within this framework.[3]

The commonsense starting point expressed by (I), then, is simply the conviction that the natures of such things as stones, tables, trees, and animals themselves are independent of the ways in which such physical objects do or may appear in anyone's experience of or thought about the world. I call the thesis that the objects of a given domain are mind-independent in this sense, *realism* about that domain. (I) is therefore an expression of realism about physical objects, which I call *physical realism*, for short.

Something else that we take for granted is that physical objects are the very things that are *presented* to us in perception. It is extremely difficult to make this very natural idea precise. Indeed, a great deal of what follows effectively concerns various fundamental controversies concerning the notion of perceptual presentation. Still, I reserve the term throughout to express the utterly uncontested sense in which we *see* and otherwise consciously perceive physical objects: they are in this sense elements of perceptual consciousness. This claim that physical objects are presented to us in perception is intended as prior, and uncommitted, to any specific controversial theoretical elucidation of what such perceptual presentation consists in.

Thus, it seems to me to be a fundamental commitment of common-sense in the area that physical objects are both presented to us in perceptual experience and have a nature that is entirely independent of how they do or might appear to anyone. That is, the very objects that are presented to us in perceptual experience are mind-independent. I call this thesis

---

[3] For a helpful and sympathetic historically informed elucidation of this notion of an object's nature, see Wiggins (1995). For a highly influential further development of his own position, see Wiggins (2001). Charles (2000) elaborates the Aristotelian source of these ideas with great force and illumination. Strawson (1959) contains important motivation for the modern relevance of the notion. Ayers (1993: ii, esp. parts I and III) offers an alternative development to Wiggins that focuses more directly on the idea of the nature of physical objects in general as causally integrated, enduring, and spatially extended material unities. Although I intend to remain neutral on this here, I am myself more persuaded by Ayers' position. See also Campbell (2002*b*: esp. ch. 4).

empirical realism. It is realism about the domain of objects that are presented to us in perception.

Now, according to the early modern empiricists, especially for my purposes Locke (1975) and Berkeley (1975*a*, 1975*b*), the nature of conscious experience in general is to be elucidated by reference to certain entities that are set before the mind in such experience. Thus, the most fundamental characterization of a specific perceptual experience is to be given by citing, and/or describing, specific such entities: the experience in question is one of encountering just those things. The notion of a most fundamental characterization of the nature of perceptual experience in general and of specific perceptual experiences in particular here is clearly crucial. Although a good deal of what follows is intended directly or indirectly to elaborate that very notion, it is sufficient for the moment to regard this as the most fruitful and comprehensive characterization of perceptual experience for the purposes of our overall theoretical understanding of such experience in the philosophy of mind, metaphysics, and epistemology of perception. I call those entities, if any, which provide the most fundamental characterization of the nature of perceptual experience in this way its *direct objects*. These identify any given perceptual experience as the specific modification of the subject's conscious mental life that it is.

So the early modern empiricist picture is this. In conscious experience, a person is related to certain entities. They are set before her mind, and their being so constitutes her being in just that conscious mental condition. The basic phenomena of consciousness are therefore relational: *S* is conscious of *e*. The identity and nature of such entities serves to characterize what it is for the subject to be so conscious. Given this general approach, the entities to which a person is related in this way in perceptual experience are its direct objects. Hence what it is for a person to have a given perceptual experience is canonically to be elucidated by citing, and/or describing, such direct objects. Throughout my discussion, I use the notion of a direct object of perception in precisely this way, as an object, if any, that plays this early modern empiricist role in the fundamental characterization of perceptual experience. I also use the term *acquaintance*, and its cognates, for the *relation* in which a person stands to the direct objects of her experience according to the early modern approach. The core idea, then, is that the most fundamental nature of perceptual experience is acquaintance with direct objects.

I am absolutely not committing myself at this stage to this early modern empiricist approach to the nature of perceptual experience, other than as part of the framework for setting up the *problem* that I wish to discuss. An important and influential response to that problem is precisely to reject the early modern framework involved in posing it as I do. I discuss this response at length in ch. 4 below. Still, I do myself believe that the best solution to my problem retains the core commitment of the early modern empiricists to the idea that perceptual experience is most fundamentally to be characterized as conscious acquaintance with certain direct objects. I elaborate and defend my own development of this approach in chs. 5–7. It is worth baldly stating right from the start, though, what strikes me as its intuitive basis.

Consider the case of vision.[4] An account of the nature of our perceptual experience is an account of the ways things are for us visually speaking, that is, an account of the ways things *look*. The early modern empiricist insight, as I see it, is to take this way of putting the problem at face value in starting to give a solution. Very crudely, the ways things look are the ways *things* look. Very slightly less crudely, the ways things look to us in vision are the ways certain specific things look that are presented to us in vision, given the circumstances of their particular presentation. This provides the most fundamental characterization of the nature of the visual experience in question. So the intuitive starting point is to take seriously what might at first sight appear to be a dummy variable, 'things', in the question 'how do things look?' In vision, there are certain specific *things* before us, and the way things are for us visually speaking is a matter of the way that those specific things *look*, given the relevant features of our particular perspective upon them. The most philosophically illuminating framework for understanding the nature of visual perceptual experience is therefore to regard this most fundamentally as a matter of our acquaintance with certain specific direct objects whose nature in turn determines the way that things look to us given the relevant circumstances of our acquaintance with them. This is certainly not intended as an argument for a precisely determinate philosophical position, and opponents of the early modern

---

[4] I concentrate throughout on the case of vision. I believe that much of what I say applies equally to the other modalities, and occasionally indicate how these may be accommodated within the general framework here, although any such generalization clearly raises many substantive isues that I do not address explicitly in this book.

empiricist approach may no doubt go along with some or all of this intuitive line of thought. I simply offer it as an articulation of what certainly strikes me as a natural inclination to characterize perceptual experience as our acquaintance with certain specific direct objects. I hope that further justification for my strategic choice to set up the problem to be addressed throughout the book on the basis of my introduction of the early modern empiricist approach will be derived from the philosophical illumination offered by the taxonomy of views induced by this formulation of the problem.

Before proceeding to that, though, it may be helpful to make explicit a couple of points about the relation between the early modern empiricist notion of a direct object of perception and other notions sometimes put in similar terms. First, the conception of a direct object adopted here is perfectly compatible with two other approaches to delineating 'direct objects' of perception: (a) as those objects about which the perception in question places a person in a position to acquire non-inferential knowledge; and (b) as those objects to which the perception in question places a person in a position to make demonstrative reference.[5] Second, a very popular contemporary approach to the nature of our perceptual relation with the physical world has absolutely no role for direct objects of perception in the technical sense invoked here, although it does insist on another prima facie legitimate sense in which we nevertheless do in appropriate circumstances perceive the mind-independent physical objects around us 'directly', without problematic metaphysical or epistemological mediation. I turn directly to views along these lines that reject the very existence of direct objects as I understand them here in ch. 4 below.

---

[5] For (a), see Snowdon (1992), Huemer (2001), McDowell (2008b), and Wright (2008). For (b) see Snowdon (1992). My own view is that it is precisely the fact that certain entities are the direct objects of perception in the technical sense that I derive here from the early modern empiricists that they may be 'direct objects' in senses (a) and (b). See ch. 6 for more on the epistemological consequences of my own approach in connection with (a). See Campbell (2002b) for a detailed discussion of the role of a relational conception of perceptual acquaintance in *grounding* demonstrative thought along the lines suggested by (b). See Brewer (1999) for the idea that the epistemological and thought-theoretic roles of perceptual experience are themselves fundamentally related, which is also of course a prominent early modern empiricist theme: perceptual experience is essential for both our grasp of the most basic empirical concepts and our acquisition of the most basic empirical knowledge.

In any case, the early modern empiricist apparatus set out above strongly suggests the following reading of the uncontroversial claim that physical objects are the very things that are presented to us in perception.

(II) Physical objects are the direct objects of perception.

Here again, in order to remain as accommodating as possible at this stage, three immediate qualifications are in order, along with a comment about how (II) interacts with explicitly factive perceptual notions.

First, the following picture is consistent with (II) as I understand it. In the most basic cases of perception, the direct objects of the experience involved are physical objects; in many cases in which a person perceives an event she does so in virtue of the fact that the physical object whose change *is* the event in question is the direct object of her experience; still there may be occasions in which we have to invoke a physical event itself as the direct object of the experience in the absence of any obvious candidate object. This may be most common in senses other than vision and touch: for example, when a person hears a clap of thunder. Second, as will be evident in ch. 2 below, in two prima facie quite different contexts, it is intended to be consistent with (II) that the direct objects of perception strictly speaking may be merely spatial and/or temporal *parts* of extended and persisting physical objects. Similarly, third, there may be other direct objects that are not themselves physical objects; for example, they may be collections of physical objects, or otherwise related to physical objects, such as their shadows. Thus, although physical objects may be fundamental amongst the direct objects of perception, (II) is intended to allow for the extension of the notion to include certain other categories of direct object.[6]

Those sympathetic with the broad spirit of (II) may also be concerned about its interaction with various explicitly *factive* perceptual notions. It is undeniable that we often perceive *that p*: I may see that the coin is circular, for example. This is certainly compatible with (II), *not* because the fact that the coin is circular is a candidate direct object of perception in my sense, though. For it is a crucial component of the early modern framework, only in the context of which my technical notion of a direct object of perception makes sense, that these are *objects*, or things, as opposed to

---

[6] See ch. 4 and below, though, for opposition to the idea that perception may be construed most fundamentally at least as a relation to worldly *facts*.

facts, propositions, or contents.[7] According to my own development of the position, factive perceptions are intelligible only in terms of more basic perceptual acquaintance-relations between subjects and physical direct objects of this kind. Normally these will be the object constituents of the facts in question, such as the circular coin itself in the example given above; but they may not be, as, for example, when I see that Anna is not at the party. As I have already indicated, there is a quite different approach that has widespread support today according to which the most funda-mental perceptual states are to be characterized in terms of relata on the fact/proposition/content side of this distinction. Even the variant of this position according to which the most basic such relata are facts about how things are in the mind-independent physical world strictly speaking denies (II). Views of this general kind are the topic of ch. 4 below.

With all the early modern apparatus in place, the conjunction of (I) and (II) offers itself as a highly natural regimentation of the empirical realist conviction that physical objects are both presented in perception and yet in themselves entirely independent of it.

Things break down for this general approach, though, when it is pointed out that the early modern empiricists themselves explicitly en-dorse the following further claim, which is evidently inconsistent with the conjunction of (I) and (II), when, as I intend throughout, objects are classified as *mind-dependent* if and only if they are not mind-independent.

(III) The direct objects of perception are mind-dependent.

Even worse, the early modern empiricists not only accept (III), but they also offer powerful arguments for it. I focus in what follows in particular on the *argument from illusion* and the *argument from hallucination*.[8]

---

[7] Once again, the distinction here is controversial. A *locus classicus* is Wittgenstein (1974: §1, esp. §1.1). See also Russell (1917), Evans (1982: ch. 1), Frege (1993), and Steward (1997, ch. 1). For its application in the philosophy of perception, see Dretske (1969), Campbell (2002b, 2009), and Cassam (2007: esp. chs. 3 and 4).

[8] My purpose here is simply to illustrate the way in which these arguments put pressure on the natural regimentation of empirical realism as the conjunction of (I) and (II), in the context of the early modern approach to conscious perception as a relation to certain direct objects of experience that provide the most fundamental characterization of the nature of conscious condition in question. I illustrate the historical options by appeal to Locke (1975) and Berkeley (1975a, 1975b). Ch. 4 provides an extended discussion of what I regard as the orthodox modern response to these problems and arguments. Chs. 5–7 set out and defend my own quite different solution to them, which is significantly more in keeping with the insights of early modern empiricism.

Very crudely, the first proceeds as follows. In cases of *illusion*, the direct object of perception has a property that no candidate mind-independent object has, and must therefore be mind-dependent; then, since every perceptual experience is subjectively indistinguishable from one in a possible case of illusion, the same goes across the board. The direct objects of any perception are bound to be mind-dependent.

This line of argument may be made precise in a number of importantly different ways. I think that Paul Snowdon (1992) is right to distinguish two phases in each of them. The first is intended to establish that the direct object of an *illusion* is mind-dependent. The second is supposed to generalize this result to all perceptual experience, including that involved in veridical perception.[9]

There are serious problems with any version of phase two that I know. It is sufficient for my purposes here in connection with the argument from illusion, though, to elaborate phase one thus:

A *visual illusion* may be characterized as a perceptual experience in which a physical object, *o*, looks *F*, although *o* is not actually *F*.[10] According to the early modern empiricist approach, the way to account quite generally for the fact that something looks *F* in an experience is to construe that experience as the subject's acquaintance with a *direct object* that provides the most fundamental characterization of that very conscious condition and that must therefore, presumably, itself *be F*. In cases of illusion, then, any such direct object is bound to be distinct from the physical object, *o*, which is not *F*, although it looks to be so. For one is *F* and the other is not. The occurrence and nature of such an illusion is manifestly independent of the accidental additional presence of any mind-independent object in the vicinity that happens to be *F*. So its direct object must be mind-dependent.[11]

---

[9] See also Smith (2002: esp. chs. 1 and 7) for a similar two-part decomposition of the argument from illusion, and also of the argument from hallucination as indicated below.

[10] Although this provisional characterization is perfectly adequate for present purposes, there are visual illusions that do not meet it. See Johnston (2006) and ch. 6 below. There may also be cases that do not obviously qualify as illusions in which this condition is met. For example, a perfect wax model may look like the Prime Minister; but it is not clear that this constitutes a visual *illusion*. Although they certainly raise interesting issues, I ignore these cases unless otherwise indicated throughout.

[11] Recall that entities are mind-dependent just if their nature is in some way a matter of how they do or might appear. The first phase of the argument from illusion as set out here assumes with Locke and Berkeley that any case of something looking *F* in an experience is

On Locke's *materialist* view, the direct object of an illusion is a mind-dependent entity, which is *F*, which nevertheless sufficiently resembles a non-*F*, mind-independent object, *o*, which is also appropriately causally responsible for its production, for the latter to *be* the physical object that illusorily looks *F*.[12] Veridical perception of *o* as *G*, say, is likewise to be construed as acquaintance with a mind-dependent direct object, which is *G*. This resembles mind-independent *o*, which is also *G*,[13] and which is causally responsible for its production. Thus, in either case, a mind-independent physical object, *o*, is *presented* in perception, in virtue of the fact that the subject has a conscious experience with a mind-dependent direct object that sufficiently resembles *o*, which is in turn appropriately causally responsible for its production.

On the most straightforward and philosophically defensible version of Berkeley's *mentalism*, on the other hand, the direct object of an illusion is a mind-dependent entity, which is a part of an equally mind-dependent composite physical object *o*. *O* is not *F*, very roughly, because most of its parts are not *F*, and it does not behave, in general, in ways characteristic of *F*s: in particular we cannot use it as we can paradigm *F*s. Nevertheless, it looks *F*, on this occasion, because a part of it that is *F* is the direct object of the relevant illusory experience.[14] Veridical perception of *o* as *G*, say, is

one of acquaintance with a direct object that *is F*. Such direct objects are therefore in this way constituted by their appearance and hence mind-dependent. See ch. 5 below for a detailed account of how the early modern empiricist insight that perceptual experience is most fundamentally a matter of acquaintance with certain direct objects may be combined with an account of illusion that explicitly rejects this assumption and is therefore compatible with the natural construal of empirical realism as the simple conjunction of (I) and (II) along with the rejection of (III).

[12] Things are of course more complicated in the case of secondary qualities, according to Locke. For, in one sense, all secondary quality perception is illusory: nothing in the mind-independent physical world is ever red, *in the basic sense in which the mind-dependent direct objects of perception are sometimes red*. Still, in having such a mind-dependent red entity before the mind, a physical object may look RED, that is, either disposed to produce red direct objects of perception in normal observers in normal conditions, or microscopically constituted in whichever way actually grounds that disposition. Mind-independent physical objects are sometimes RED. So some, but not all, such perceptions may then be illusory in a derived sense. In such cases, a physical object, *o*, looks RED, although *o* is not actually RED. For the direct object of experience is a mind-dependent red entity that nevertheless sufficiently resembles *o* and is appropriately caused by that very mind-independent object. None of these details are relevant for present purposes, although they effectively come to the fore in ch. 3.

[13] Modulo the point in n. 12 above concerning secondary qualities.

[14] See Stoneham (2002) for a compelling presentation of this account of Berkeley. Note, as with Locke's account of the secondary qualities, predicates apply to persisting physical objects,

likewise to be construed as acquaintance with a mind-dependent direct object, which is G. This is again part of an equally mind-dependent composite physical object, *o*, which is itself G, roughly, because most of its relevant parts are G. Thus, in either case, a mind-dependent physical object, *o*, is *presented* in perception, in virtue of the fact that the subject has a conscious experience with a mind-dependent direct object that is part of *o*.

Hallucination presents related problems for any attempt to maintain empirical realism as the conjunction of (I) and (II) above within the early modern empiricist framework. The structure of the argument from hallucination is similar to that of the argument from illusion. In cases of *hallucination*, there is no plausible candidate mind-independent direct object of perception, so this must be a mind-dependent thing. Then, since every perceptual experience is subjectively indistinguishable from one in a possible case of hallucination, the same goes across the board. The direct objects of any perception are bound to be mind-dependent.

Again there are two phases to the argument. The first is intended to establish that hallucinatory experience must be construed as a relation to a mind-dependent direct object. The second is supposed to generalize this result to all perceptual experience, including that in veridical perception. My current concern is simply to illustrate Locke's and Berkeley's contrasting implementations of the first phase of the argument.

Thus, according to Locke's materialism, hallucination consists in acquaintance with a mind-dependent direct object of experience that is either not appropriately caused by any mind-independent physical object, or insufficiently resembles any mind-independent physical cause it may have to qualify as its perceptual presentation. According to Berkeley's mentalism, on the other hand, hallucination consists in acquaintance with a mind-dependent direct object of experience, which fails to qualify as a part of any composite mind-dependent physical object because it is not appropriately related to a suitable series of distinct such object-parts.

Locke and Berkeley both endorse (III) above, then, which is evidently inconsistent with the conjunction of (I) and (II). They both also acknowledge that physical objects are presented to us in perceptual experience.

according to Berkeley, in a way that is derivative of their more basic application to our fleeting ideas, which are, according to this version of his view, their temporal, and 'personal', parts. A number of issues arising here receive more extended treatment in ch. 2.

Locke accepts (I) and therefore denies (II). Nevertheless, he hopes to rescue empirical realism by offering an alternative construal of the way in which physical objects are presented in perception to their actually being the direct objects that provide the most fundamental characterization of the nature of perceptual experience itself. This crucially depends upon a notion of *resemblance* between the mind-dependent such direct objects and mind-independent physical objects themselves. Berkeley argues that any such proposed resemblance is fatally flawed. So he reverts to a more natural conception of perceptual presentation, on which a physical object is presented in perception when one of its parts is the direct object of the experience in question. Given his endorsement of (III), he therefore derives his anti-realist rejection of (I): physical objects are mind-dependent.

My discussion throughout the book is organized around the *Inconsistent Triad*.

(I)   Physical objects are mind-independent.
(II) Physical objects are the direct objects of perception.
(III) The direct objects of perception are mind-dependent.

Chapters 2 and 3 elaborate Berkeley's and Locke's accounts in turn. Their main concern is to derive general lessons for my own resolution of the inconsistency between (I), (II), and (III) above. I reject (III). This is the response of most philosophers today. What I hope to demonstrate, though, is that there are two quite different ways in which (III) may be denied. My contention is that the standard approach amongst philosophers today involves a denial of (III) that shares with Locke's rejection of (II) closely related problems to those that motivate Berkeley's rejection of (I). Berkeley has compelling arguments that Locke's attempted defence of empirical realism succeeds in sustaining realism for physical objects, *at best*, only at the cost of distinguishing these from anything genuinely presented to us in perception. Given their shared commitment to (III), the only possible attitude towards the physical objects that really are presented in perception, according to Berkeley, is therefore to regard these as mind-dependent. I argue that something very similar goes wrong with the orthodox denial of (III) today. Perhaps this succeeds in delineating a domain of mind-independent objects; and these may be *called* 'physical objects' if proponents of the position so choose. Still, they are absolutely not the objects that are in any satisfactory sense actually presented to us in perception. The resultant physical realism is no defence of *empirical* realism at all.

In contrast, I insist that the idea that physical objects are genuinely *presented* to us in perception plays an ineliminable role in identifying the domain of objects whose status as mind-independent is of fundamental philosophical concern in debates over realism with respect to the familiar physical world of stones, tables, trees, and animals. My central thesis is that defence of a genuinely *empirical* realism concerning this world that we all know and love depends upon a denial of (III) that ironically shares a good deal more with early modern empiricism than is normally even countenanced by current philosophical orthodoxy.

Chapter 4 outlines the standard approach taken towards these issues today. This involves a wholesale rejection of the early modern notion of direct objects of perception. Instead of regarding perceptual experience as acquaintance with particular entities whose identity and nature character-ize the experience in question as the specific conscious occurrence that it is, current orthodoxy approaches the understanding of perceptual experi-ence in terms of its representational content: the way it represents things as being in the world around the subject. Thus, (III) is effectively denied by insisting that there are no direct objects of perception in the early modern empiricist sense. This revision is intended to provide a sense in which physical objects are nevertheless presented to us in perception that avoids the deeply unattractive choice instantiated by Locke and Berkeley be-tween a realism that changes the subject altogether away from the familiar world of objects that really are presented to us in experience, on the one hand, and an explicit endorsement of the mind-dependent status of the stones, tables, trees, and animals that we genuinely do perceive, on the other. I argue at length that this attempt is a failure. The initial assimilation of perception to thought involved in the contemporary move towards a characterization of our fundamental perceptual relation with the world in terms of representational *content* excludes any proper recognition of the status of perceptual experience as the conscious presentation to a person of a world of physical *objects*.

Chapter 5 sets out my own elaboration of the early modern empiricist insight that perceptual experience is most fundamentally to be construed in terms of a relation of acquaintance with certain direct objects, whose identity and nature provide the most basic elucidation of what it is to be in the relevant conscious experiential condition. I explain in detail how the dependence of a person's perceptual experience of a given object upon her point of view and other circumstances of perception, and also the possibility of illusion and hallucination, all entirely fail to establish that such direct objects of perception are absolutely bound to be mind-dependent things. The idea that persisting mind-independent physical objects themselves are the direct objects of perceptual experience is perfectly compatible with the existence of such phenomena. I go on to provide a detailed account of how to make sense of the many and varied ways that such mind-independent physical objects look in visual perception on this basis.

The focus of ch. 6 is epistemological. The position advanced in ch. 5 has certain features that may provoke concerns under the head of the Myth of the Given. I set out Sellars' own (1997) formulation of the objection. Then I give an extended sketch of how the positive epistemology of empirical knowledge might proceed in the context of my own position illustrating at various points how further objections motivated at least in part by Sellars' discussion may be handled. I also provide a brief comparison between this account and my own earlier views (Brewer, 1999).

In ch. 7 I complete the defence of my own positive position by explaining in detail how the *mind-independence* of the direct objects of perception that I insist upon shows up from the subject's own perspective. Our account as theorists of the direct objects of perception is responsible at least in part for how things are from the subject's own perspective. I explain the role in bringing their mind-independence to light *for the subject* of certain commonsense explanations of the actual and counterfactual order and nature of experience of physical objects on the basis of the perceptible natures of the particular objects perceived.

Thus, I reject (III) outright: there are direct objects of perception; but these are the familiar persisting mind-independent physical objects that we all know and love. Empirical realism is indeed sustained as the perfectly natural simple conjunction of (I) and (II).

Put slightly differently, a key message of the book is that the early modern empiricists were absolutely right to focus their attention on a fundamental tension inherent in the empirical realist conception of physical objects as both the very things that are subjectively presented to us in perception and yet also entirely independent in themselves of any thought or experience of them. This tension is not to be avoided by today's alternative construal of the fundamental nature of perceptual experience in terms of some kind of representational content. What is required instead is a radical reconfiguration of the early modern empiricist conception of perception as a direct acquaintance-relation with its objects that is nevertheless entirely in line with our pre-philosophical commonsense expressed in the conjunction of (I) and (II). This is what I offer here.

2

Anti-Realism

Berkeley's response to the Inconsistent Triad identified in ch. 1 is to reject that

(I) Physical objects are mind-independent.

In ch. 3 I develop my own version of what I regard as his most powerful argument for this rejection of (I) as an argument against Locke's indirect realism. In the context of the early modern approach to perception, then, on which our most basic experiential condition consists in our acquaintance with mind-dependent direct objects, indirect realism is unstable according to this Berkeleian argument and some form of anti-realism is inevitable. A central component of the view that I present over the course of the book is that a line of thought that has certain fundamental features in common with Berkeley's objection to Locke also threatens a great deal of contemporary work on perception.[1] My most important proposal is that this is only ultimately avoided by the position that I develop on my own account in chs. 5–7. The topic of the present chapter, though, is the rejection of (I).

Notoriously, Berkeley (1975a, 1975b) combines this denial of the existence of mind-independent matter with the insistence that most of what commonsense claims about physical objects is perfectly true.[2] As I explain (§2.1), he suggests two broad strategies for this reconciliation, one of which importantly subdivides. Thus, I distinguish three Berkeleian metaphysical views, and explain how the real distinctions between them are ultimately semantic rather than ontological.

---

[1] See especially ch. 4 below.
[2] My discussion of Berkeley throughout draws most heavily on these two primary texts. I make no further specific reference to them, and make only sparing reference to the secondary literature where necessary.

Important recent work by David Lewis (esp. 1998, 2009) provides a framework for articulating three far more modern-looking metaphysical options, between which I argue that the real distinctions are again semantic rather than ontological (§2.2). This highlights a striking isomorphism between the two trios of views.

All six views share a fundamental assumption that the explanatory grounds of the actual and counterfactual nature of our experiences of physical objects are distinct from any *direct objects* of those experiences, in the technical sense that I introduced in ch. 1 as part of my explication of the early modern empiricist approach to the identification and fundamental categorization of conscious experience in general. Let me explain this idea a little here. It should come into increasing focus as my discussion proceeds throughout the book.

According to the early modern empiricists, the most basic characterization of perceptual experience is to be given by citing and/or describing certain *direct objects* with which the subject is *acquainted* in such experience. When a person perceives a specific physical object of a certain kind there is also an *explanation* to be given of why he is having an experience of just the kind that he is having, and of what various other possible experiences of that same physical object would be like from different points of view and in different circumstances of perception.

Examples of phenomena to be explained here would be the following. The fact that a coin looks circular from head on; and the fact that it would look increasingly elliptical as one's angle of view increases away from head on; the fact that a given jumper looks red outdoors; and the fact that it looked mauve in the store; and so on.

All six of the views that I am concerned with in this chapter distinguish the fundamental explanatory grounds in terms of which such explanations are to be given, on the one hand, from any direct objects with respect to which those experiences themselves may be characterized according to the early modern approach, on the other. As a result, I argue, they all struggle seriously to sustain our intuitive commitment to *empirical realism*, the thesis that physical objects are both presented to us in perceptual experience and have a nature that is entirely independent of how they do or might appear to anyone (§2.3).

I conclude (§2.4) by proposing the denial of this shared assumption as the fundamental starting point for any stable and fully satisfying defence of empirical realism. The ultimate explanation of the actual and counterfactual nature of my experience when perceiving a specific physical object of a given kind is that very object, which also constitutes the direct object with which I am acquainted in each of the various experiences that I may have of it.[3] This sets my agenda for the remainder of the book.

Recall that I identify *physical objects*, in the first instance, by extension, as things like stones, tables, trees, and animals: the persisting macroscopic constituents of the world in which we live. *Physical object language* is the language in which we speak and write about physical objects. For the entities of a given kind to be *mind-independent* is for them to have a nature that is entirely independent of how they do or might appear to anyone. Otherwise they are *mind-dependent*.

On the early modern empiricist approach that I take as my starting point here, the nature of conscious experience is to be elucidated by reference to certain entities that are set before the mind in such experience. Thus, the most fundamental characterization of a specific perceptual experience is to be given by citing, and/or describing, specific such entities: the experience in question is one of *acquaintance* with just those things. I call those entities, if any, which provide the most fundamental characterization of the nature of perceptual experience in this way its *direct objects*. These identify any given perceptual experience as the specific modification of consciousness that it is.

Of course there are many who reject altogether the idea that the most fundamental characterization of perceptual experience is to be given relationally by reference to direct objects of this kind. Chapter 4 below comprises a sustained critical discussion of what I regard as the most significant modern approach to the issues here along precisely these lines. For the purposes of the present chapter, though, I assume the early modern empiricist approach for the following four reasons. First, Berkeley himself clearly makes this assumption, and the options for his own metaphysical system are quite clear in this context. Second, the modern metaphysical views with which I am concerned here are to my mind also most clearly defined and distinguished in the context of this assumption, although their actual proponents may more or less explicitly distance themselves from it. Third, the assumption facilitates and clarifies my general assessment and articulation of the prospects and preconditions for

---

[3] See Fine (1994) for the idea of the nature of a given object as the explanatory ground of various modal truths.

empirical realism in the present chapter. Fourth, the early modern relational approach to the fundamental characterization of perceptual experience by reference to its *direct objects* is I believe ultimately correct, although
not of course in the form adopted by its early modern proponents themselves, governed as this is by the conviction that the direct objects of
perception are bound to be mind-dependent. This is perhaps the most
important contention of the book as a whole.

2.1 Berkeley's options

Berkeley begins Part I of the *Principles* (1975*b*) with an explicit endorsement of the widely held assumption at the time that the direct objects of
perception are mind-dependent. This is the conclusion of the arguments
from illusion and hallucination that I set out in ch. 1, and forms claim (III)
of the Inconsistent Triad.

In what follows he is scrupulously attentive to the fact that physical
objects, such as stones, tables, trees, and animals, are in some way *presented*
to us in perception in a sense in which it follows that perception provides
some conception of what physical objects are: perception provides our
indispensable initial identification of the domain that constitutes the subject
matter for any subsequent theoretical investigation into their fundamental
natures. He concludes that physical objects must be *appropriately related* to
the direct objects of perception. Berkeley's many, varied, and powerful
arguments against Locke's materialism aim to establish that physical objects
are therefore likewise mind-dependent. Given crucial constraints upon
the appropriate relations that physical objects must bear to the mind-
dependent direct objects of perception, any conviction that such objects
have mind-independent material natures cannot, he argues, be sustained.[4]
Nevertheless, as I say, he insists that much of our commonsense conception
of the physical world is correct. This much I take for granted as familiar
background concerning Berkeley.

He has two broad strategies for developing the overall position.[5]

---

[4] My extended discussion in ch. 3 of the difficulties faced by philosophers responding to
my opening Inconsistent Triad by rejecting (II) in a way that introduces strong structural
similarities with Locke's indirect realism effectively articulates and develops this Berkeleian
objection.

[5] I first encountered this basic distinction in Foster (1985). I have also been helped in my
understanding of Berkeley's options by Stoneham (2002).

Idealism (I), identifies physical objects with mereological sums of mind-dependent direct objects of perception.[6] Here there are two varieties. *G-idealism* (GI), identifies physical objects with mereological sums of mind-dependent direct objects of *God's* experience.[7] *H-idealism* (HI), identifies physical objects with mereological sums of mind-dependent direct objects of *humans'* experience.[8]

Phenomenalism (P), systematically analyses whole sentences of physical object language in terms of sentences concerning various patterns amongst the actual and possible mind-dependent direct objects of perception, without asserting numerical identities between particular physical objects and anything mind-dependent. Strictly speaking, and notwithstanding the surface structure of the sentences of physical object language, we do not make genuine (*objectual*) reference to physical objects at all. Rather, truth-conditions are given for whole physical object language sentences by truth-functional constructions of sentences concerning the actual and counterfactual course of human experience.[9]

One way to articulate the basic contrast between the idealist and phenomenalist strategies is as a disagreement about what constitute the *semantic primitives* of physical object language.[10] These are the basic units of the language to which semantic assignments are made, on the basis of which assignments truth conditions may systematically be determined for all the well-formed sentences of the language. According to (I), the semantic primitives of physical object language include referring expressions and predicates; according to (P), they include instead whole atomic sentences.

Thus, according to (I), referring expressions of physical object language, such as 'that table', are assigned mereological sums of mind-dependent objects as their *reference*: (sums or parts of) *ideas* in God's mind, according to (GI),

---

[6] This is Foster's (1985) '*mentalistic realism*'.

[7] Strictly speaking, this is not *perceptual* experience, since God is active in its production rather than passive in its reception. Furthermore, the most plausible reading of Berkeley's gestures in this direction identifies each physical object with a *single* such '*idea*' in God's mind, or perhaps even with a single element of one overall idea which *is* the whole physical world. Thus, according to (GI), physical objects are (mereological parts of) mind-dependent objects of God's active-creative experience.

[8] See Stoneham (2002, ch. 8) on this distinction between (GI) and (HI). I agree with Stoneham that (HI) is the most straightforward and philosophically defensible version of Berkeley's *mentalism*.

[9] This is Foster's '*mentalistic reductionism*'.

[10] The remainder of the present section elaborates my earlier claim that the real distinctions between all three Berkeleian views are ultimately semantic rather than ontological.

and sums of direct objects of human perception, according to (HI). *Satisfaction* clauses for predicates are not straightforward; but the basic idea would be that a physical object language predicate, such as 'x is brown', is satisfied by an object iff that object has enough (of the right kind of) brown-type mind-dependent direct objects of experience as parts.[11]

According to (P), on the other hand, truth conditions will be given directly for whole atomic sentences of physical object language *roughly* along these lines:

'That table is brown' is true iff my current perceptual experience has a brown-table-type direct object, and I would have experiences with brown-table-type direct objects in certain different circumstances, and your perceptual experience would have a brown-table-type direct object if you were in my study, and...[12]

The truth-functors of physical object language are given standard treatment on both accounts. Notice, though, that physical object language quantification is *objectual* according to (I), whereas it is *substitutional*, according to (P).

On both Berkeleian strategies—indeed, on all three of the Berkeleian metaphysical options that I have distinguished—the actual and counterfactual nature of all human perception is ultimately explained by God's free volitional strategy: the very volitional strategy by which He effectively creates the physical world itself.[13] The only cognitive access that we have to this explanatory volitional strategy is essentially *indirect*, though, as the strategy that results in just *these* patterns in perceptual experience. Crucially, for my purposes, this explanatory ground of the actual and counterfactual nature of our experience of physical objects—God's will—is quite distinct

---

[11] Note, as I mentioned in ch. 1 n. 14 above, that on all three of Berkeley's accounts predicates apply to physical objects themselves only derivatively. Their primary application is to mind-dependent direct objects of experience.

[12] This account is very rough indeed, and it may be a serious objection to (P) that it cannot ultimately be made completely satisfactory without some kind of circularity. For clauses are required to allow for the fact that there may be misleading perceptions of brown tables in unusual lighting conditions, say, and also for the fact that brown tables might have been different colours in some different circumstances. These possibilities raise many difficult issues that I pass over here for current purposes.

[13] Although this is of course crucial to *Berkeley's* metaphysics, I outline and discuss below variants of all three positions on which the explanatory ground of our perceptions is supposed to be quite different.

from any *direct object* of that experience, by reference to which the fundamental characterization of the experience itself is to be given.

All three Berkeleian metaphysical views share a single fundamental ontology. God's free creative volitional strategy constitutes the fundamental explanatory ground of the actual and counterfactual nature of human perceptual experience of physical objects, which consists in subjects' actual and counterfactual relations of acquaintance with mind-dependent direct objects. This is all that there most fundamentally is: minds and their ideas. The metaphysical distinctions between the views are due ultimately to their different semantics for physical object language.

First, according to (GI), everyday terms for particular physical objects, such as 'that book' and 'my laptop', are to be construed as genuinely referring expressions, whose referents are particular direct objects of God's creative volitional experience. Second, according to (HI), such everyday terms for particular physical objects are again to be construed as genuinely referring expressions. Their referents in this case are mereological sums over time and over various human subjects of certain mind-dependent direct objects of perceptual experience. Third, according to (P), everyday terms for particular physical objects are not to be construed as genuinely referring expressions at all. Rather, whole sentences containing such terms are to be given truth conditions by logical constructions of sentences referring to human beings and the mind-dependent direct objects of their actual and possible perceptual experiences.

Thus, although *the metaphysics of physical objects* is quite different on each of the three Berkeleian options that I have been discussing, these differences are the product of a single *underlying* ontological picture and a range of alternatives concerning the semantics of ordinary physical object language.[14]

---

[14] Again many issues are raised here that I pass over for current purposes. One concerns the way in which proponents of the three Berkeleian metaphysical views interpret and answer the question 'are there physical objects?'. On one natural reading, the answer is 'yes' according to (GI) and (HI) and 'no' according to (P). The first two affirmative answers assume the existence of mereological sums, though, which is not obviously uncontroversial. Furthermore, (P) might argue for its own affirmative answer as follows. There are physical objects because 'physical objects exist' is true. This consists in the truth of such sentences as 'that table exists', which is in turn secured by the truth of such things as 'that table is brown'. For an excellent collection of essays addressing this kind of issue, see Chalmers, Manley, and Wasserman (2009). I do not take a stand here. My point is simply that a shared fundamental ontology of minds and their ideas conjoined with different physical object language semantics yields different metaphysical views.

2.2   Three more modern metaphysical views

The central argument of David Lewis's influential paper 'Ramseyan Humility' (2009) provides a framework for articulating three far more modern-looking metaphysical options. I begin with the argument and move on to the options.

According to Lewis, the 'final theory' to which scientific research ideally tends ought to deliver a complete inventory of the fundamental intrinsic properties that play an active role in the actual workings of nature.[15] Call the true and complete such final theory T. This contains a good deal of our old *O-language*, which is available and interpreted independently of T, and which suffices to express all possible observations. T also contains its own theoretical *T-terms*. These are implicitly defined by their role in the overall theory and name the fundamental properties in question. Furthermore, Lewis (2009: 206) assumes that none of these causally basic intrinsic properties are named in O-language, 'except as occupants of roles; in which case T will name them over again, and will say that the property named by so-and-so T-term is the occupant of such-and-such role'.

Suppose that $T(t_1 \ldots t_n)$ is the simplest form of T, where $t_1, \ldots t_n$ are the T-terms, thereby implicitly defined in terms of the O-language that constitutes the remainder of this expression for T. The *Ramsey sentence* of T is $\exists x_1 \ldots \exists x_n T(x_1 \ldots x_n)$. This logically implies all and only the O-language sentences that are theorems of T. Call this Ramsey sentence R. Since O-language alone suffices to express all possible observations, every possible observable prediction of T is equally a prediction of R. Thus, any evidence for T is equally evidence for R: evidence for T cannot go beyond evidence merely for R.

Now, it is extremely likely that, if there are any, then there will be more than one fundamental property in at least the most basic ontological categories: monadic properties, dyadic relations, and so on. That is to

---

[15] There are substantive and controversial issues concerning the correct precise characterization of *intrinsic* properties. See e.g. Lewis (1983*a*, 1983*b*), Sider (1993, 2001), Langton and Lewis (1998, 2001), Yablo (1999), Hawthorne (2001), Marshall and Parsons (2001), and Weatherson (2001). It is unnecessary for my purposes in what follows to engage with these debates in detail. The provisional characterization of intrinsic properties as those that an object has *of itself*, independently of any other thing, those it would retain, or retain the lack of, if it were the only thing that existed, should suffice.

say, if there are any monadic fundamental properties, then there are very likely to be more than one. Similarly for dyadic relations, and so on. Suppose that $\langle a_1 \ldots a_n \rangle$ is the n-tuple that actually realizes T; and suppose that $\langle b_1 \ldots b_n \rangle$ is any n-tuple which results from permuting some of the pairs $\langle a_i, a_j \rangle$ in which a_i and a_j are of the same ontological category. In other words, supposing that a_p and a_q are both monadic fundamental properties in the n-tuple $\langle a_1 \ldots a_p \ldots a_q \ldots a_n \rangle$ that actually realizes T, let $\langle b_1 \ldots b_n \rangle$ be the n-tuple $\langle a_1 \ldots a_q \ldots a_p \ldots a_n \rangle$. *Combinatorialism* is the thesis that possibility is preserved under permutation or replacement of co-categorial items. So, on the assumption of combinatorialism, $\langle b_1 \ldots b_n \rangle$ is a *possible* realization of T. *Quidditism* is the thesis that possibilities which differ simply by the permutation or replacement of properties are genuinely *distinct*. So, on the additional assumption of quidditism, $\langle b_1 \ldots b_n \rangle$ is a *distinct* possible realization of T from the actual realization $\langle a_1 \ldots a_n \rangle$. Furthermore, since any evidence for T is evidence for R, and R is true in both the actual case, in which $\langle a_1 \ldots a_n \rangle$ realizes T, and in the distinct possible case in which $\langle b_1 \ldots b_n \rangle$ realizes T, then no possible evidence can tell us that $\langle a_1 \ldots a_n \rangle$ is the actual realization of T, as opposed to $\langle b_1 \ldots b_n \rangle$.[16]

Though our theory T has a unique actual realization . . . it has multiple possible realizations. . . . no possible observation can tell us which one is actual, because whichever one is actual the Ramsey sentence will be true. There is indeed a true contingent proposition about which of the possible realizations is actual, but we can never gain evidence for this proposition, and so can never know it. . . . Humility follows. (Lewis, 2009: 207)

The Humility Thesis (HT) that follows, according to Lewis, is the thesis that we are irremediably ignorant of the fundamental properties of the world: we cannot possibly know the intrinsic nature of physical reality itself. Provided only that a fundamental property is not a categorial singleton—that is to say that there are others of the same category[17]— then we can never have any evidence that *it*—as opposed to any of these

---

[16] Combinatorialism and quidditism are both substantive assumptions that may be questioned. I abstain from such questions here.

[17] Later in the paper Lewis introduces additional assumptions that enable him to extend the argument to all fundamental properties; but it is unnecessary for my purposes to get involved with the additional complications.

others—is the actual realizer of the theoretical role definitive of its name. We know that there is *a* property, so-named, that does just that; but we cannot possibly know which it is, what the intrinsic nature of the property so-named actually is. Since all intrinsic properties supervene upon these fundamental properties, we are in this sense irremediably ignorant of the intrinsic nature of mind-independent reality itself.

From this point forward I go beyond anything that Lewis actually says in order to explore a possible account of how perception fits into the picture that is at least suggested to me by his discussion. My purpose is to clarify further what is at stake in philosophical debates concerning empirical realism.

According to Lewis, independently interpreted O-language suffices to express all possible observations, and certainly, therefore, the way things appear to subjects in perception. According to the early modern approach to perception, the most fundamental characterization of any specific perceptual experience is to be given by citing, and/or describing, its mind-dependent direct objects. The way things appear to subjects in perception is precisely a matter of the intrinsic natures of the relevant mind-dependent objects of acquaintance. Putting the two ideas together suggests that O-language suffices to characterize the natures of the mind-dependent direct objects of all perception. Lewis also explicitly assumes that no fundamental properties are named in O-language, except as the occupants of roles, presumably such as the role of being systematically causally explanatory of such and such observations. Thus, the intrinsically unknowable fundamental explanatory grounds of the actual and counterfactual nature of our perceptual experience of physical objects are quite distinct from any direct objects of perception themselves that provide the most fundamental relational characterization of such experience.[18]

According to this composite picture, perception consists in our acquaintance with certain mind-dependent direct objects whose nature

---

[18] Lewis's discussion of qualia (2009: §8) resists the idea that we have knowledge of which properties even these are simply in virtue of our experiential acquaintance with them. We know them instead only as the occupants of psychological roles that 'confer on us abilities to recognize and imagine what we have previously experienced' (p. 217). For my own illustrative purposes in what follows I impose upon his position the early modern construal of perception by postulating mind-dependent direct objects with their own natures as the experiential foundation of all possible observation expressed in O-language. It may well be that Lewis's own position here is closer to the Content View (CV), discussed below in ch. 4.

determines the way things appear to us. The actual and counterfactual course of such perceptual experience, like everything else, is ultimately to be explained by the fundamental nature of mind-independent physical reality of which we are irremediably ignorant. This single underlying ontology once again offers three possible metaphysical options for physical objects depending crucially upon the semantics for physical object language that are imposed upon it.

First, according to *Scientific Realism* (SR), physical objects, like stones tables, trees, and animals are mereological sums, over space and time, of the constituents of an intrinsically unknowable mind-independent reality, which is the subject matter of fundamental physics, and which constitutes the explanatory ground of all human perceptual experience. Such experience, in turn, constitutes the various ways that physical objects *appear* to us. According to (SR), then, everyday terms for physical objects, such as 'that book' and 'my laptop', are to be construed as genuinely referring expressions, whose referents are mereological fusions of intrinsically unknowable mind-independent fundamental physical constituents.

According to *Modern Transcendental Idealism* (MTI), physical objects are mereological sums of the mind-dependent direct objects of various humans' perceptual experiences over time. The actual and counterfactual nature of these experiences is explanatorily grounded in the intrinsically unknowable mind-independent reality that is the subject matter of fundamental physics. Although this position is idealist about physical objects themselves, the stones, tables, trees, and animals that we all know and love, it insists, in opposition to Berkeley's appeal to the volitional strategy of God's infinite mind, that the explanatory ground of the nature of human experience is mind-independent, although intrinsically irremediably unknowable. It is not a view that is often endorsed explicitly today; but I do believe that some temptation towards it is evident in much modern metaphysics, given the alternatives available once (HT) is in place alongside the early modern approach to perceptual experience. I give an example of this temptation in Lewis below. According to (MTI), then, everyday terms for particular physical objects are again to be construed as genuinely referring expressions. Their referents in this case are mereological fusions of mind-dependent direct objects of human perceptual experience.

According to *Reductionism* (R), there are, strictly speaking, no persisting physical objects, such as stones, tables, trees, and animals. Sentences 'about' such things are reducible to sentences about the actual and counterfactual order and nature of various humans' perceptual experiences over time, where the truth of these sentences is in turn grounded in the way things are in the intrinsically unknowable mind-independent reality which is the subject matter of fundamental physics. According to (R), then, everyday terms for particular physical objects are not to be construed as genuinely referring expressions at all. Rather, whole sentences containing such terms are to be given truth conditions by logical constructions of sentences referring to the fundamental constituents of physical reality that are explanatory of certain characteristic patterns in the mind-dependent direct objects of human beings' actual and possible perceptual experiences.

Lewis himself presents (HT) as a thesis concerning our epistemological relation with the fundamental constituents of *physical objects* themselves, such as stones, tables, trees, and animals. This identifies his metaphysical position as a version of (SR), which is surely his official view.

Consider his argument for a perdurance account of the persistence of such physical objects, though (Lewis, 1998).

> The principal and decisive objection against endurance, as an account of the persistence of ordinary things such as people or puddles, is the problem of temporary intrinsics. Persisting things change their intrinsic properties. For instance, shape: when I sit, I have a bent shape; when I stand, I have a straightened shape. Both shapes are temporary intrinsic properties; I have them only some of the time. How is such change possible? I know of only three solutions. (Lewis, 1998: 205)

Lewis's argument is that two of these 'solutions' are untenable. The first denies that shapes are intrinsic properties of physical objects. 'They are disguised relations, which an enduring thing may bear to times' (ibid.). Lewis objects that this is 'simply incredible, if we are speaking of the persistence of ordinary things. . . . If we know what shape is, *we know that it is a property, not a relation*' (ibid., my emphasis). The second 'solution' is to claim that 'the only intrinsic properties of a thing are those it has at the present moment. Other times are like false stories' (ibid.). Lewis objects here that this 'rejects persistence altogether. . . . In saying that there are no other times, as opposed to false representations thereof, it goes against what we all believe' (p. 206). The third possibility, which must therefore be the correct solution, is to invoke *perdurance* as an account of the persistence of physical objects: 'different temporary intrinsics ... belong to different ... temporal parts' (ibid.).

The crucial premiss for my purposes is that bent and straightened, the very properties that we know on the basis of everyday observation, are different intrinsic shape properties of ordinary physical objects, or at least of their distinct perceptible temporal parts. This is surely incompatible with (SR), though. For, recall that, according to (SR), all the properties of physical objects that we know on the basis of perception are relational: they are their dispositions to produce various experiences in us, which present us merely with their *appearances*. For all intrinsic properties of physical objects supervene upon their fundamental nature of which we are irremediably ignorant. It is therefore such appearances that change from bent to straight as we perceive shape to change when Lewis stands up. That is to say, in so far as *bent* and *straightened* are construed as intrinsic properties that we know on the basis of perception, they must be construed by the proponent of (HT) as intrinsic properties of mind-dependent direct objects of experience: as the early modern conception of experience contends, the way things appear to subjects in perception is precisely a matter of the intrinsic natures of the relevant mind-dependent objects of acquaintance. Thus, identifying physical objects with those objects of which the shapes that we perceive to change in this way are intrinsic properties, assimilates the position to a version of (MTI), as opposed to (SR).[19]

Perhaps Lewis's reply would be that the properties which shape terms such as 'bent' and 'straightened' actually name are instead certain intrinsic properties of intrinsically unknowable physical objects, as these are understood according to (SR), of which the so-called 'bentness' and 'straightenedness' *that we perceive* are the mere appearances to us. Intrinsic shape, on this view, is that determinable property which causally grounds the change in appearance that we experience when Lewis stands up, whatever property that may be. Strictly speaking though, we have no conclusive reason to regard standing as a *change* in that intrinsic property of physical objects on this construal. More importantly, this response is inconsistent with

---

[19] The assimilation is not irresistible, but intended rather as illustrative. See my extended discussion of the scientific implementation of my *Explanatory Proposal* (EP), in ch. 7 below for critical consideration of what is effectively an attempt to resist it.

Lewis's firm implication, in rejecting the first purported solution to the problem of temporary intrinsics above, that we *do* 'know what shape is' (p. 205). For the consequence of Lewis's envisaged reply would be precisely that we do not: we know only the appearance that it produces in us, which we are misleadingly inclined to call by the same name.

Put succinctly, the problem for the Lewisian position under consideration is that (SR) entails that every property of physical objects that we know on the basis of perception is relational, a matter of their disposition to produce certain mind-dependent objects of acquaintance whose intrinsic nature constitutes the way things appear to us in perception; yet the argument for a perdurance account of the persistence of physical objects requires that some of their properties that we know on the basis of perception should be intrinsic, and that this should itself be perceptually evident to us.

In any case, my point at this stage is not so much to accuse Lewis himself of inconsistency, but rather to illustrate the temptation, even amongst explicit proponents of (SR), towards the idea that physical objects such as stones, tables, trees, and animals are presented to us in perception, *in a sense that most naturally suggests (MTI) rather than (SR)*. The idea is that physical objects themselves are the objects that we all know and love, as it were, in the sense that we know at least some of their intrinsic properties on the basis of our perception of them. Given (HT), this is inconsistent with the (SR) identification of physical objects with mereological fusions of intrinsically unknowable fundamental physical constituents. We must think of physical objects instead along the lines of (MTI), as mereological sums of the mind-dependent direct objects of various humans' perceptual experiences over time, where the nature of these experiences is explanatorily grounded in the intrinsically unknowable mind-independent reality that is the subject matter of fundamental physics.[20]

---

[20] The idea that physical object are presented to us in perception in this sense is also crucial to Berkeley's (1975*a*, 1975*b*) argument against Locke's (1975) materialism. Like Lewis, Locke wishes to secure some perceptual acquaintance with the intrinsic properties of physical objects, through his thesis that our ideas of primary qualities at least *resemble* those qualities in the objects themselves. Just as this is strictly incompatible with Lewis's official (SR), Berkeley argues that it is inconsistent with Locke's distinction between the mind-dependent ideas that are the direct objects of our perceptions and the purportedly mind-independent physical objects themselves that are supposed to be their causes. See ch. 3 for further development of this argument.

All three modern metaphysical views endorse (HT). They all construe fundamental physics as a merely *relational* identification of the intrinsically unknowable mind-independent reality that constitutes the fundamental explanatory ground of the nature of our actual and counterfactual perceptual experience of physical objects. According to Berkeley, on the other hand, scientific investigation provides an increasingly general, detailed, and accurate characterization of the content of God's intention in creating the observable physical world as He does, which is nevertheless bound to concern itself only with His means rather than His ultimate end. So fundamental physics is to be construed as a merely relational identification of the intrinsically unknowable *volitional strategy of God* that constitutes the fundamental explanatory ground of the nature of our actual and counterfactual perceptual experience of physical objects. By mapping the modern metaphysician's intrinsically unknowable mind-independent reality onto Berkeley's intrinsically unknowable divine intention we therefore have this general isomorphism between Berkeleian and more modern metaphysics:

$$(GI) \equiv (SR)$$
$$(HI) \equiv (MTI)$$
$$(P) \equiv (R)$$

All six accounts as I construe them here endorse the early modern empiricist thesis that the most fundamental characterization of perceptual experience is in terms of the subject's relation of acquaintance with certain specific mind-dependent direct objects whose intrinsic nature constitutes the way that things appear in perception. On the Berkeleian left-hand sides of the three isomorphisms set out above, the fundamental explanatory ground of the actual and counterfactual nature of such perceptual experience is God's volitional strategy. On the more modern right-hand sides this explanatory ground is the fundamental nature of mind-independent physical reality. On both sides we are irremediably ignorant of the intrinsic nature of this explanatory ground that is knowable only relationally in terms ultimately of its observable effects.

According to (GI), physical objects are particular direct objects of God's creative volitional experience. According to (SR), they are mereological sums of the constituents of fundamental mind-independent reality. Correlating these two intrinsically unknowable explanatory grounds across the Berkeleian–modern divide yields the first isomorphism above. Both (HI) and (MTI) offer the same account of physical objects as mereological sums of mind-dependent direct objects of human perceptual experience. Correlating their two quite different intrinsically unknowable fundamental explanatory grounds of such experience yields the second isomorphism above. Similarly, (P) and (R) offer the same account of the semantics of physical object language, on which sentences superficially 'about' physical objects are reducible to sentences about the actual and counterfactual order and nature of various humans' perceptual experiences over time. Again, correlating their different intrinsically unknowable explanatory grounds of such experience yields the third isomorphism above.

2.3   Empirical realism

Intuitively, none of the six views that I have been discussing sustain *empirical realism*, the thesis that physical objects are *both* the very things that are presented to us in perception *and* have a nature that is entirely independent of how they do or might appear to anyone. In the context of the early modern empiricist assumption, operative throughout this chapter, that the correct way to construe perceptual experience in general is in terms of a relation of acquaintance with certain specific direct objects whose nature constitutes the way things appear in perception, it is natural to identify the objects that are *presented* in experience in this sense precisely with such direct objects of experience. Let us say that a domain of objects is *primary-empirical*, then, if its elements are either identical to or mereologically composed of direct objects of human perceptual experience in the early modern sense. Thus, the shortcomings of the six views under consideration may be expressed as follows.

(GI) Physical objects are neither primary-empirical nor mind-independent. They are the direct objects of God's active-creative experience. These are explicitly mind-dependent in nature. They may still be presented to us *in some sense* in perception, since the direct objects of our own perceptual experiences may *resemble* those of God's creative experience, which are the physical objects themselves. For they are both fundamentally the same kind of entity: mind-dependent direct objects of experience. Still, since such mind-dependent entities are mind-specific in the sense that no mind-dependent direct object of one subject's experience is identical to any direct object of a distinct subject's experience, no physical object itself is primary-empirical.

(SR) Physical objects are mind-independent, since their fundamental physical parts are mind-independent; but they are not primary-empirical. For physical objects on this view are not identical to or mereologically composed of the mind-dependent direct objects of acquaintance whose nature constitutes the way things appear in perception. It may be claimed that mind-independent physical objects are nevertheless still *presented* to us in perception, in virtue of their resemblance, in respect of the primary qualities at least, to the mind-dependent direct objects of our perceptual experiences. I argue in ch. 3 below, though, that Berkeley (1975a, 1975b) is absolutely right in his objection to Locke (1975), that this resemblance thesis cannot be sustained in this context. Very crudely, as Berkeley puts it: 'an idea [or *mind-dependent* direct object of experience] can be like nothing but an idea' (1975b, §8). A closely related alternative suggestion would be that mind-independent physical objects are *presented* to us in perception, according to (SR), in spite of their not being primary-empirical, in virtue of the fact that perception acquaints us with the natures of the particular mind-dependent direct object of experience to which such objects are disposed to give rise in subjects like us in the circumstances in question. This is the position into which Berkeley's argument forces Locke as I develop this dialectic in ch. 3. I argue that it is incompatible with the principle that their subjective presentation in perception provides us with a genuine conception of what mind-independent physical objects actually *are*. This principle may be rejected; but I suggest that there are serious costs to doing so.

(HI)/(MTI) Physical objects are primary-empirical, since they are composed of direct objects of human perceptual experience; but physical objects are not mind-independent: they are simply mereological sums of these mind-dependent parts.

(P)/(R) There are no physical objects. Physical object language sentences are analysed in terms of sentences concerning what is primary-empirical, whose truth values are in turn explanatorily grounded in the intrinsically unknowable reality relationally described by the fundamental physics. According to (P), what is primary-empirical may resemble key components of this reality (the direct objects of God's active-creative experience); but the reality is itself mind-dependent. According to (R), this reality is mind-independent; but any claims of its resemblance to anything primary-empirical are, for that very reason, as with (SR), untenable.

In any case, nothing is both primary-empirical and mind-independent. Furthermore, it is a consequence of my anti-Lockean argument in ch. 3 that nothing mind-independent may on any of these views be construed as presented in perception in some less direct way by appeal to the notion of resemblance.

The underlying isomorphism between Berkeleian and modern metaphysical views, and the semantic, rather than ultimately ontological, conception of the variation amongst the views within both of these ranges of options, strongly suggest a diagnosis for this universal failure. All six views insist upon a strict distinction and independence between the explanatory grounds of the actual and counterfactual nature of our perceptual experience of physical objects, on the one hand, and the direct objects of those experiences that provide their most fundamental relational characterization according to the early modern approach, on the other. It is this distinction that I claim constitutes a fundamental obstacle to any adequate defence of empirical realism.

2.4 Conclusion

If my diagnosis is correct, then a crucial necessary condition for sustaining empirical realism is the identification of the explanatory grounds of the actual and counterfactual nature of human perceptual experiences of physical objects with their direct objects, in my sense, namely those objects with which the subject is acquainted in perception and that therefore provide the most fundamental characterization of the nature of the experiences themselves. Thus, the core of empirical realism is the idea that physical objects are the enduring explanatory grounds of the actual and counterfactual nature of our perceptual experiences of those very things, which are also the direct objects of such experiences. They are therefore, I shall argue, both independent of our, or anyone else's, thoughts or experiences of them, and also the very things that are presented to us in our perceptual experience of the world around us. My agenda for the remainder of the book is an extended elaboration, further motivation, and defence of this identification.

3

Indirect Realism

Locke's response to the Inconsistent Triad identified in ch. 1 is to reject that

(II) Physical objects are the direct objects of perception.

Although it is quite difficult to articulate the resultant view precisely, this leads to what is historically perhaps the most familiar realist strategy.

Accordingly, there are supposed to be persisting *mind-independent* physical objects such as stones, tables, trees, and animals. This registers commitment to the first claim of the Inconsistent Triad.

(I) Physical objects are mind-independent.

The nature of perceptual experience is to be elucidated by reference to certain *direct objects* that are set before the mind in such experience. Thus, the most fundamental characterization of any specific perceptual experience is to be given by citing, and/or describing, specific such entities. The experience in question is one of acquaintance with just those things, which identify it as the specific modification of consciousness that it is. In line with claim (III) of the Inconsistent Triad, such direct objects of experience are bound to be *mind-dependent* things that are therefore distinct from mind-independent physical objects. Still, we see and otherwise consciously perceive physical objects themselves. They are in this quite uncontroversial and theoretically neutral sense *presented* to us in perception. Our experiential relation with them is therefore *indirect*. It obtains in virtue of a direct conscious acquaintance with certain mind-dependent objects, along with the fact that the mind-independent physical objects in question are appropriately related to these mind-dependent direct objects of perception. I follow standard usage in referring to this strategy as *indirect realism*.

3.1 Preliminary concerns

A standard preliminary worry about indirect realism is epistemological. If the nature of perceptual experience is constituted by the subject's acquaintance with mind-dependent direct objects distinct from mind-independent physical objects, then how is such experience supposed to constitute a source of knowledge about the presence and nature of any such physical objects themselves? The only resource available to the indirect realist in response is to cite the relation between direct and indirect objects in virtue of which a person's experiential encounter with the former purportedly constitutes her perception of the latter. This is generally supposed to have two aspects: causation and resemblance. Mind-independent physical objects of certain specific kinds and qualities are the *normal causes* of a person's acquaintance with *appropriately resembling* mind-dependent objects. When this normal explanation obtains, then she (indirectly) perceives the physical object in question.

The objection is thus: the fact that this normal causal explanation actually does obtain in any particular case makes no difference whatsoever to the nature of the subject's experience. For her acquaintance with just such a mind-dependent direct object is supposed to be the common element between veridical perception and appropriate illusion and hallucination. This is the primary motivation for the indirect realist's endorsement of (III), to accommodate the subjective similarities between veridical perception and appropriate illusion and hallucination. So the subject cannot know in any particular case that the relevant relation between direct and indirect objects of perception does indeed obtain. For all she knows in any particular case, then, she might be subject to illusion or hallucination. Thus, she can never know such things as that there actually is a mind-independent physical object of any specific kind or quality before her.

As things currently stand, this purely epistemological objection is quite inconclusive, and I myself see little hope of any fatal blow to indirect realism on these grounds alone. For two broad lines of reply are forthcoming, and appear capable of unlimited revision under pressure.

The more ambitious reply contends that a person can know, either by inference to the best explanation or by some kind of transcendental argument, that appropriately resembling mind-independent physical objects provide the *normal* causal explanation of her direct perceptual encounter with certain mind-dependent objects; and that this is sufficient for her experience on any particular occasion on which this is the actual explanation to constitute a source of knowledge about the physical objects in question.[1]

The more cautious reply contends that such knowledge of normal causes is entirely unnecessary. All that is required if indirect perception along these lines is to constitute a source of knowledge about the physical world is that it be de facto true that appropriately resembling mind-independent physical objects provide the normal causal explanation of perceivers' direct experiential acquaintance with certain mind-dependent objects, which in turn prompts relatively reliable beliefs about the physical world around them. People need not be epistemologists of their own situation in order for their perceptual experience to provide them with knowledge of the physical world.[2]

As it turns out, both of these replies *may* be combined with the claim that a person is, after all, in a position to know, even on a particular occasion on which this is the case, that she is in fact perceiving the world around her, and not subject to illusion or hallucination. For if it really is correct on either ground to insist that indirect perception is a source of specific knowledge of the physical world, then subjects in any such case may infer from such knowledge, of the fact that there is a mind-independent physical object of such and such kind or quality before them, say, that they are therefore not subject to illusion or hallucination on that score. Thus, the initial objection is mistaken, not only in its conclusion that indirect realism is incompatible with perceptual knowledge of the physical world, but also in claiming that, on any particular occasion, for all the subject knows, she might be subject to illusion or hallucination.[3]

---

[1] See Alston (1993) and Brewer (1999: §4.2) for outlines of both these strategies for securing our knowledge that appropriately resembling mind-independent physical objects are the *normal* cause of our perceptual acquaintance with certain mind-dependent objects, and also of some of their major problems. It is unnecessary to get into these details in the current context.

[2] This basic *reliabilist* idea is extremely popular in current epistemology. Nozick (1981: ch. 3) is a very influential source, although there are antecedents in Goldman (1967), Armstrong (1973), Ramsey (1990a), and others. For more recent critical discussion and defence, see Foley (1985), Sosa (1991, 2007), Plantinga (1993), Conee and Feldman (1998), Brewer (1999: §4.1), Vogel (2000), Kvanvig (2003), and Goldman and Olsson (2008).

[3] I believe that these replies on behalf of the indirect realist are ultimately unsatisfactory; but I am inclined to make the fundamental objection on the grounds set out below rather than on a purely epistemological basis.

The situation here has all the familiar hallmarks of a philosophical stand-off. One side claims that indirect realism condemns perceivers to a position in which they can never knowledgeably rule out the possibility that they are subject to illusion or hallucination. It goes on to claim that indirect realism is therefore incompatible with the status of perception as a source of specific knowledge about the mind-independent physical world. The other side insists that indirect realism is perfectly compatible with the status of perception as a source of specific knowledge about the physical world. For opponents place excessive conditions on what is to count as an adequate source of such knowledge. It goes on to claim that indirect realism therefore places reflective perceivers in a position in which they can after all know in particular cases that they are not subject to illusion or hallucination. Given the availability of these alternatives, and their elaborate and varied development in the literature, there is little hope of a conclusive refutation of indirect realism on purely epistemological grounds.

A more fundamental objection to indirect realism concerns its compatibility with the very idea of empirical content, with our capacity to grasp thoughts at all that are genuinely about the mind-independent world around us (McDowell, 1982, 1986; Child, 1994: ch. 5; Brewer, 1999: ch. 3).[4] According to this line of objection, thought determinately about *F*s depends upon either direct cognitive contact with *F*s or the construction of a way of thinking of *F*s from concepts of kinds of thing that one has (had) direct cognitive contact with. The notion of *direct cognitive contact* clearly requires elucidation, in the light of which this first premiss of the objection is equally clearly in need of extended motivation and defence. My own critical discussion of indirect realism to follow avoids the need to take a stand on these issues, though; and my point in mentioning the current line of objection is to lead us into that discussion. So it is sufficient for present purposes to think of 'direct cognitive contact' as a placeholder for the mental relations grounding the possibility of demonstrative thought about *F*s, where I take it that the natural assumption would be that these include at least certain relations involved in perception and also in testimony.

This apparently offers the indirect realist two alternatives. First, it may be said that the direct cognitive contact essential for thought about *F*s

---

[4] I draw heavily on Child's (1994: 147–8) presentation of the objection in what follows.

requires acquaintance with *F*s themselves. In that case the indirect realist denies that we have direct cognitive contact with mind-independent physical objects. So it must be shown how we may construct a way of thinking of such things from concepts simply of the mind-dependent direct objects of our perceptual experience according to the indirect realist account. The obvious proposal is that we may think of mind-independent *G*s, for example, descriptively, as the kinds of thing normally perceptually presented in experiences with *F*-type direct objects. Second, it may be said that perceptual presentation of mind-independent physical objects as the indirect realist conceives of this itself constitutes direct cognitive contact of the kind required by the current argument for thought about them. Thus, indirect perception of mind-independent physical *G*s itself grounds the possibility of demonstrative thought about them, without any need for our reflective descriptive conception of such things *as* the indirect objects of perceptions with such and such mind-dependent direct objects.

Both of these alternatives sound quite plausible on the perfectly natural assumption that the presentation to us of stones, tables, trees, animals, and so on, in perception, however exactly this is to be elucidated, provides us with a conception of what such mind-independent physical objects are, at least a very rough and provisional conception of them as something like persisting, unified, extended space occupants. Without this assumption, though, neither seems to me defensible. For, in that case, the second option clearly fails to meet what is surely a necessary condition on our possession of concepts of mind-independent physical objects, namely that we do indeed grasp at least roughly and provisionally what such objects are.[5] This, I take it, is the whole point of the requirement for direct cognitive contact with such things as it figures in the first premise of the objection under consideration. The current variant of indirect realism asserts that this is indeed provided by perceptual presentation itself, yet, if the assumption above is unwarranted, then this is precisely what is denied. Similarly, without the assumption that perceptual presentation provides us with a conception of what mind-independent physical objects

---

[5] There are of course philosophers who reject such conditions upon concept possession altogether, and the *cognitive* contact requirement intended to meet them too, although they may insist upon various causal conditions. See e.g. Mill (1867), Kripke (1980), Salmon (1986), Fodor (1987, 1998), and Kaplan (1989). I offer below a more direct objection to indirect realism that is not bound by any such thought-theoretic commitments.

are, the recipe offered by the first option above for the construction of a descriptive way of thinking about such things on the basis of our more basic thought about the mind-dependent direct objects of perception is equally ineffectual. The proposal is that we think of certain mind-independent physical objects as the kinds of thing normally perceptually presented in experiences with F-type direct objects, say. Yet, absent the assumption in question, this actually gives us no idea whatsoever of what such things are. The crux of the current line of objection to indirect realism is therefore the contention that its own elucidation of perceptual presentation is entirely incapable of sustaining the assumption that such presentation provides us with at least a provisional conception of what mind-independent physical objects are.

Indeed, if the present objection succeeds on that basis, then on plausible further assumptions a more straightforward challenge may be made to the indirect realist strategy of rejecting (II) as elucidated above. For it is a plausible necessary condition upon *any* satisfactory account of perceptual presentation that this provides us with an initial conception at least of what mind-independent physical objects *are*. It is a necessary condition on any relation between us and the physical objects around us being genuinely one of *perceptual presentation*—however directly or indirectly this is ultimately philosophically to be elucidated—that it provides us with some conception of what such physical objects are. Perception of physical objects displays their nature, not in the sense that we may read a complete correct metaphysics of the physical world off our perceptual experience; but this must at least fix for us the domain that is the concern of such metaphysics. We must have a provisional conception of what mind-independent physical objects are. In that case, the crux of the current thought-theoretic objection constitutes a more straightforward challenge to indirect realism as a theory of our perceptual experiential relation with such things. So I focus the remaining discussion directly upon the key question of whether the indirect realist account of perceptual presentation is compatible with the claim that this provides us with such a conception of what mind-independent physical objects are.

If, as I argue, it is not, then there are a number of possible responses. I myself propose that we conclude immediately that indirect realism should therefore be rejected. For I contend that any adequate account of perceptual presentation must indeed provide us as subjects of perception with at least a provisional conception of what physical objects are. I also argued above that this is a necessary condition upon any satisfactory account of the role of perceptual experience in yielding a form of cognitive contact with its objects that plausibly grounds the possibility of our thought about those very things. Of course it is open for others simply to reject this idea that perceptual presentation provides us with a genuine conception of what physical objects are altogether. Some philosophers explicitly do so.[6] I cannot respond conclusively to all the issues raised here. Instead I offer a more explicit and nuanced statement of what I do and do not take for granted throughout my discussion, and of why I do so.

First, I claim that the basic idea that perceptual experience of physical objects provides us with a provisional conception of what such things are has powerful pre-theoretical intuitive force. This claim itself needs some unpacking. One debate in the area is between what might be called *empiricism* and *innatism* about physical object concepts. Both parties agree that we conceive of physical objects as persisting, unified, extended space occupants. The empiricist holds that this conception must, like all our genuine concepts of anything, be derived in some way from experience. The innatist, on the other hand, holds that we are hardwired from birth, and certainly independently of any of our perceptual experience, to think about the physical world in terms of persisting, unified, extended space occupants, perhaps as a result of natural selection. My claim is not that the empiricist side of this philosophical debate is more intuitive in advance of any relevant theoretical consideration. It is rather that we have a pre-theoretical grasp of what kind of phenomenon *perceiving* something is. Of course this is subject to revision in the light of evidence and argument; but I claim that we at least start with the idea that something that we *perceive* is something whose nature is *thereby* at least to some extent evident to us: we have at least a rough initial conception of what kind of thing it is.[7] As we will see, the indirect realist is explicitly driven by this idea, in the insistence that indirect perception at least displays physical objects as they

---

[6] Here I have in mind specifically Langton (1998) and Lewis (2009).

[7] I grant entirely that this claim is more immediately compelling in connection with sight and touch; but I would also insist that the nature of *our own* experience in the other modalities is heavily dependent upon their integration with sight and touch. What conception of the physical world, if any, might be available to imaginary perceivers entirely lacking in sight and touch is certainly an interesting question. It is nevertheless one that I do not address here. See Strawson (1959: esp. ch. 2; 1980) and Evans (1980) for seminal discussion in connection with hearing that also engages with the question to what extent the objectivity of our conception of the physical world is dependent upon its spatiality.

are in respect of their primary qualities. My objection is that he fails in precisely this regard. The attempt is revealing though, and supports my contention that an intuitive starting point in the area is the idea that perceptual presentation provides us with a provisional conception at least of what physical objects are.[8]

Second, there is a perspective from which this idea that perceptual presentation provides us with at least our initial starting conception of what physical objects are really is non-negotiable. For it plays an absolutely fundamental role in setting the *domain* for the whole debate about realism. The question that we are interested in as perceivers of the physical world of stones, tables, trees, and animals around us, and, indeed, as philosophical theorists who are also perceivers of such things, is what the metaphysical status is of *those very things*: the very things *of which we have our initial conception precisely through such perception*. Arriving at the conclusion that some quite distinct domain of entities may be truly mind-independent, for example, is of little or no significance to us. The constraint here is not simply that the metaphysical debate should concern those things that we perceive, *whatever* 'perceiving' may be said to be. It is rather that our metaphysical attention is focused from the outset precisely upon the things with which perception makes us familiar, of whose basic nature we are provided with at least a provisional conception directly on the basis of our perceptual experience of them: the very physical objects, as we might say, that we all know and love.

Third, my own positive position developed in chs. 5–7 succeeds in my view in *explaining* how perception does indeed provide us with a conception of what mind-independent physical objects are in this sense. So I reject any suggestion that, regardless of its intuitive pre-theoretical appeal, it is simply not possible to accommodate this basic idea in any developed philosophical theory of the nature of our perceptual relation with such things. This *is* impossible, in my view, given the third claim (III),

---

[8] Notice that this intuitive conception of perception as revelatory to some extent of the nature of its objects is not *independent* of the empiricism/innatism debate concerning the source of our physical object concepts. For if the intuitive conception of perception is vindicated, and perceptual presentation does indeed provide us with a provisional conception of what physical objects are, then there will be correspondingly less *need* for any appeal to innate endowment in explanation of the evident fact that we *think* of physical objects as persisting, unified, extended space occupants. See Ayers (1993: i) for development of this kind of argument in Locke against the *need* for innate concepts and knowledge.

from my opening Inconsistent Triad. That is effectively my conclusion from chs. 2 and 3 taken together. Chapter 4 presents the familiar orthodox alternative to (III) and finds this also wanting. Chapters 5–7 develop and defend my own alternative rejection of (III) that I believe avoids all these objections and vindicates the initial intuitive idea that perceptual presentation provides us with a provisional conception of what mind-independent physical objects are.

Fourth, and relatedly, there are also more specific philosophical arguments aimed directly against this starting point. In particular, there is Lewis's argument for (HT) set out in ch. 2 above (Lewis, 2009) and Langton's Kantian argument (Langton, 1998) for a similar humility thesis that she regards as an elucidation of Kant's claim that we are irremediably ignorant of the nature of 'things-in-themselves' (Kant, 1929). I explain in ch. 7 how I think that these arguments should be resisted. Very briefly, against Lewis I claim that my own account of perception explains how it is that we are in a position to know some at least of the relatively intrinsic properties of physical objects that play an ineliminable active role in the workings of the world directly on the basis of perception. This contradicts his premiss that none of the intrinsic properties that play an active role in the actual working of the physical world are named in O-language, 'except as occupants of roles' (Lewis, 2009: 206). Similarly against Langton's Kant I argue that the *receptivity* involved in our perceptual relation with mind-independent physical objects is perfectly compatible with all that is required for our knowledge of their intrinsic nature on the basis of our perception of them.

In the light of all of this, for present purposes and in what follows, I take for granted the basic idea that the presentation to us in perception of mind-independent physical objects, whatever exactly this may involve, at least provides us with a provisional conception of what such objects *are*.

3.2 The objection

On the assumption that any adequate account of perceptual presentation must indeed provide us with a provisional conception at least of what physical objects are, then, the key question is whether the indirect realist construal of perceptual presentation is capable of providing such a conception.

To make proper progress with this question we first need an explicit elucidation of the core indirect realist idea that the direct objects of perception are *mind-dependent* entities that are therefore distinct from the *mind-independent* physical objects that are nevertheless presented to us in such experiences. This is certainly not straightforward; but I begin with a relatively familiar conception of the distinction between primary and secondary qualities, for example between the shapes and colours of physical objects respectively (Locke, 1975). The approach that seems to me both faithful to the key historical arguments in the area and is in any case most useful for my purposes here characterizes this as a distinction between the relations that the relevant properties of physical objects bear to the perceptual appearances to which they may give rise in the two cases. I call this the *standard account*.[9]

Thus, the most basic distinctions concerning secondary qualities are between, say, red-type and green-type *appearances*, and the rest, conceived quite independently of the question of what their worldly correlates, if any, may be. The characterization of such appearances is prior to, and independent of, any characterization of the worldly properties that may in some way be presented or indicated by them. Having given such a characterization, of red-type appearances, say, we may then define a property—*redness*—which applies to mind-independent objects, as that of being disposed to produce those kinds of appearances—red-type ones—or, alternatively, as the property of having whatever underlying physical constitution happens in the actual world to ground that disposition.

In contrast, the most basic distinctions concerning the primary qualities are those between, say, squareness and circularity, and the rest, *as properties of mind-independent things themselves*, conceived quite independently of the question of what appearances, if any, they might produce. Having first identified which property squareness is, we can then identify square-type appearances as those that present something as having *that property*—squareness. So, the relevant appearances are to be characterized only by appeal to a prior, and independent, characterization of the worldly properties that they may present.

Generalizing this basic idea, in line with my opening characterization of mind-independence and mind-dependence set out in ch. 1,

---

[9] I should say that I do not myself endorse the following characterization of secondary qualities and our perceptions of them. See Campbell (1993) for an alternative that I prefer.

then, I propose that the *mind-independence* of the objects that we perceive consists in the individuative priority of their nature over the various appearances that show up in our perception of them. Correlatively, the *mind-dependence* of the indirect realist's direct objects of perceptual experience consists in their individuation and characterization prior to and entirely independently of the natures of any mind-independent physical objects that experiences with such direct objects may indirectly present to us. Their natures are in this way at least to some extent dependent precisely upon their appearance in those experiences. Such mind-dependent direct objects have natures that are therefore quite silent on the question of what any mind-independent objects may be that experiences with those direct objects somehow supposedly present to us.

On the assumption that there are mind-independent physical objects such as stones, tables, trees, and animals, the indirect realist may then go on to identify specific such things as the indirect objects of perception: the mind-independent causes of experiences with such and such kinds of mind-dependent direct objects. Thus, an experience with mind-dependent direct object d constitutes a perceptual presentation of mind-independent physical object p, very crudely, provided that it is caused by p, where this is of the kind P that normally causes experiences with direct objects of the same kind, D, as d. The central question to be considered in the remainder of the present chapter is whether this approach is really compatible with the claim that perceptual presentation provides us with a conception of what mind-independent physical objects are. I will argue that it is not.

Before proceeding with that main argument, though, it may be helpful to clarify some issues concerning my characterization of mind-independence and mind-dependence.

First, whatever the merits may be of my elucidation of the familiar distinction between primary and secondary *qualities*, it is surely a further question how the distinction between mind-independence and mind-dependence is to be construed in connection with various *objects*. I agree that this is a further question but defend my generalization of the distinction with the insistence that the objects in question are precisely those whose natures are to be construed in terms of the very properties to which the initial distinction applies. The mind-(in)dependence of the various objects of perception that I claim is of interest to us, or at least is of focal interest to me here, is on this account the mind-(in)dependence of their nature that provides the most fundamental answer to the question of what such things are.[10]

Second, the concepts of mind-independence and mind-dependence in question here are in my view specific concepts that apply in a specific context. There may well be other equally legitimate concepts of mind-independence and mind-dependence that are appropriate to consider in other contexts. Here our concern is with the mind-(in)dependence of the objects of *perception*—direct and indirect in the case of indirect realism where such a distinction is applicable; but objects of perception throughout. These objects *appear* to us in various ways in our perception of them. Our fundamental question as I understand it is whether their nature is entirely independent of those appearances or whether it is in part in some way constituted by them. Thus, regardless of the possibility of other legitimate ways to understand these notions, I propose for my own concerns here and throughout to employ the concepts of the mind-independence and mind-dependence of various objects of perception in line with the elucidation given above.[11]

I return now to the crucial question of whether the indirect realist conception of our perceptual experience as acquaintance with mind-dependent direct objects appropriately caused by mind-independent physical objects is really compatible with the claim that perceptual presentation provides us with a genuine conception of what such mind-independent physical objects are. Locke certainly thinks that it is, and the key for him consists in the *resemblance* between our ideas of primary qualities and those qualities in mind-independent physical objects themselves. He famously writes: 'The *Ideas of Primary Qualities* of Bodies, are *Resemblances* of them, and their Patterns do really exist in the Bodies themselves; but the *Ideas, produced* in us *by* these *Secondary Qualities, have no resemblance* of them at all' (Locke, 1975: I. viii. 15). And Michael Ayers (1997: 17–18) develops the point on his behalf: 'What calls for justification . . . is . . . the assumption that ideas of primary qualities are *more* than merely causally correspondent to certain unknown attributes of things. Locke's response is his claim that

---

[10] See ch. 7 below for further details about the mind-independence of the physical objects that we perceive and how this is evident to the subject himself in his perceptual experience of them.

[11] I raise and respond to further questions about these notions in the context of an extended discussion of the way in which the mind-independence of the objects of perception in my view comes to light *from the point of view of the subjects of perception themselves* in ch. 7.

the primary qualities supply our only understanding both of what external objects actually *are* and of what they *do*.' The proposal is that, in virtue of this resemblance, our perception of their primary qualities somehow offers us illumination as to what physical objects are.[12] The difficulty, I argue, is that this depends upon the standard primary quality model of the relation between mind-independent physical objects and the perceptual appearances we have of them, which is inconsistent with the mind-dependence of the indirect realist's direct objects of perception that figure in such appearances. There is a contradiction at the heart of the Lockean indirect realist account of the place of primary qualities in our perceptual relation with physical objects.

Recall the standard account of primary qualities. The most basic distinctions are made between properties of mind-independent objects themselves: squareness is this shape property, and circularity that one, where these are conceived quite independently of any question as to what perceptual appearances such properties may produce in us. Square-type appearances are then individuated as those that present something as having *this shape*—squareness. So the nature of squareness itself is evident from the fundamental nature of our experience of squareness: that experience just is the kind that presents something as having just that shape. Thus, perceptual presentation provides us with a conception of what mind-independent physical squares are. They are extended space occupants shaped like *this*; and similarly for the other properties to which the standard primary quality model applies. Generalizing this basic idea, provided that the natures of the physical objects that we perceive are individuated prior to and independently of the various appearances to which they may give rise in perception, which are to be individuated

---

[12] The source of our knowledge and understanding as theorists of the status of our ideas of primary qualities as revelatory in this way of the natures of physical objects themselves and what they do is a delicate issue in Locke. It is unclear whether this knowledge and understanding is supposed to be derived from a priori philosophical argument and reflection upon the nature of our perceptual experience of mind-independent physical objects or from some kind of deference to the best scientific theories of the day that apparently retain the primary qualities at least in their fundamental characterization of such objects. Descartes of course clearly thought the former (1986: esp. Meditations II and V). Locke's official view may well be the latter; but there is I believe a significant residue of Cartesian rationalism in Locke's thinking in this area that leads to a certain amount of tension throughout the *Essay*. See Ayers (1993) for highly illuminating extended discussion of many aspects of this combination of radical empiricism with elements of rationalism in Locke.

precisely as the presentation of objects *of those kinds*, then such appearances evidently provide us with a conception of what such physical objects are: persisting, unified, extended space occupants, modified with such shapes as *these*, for example.

The core of the current objection is that there is a contradiction between two essential components of the indirect realist's overall position. First, the feature of the standard account of the relation between the individuation of the primary qualities of physical objects and the individuation of the perceptual appearances to which they may give rise that makes it possible to think in the required way of the perceptual presentation of physical objects as the source of our conception of what such mind-independent objects are. Second, the crucial distinction between the mind-dependent direct objects of perception and any mind-independent physical objects that may be supposed somehow to be its indirect objects. Grasp along the lines set out above of what mind-independent physical objects are depends upon the fact that appearances of physical objects on this model make absolutely evident the natures of the physical objects themselves. They do so only because the former appearances are individuated precisely in terms of the latter objects, as presentations of things as *just such things*. This is what the crucial resemblance thesis *means* here, in my view, in so far as such resemblance really is helpful in the way that Locke so clearly intends. Yet the defining feature of indirect realism as I have characterized it is a quite general commitment to precisely the reverse order of individuation that is associated by the standard model with the *secondary* qualities. Mind-dependent direct objects of perception are to be individuated and characterized prior to and entirely independently of any reference whatsoever to the natures of any mind-independent physical objects that experiences with such direct objects may indirectly present to us. Thus, the natures of any mind-independent physical objects that may be identified as the causes of such experiences are absolutely not evident in any way whatsoever from the fundamental nature of those experiences. The fact that physical objects of certain kinds regularly cause experiences with one or another kind of mind-dependent direct object does nothing to explain how, on any particular occasion on which this is the case, the subject might be supposed to grasp what on earth such mind-independent objects are. Indirect realism is therefore incompatible with any appeal to resemblance along the lines set out above in explanation of how perceptual presentation provides us with even a rough provisional conception of what mind-independent physical objects are.

Two lines of responses deserve immediate consideration.

First, the standard model of the *distinction* between primary and secondary qualities surely offers an obvious solution for the indirect realist. According to this proposal, the order of individuation from appearances to objects in connection with *secondary* qualities captures the mind dependence of the direct objects of perception; and the order of individuation from objects to appearances in connection with *primary* qualities provides the necessary resemblance to sustain the idea that perceptual presentation provides us with a conception of what mind-independent physical objects are. This is indeed an orthodox reading of Locke's (1975) own version of the view.[13] It is in my view simply inconsistent though, in ways that are fundamental to his whole metaphysical and epistemological system.

The indirect realist is committed to the early modern relational approach to perceptual consciousness elucidated in ch. 1. Accordingly, the most fundamental characterization of any specific perceptual experience is to be given by citing, and/or describing, specific direct objects that we are acquainted with in perception. The identity and nature of such direct objects characterize what it is for the subject to be in just that conscious experiential state. Thus, the question of the order of individuative priority between appearances and physical objects is a question of whether, on the one hand, the direct objects of perception are to be characterized prior to and entirely independently of any reference to the natures of any mind-independent objects that may be related to them, or, on the other hand, those very direct objects are essentially to be characterized only in terms of the natures of mind-independent physical objects themselves. To say, as the indirect realist definitively does, that the direct objects of perception are mind-dependent is to say that those objects are to be characterized as the specific subjective phenomena that they are without any reference to the nature of anything that may or may not exist in the mind-independent world. To insist simultaneously that the direct objects of perception are to be characterized in terms of the primary qualities of mind-independent physical objects in order to maintain the relevant resemblance thesis is simply inconsistent.

---

[13] See also Baldwin (1992).

What the indirect realist really needs at this point is appeal to something like the Cartesian distinction between the *formal* and *objective* reality of ideas (1986: III). As I understand it, the formal reality of an idea is its nature in itself as the particular modification of consciousness that it is. Its objective reality is its nature as a presentation or representation of a more or less specific (normally non-mental) worldly phenomenon: its nature as an idea *of X*, say. Formally speaking, according to indirect realism, perceptual experience is simply acquaintance with specific mind-dependent direct objects whose nature is to be characterized entirely independently of anything mind-independent. Objectively speaking, our acquaintance with such things nevertheless presents or represents mind-independent objects as being certain specific ways supposedly such as to ground some kind of resemblance between the two. The difficulty brought out by my argument above, though, is that, given the indirect realist's definitive account of the formal reality of perceptual experience as a matter of acquaintance with mind-dependent direct objects, the proposed account of its objective reality is absolutely incompatible with the required resemblance. According to the indirect realist, perception presents a mind-independent object, *o*, as *F*, very roughly, just if it is a case of acquaintance with a mind-dependent direct object of a type that is normally caused by mind-independent *F*s that is on this occasion caused by *o*. The mind-dependence of direct objects consists in the fact that they are typed by their nature—that is, formally—entirely independently of any question of the mind-independent nature of such normal causes. Yet the required resemblance as I have been elucidating it depends essentially upon the characterization of the very nature of perceptual appearances by reference to the specific ways that they present mind-independent physical objects as being.

I can see two very different ways in which the Cartesian distinction has a more promising application in this context. On one, perceptual appearances are characterized *as* mental representations of specific ways a mind-independent world might be: this is the most fundamental way of elucidating which perceptual experience is in question. On the other, perceptual appearances are most fundamentally cases of standing in an essentially experiential relation of acquaintance with specific mind-independent physical objects themselves. Very crudely, these are the Content View (CV) and the Object View (OV) that are the topics of chs. 4 and 5 respectively. Indirect realism as I conceive of it is an explicit rejection of both. It retains the early modern approach of offering direct objects of acquaintance as characteristic of the fundamental nature of perceptual experience, rather than as (CV) representations of ways a mind-independent world might be; and it insists as against (OV) that these direct objects are themselves mind-dependent entities quite distinct from any mind-independent physical objects. Thus, I conclude that the orthodox Lockean version of indirect realism is absolutely untenable notwithstanding its manifest desirability at precisely this point in the dialectic.

The second line of response to my core objection insists that the universal application of the order of individuation from properties of perceptual appearances to properties of physical objects definitive of indirect realism is perfectly compatible with an account of appearance-object resemblance adequate to sustain perceptual presentation as the source of our conception of what mind-independent physical objects are. In order to do so it adopts a generalization of a claim sometimes made on behalf of dispositional theories of secondary qualities.

According to a very crude dispositionalism, physical objects cause certain experiences in us that may be categorized purely on the basis of their subjective type, as red-type, green-type, and so on, quite independently of the question of what their worldly correlates, if any, may be. Colour properties of the physical objects themselves are then defined along the following lines. *Redness* is the property of being disposed to produce red-type experiences in normal subjects in normal circumstances. A question then comes up: in what sense, if at all, are red-type experiences genuinely *appearances that something is red*, given how redness is defined? McDowell (1985b: 112) answers rhetorically on behalf of the dispositionalist: 'what would one expect it to be like to experience something's being such as to look red if not to experience the thing in question (in the right circumstances) as looking precisely red?'. In our terms, the claim is that having red-type experiences just is a matter of things looking red. For being red is being disposed to produce red-type experiences (in the right circumstances) and so looking red could be nothing but having red-type experiences (in the right circumstances).

Indirect realism may be construed as a generalized dispositionalism of this kind. We have perceptual experiences in which we are acquainted with various mind-dependent direct objects whose nature consists simply in being the specific subjective entities that they are, entirely neutral on what their physical causes, if any, may be. Still, physical objects *are* precisely the normal causes of such experiences; and, being subject to those very experiences, we are thereby presented with physical objects *as* whatever normally causes experiences of our acquaintance with such and such mind-dependent direct objects. 'What would one expect it to be like to experience something's being the normal cause of experiences with such and such mind-dependent direct objects if not to have in the right circumstances experiences with precisely those mind-dependent direct objects?' Thus, it may be contended, perceptual presentation does after all provide us with a conception of what mind-independent physical objects are.

My counter to this line of response is simply to deny that the proposed dispositionalist manoeuvre really succeeds at all in meeting the requirement that the perceptual presentation of mind-independent physical objects provides a substantial, if provisional, conception of what such mind-independent objects are. Being in a position to think of physical objects simply as the causes we-know-not-what of such and such mind-dependently characterized perceptual experiences, as the current response suggests, is not yet to know in the relevant sense what mind-independent stones, tables, trees, and animals are. It is far harder to give an explicit characterization of precisely what is required than to assert that something fails to provide it; and I do not offer any precise such characterization here. The guiding intuition, though, is the one that surely moved Locke in his insistence that perception of such objects as bearers of the primary qualities provides us with a conception of what physical objects are and what they (can) do (Locke, 1975: I. viii; Ayers, 1997: 17–18). For present purposes it is sufficient to insist that perceptual presentation should be the source of something along the lines of our commonsense conception of physical objects as persisting, unified, variously extended space occupants: certainly something far more than a conception of them simply as whatever causes these sensations. The key claim is that perceptual presentation provides us with a conception of physical objects, not merely as whatever gives rise to certain experiences in us and the familiar patterns amongst them, but as things evidently constituted more or less thus and so, in virtue of which they explanatorily do so.[14]

---

[14] See ch. 7 for more on the role of physical objects as the perceptually presented explanatory grounds of the order and nature of our perceptual experience.

My counter to the present line of response therefore stands: the dispositionalist manoeuvre simply fails to vindicate this key claim.

I have considered two lines of response to my objection to indirect realism. Neither is in my view successful. The notion of resemblance that underwrites the idea of perceptual presentation as the source of our conception of what mind-independent physical objects are depends upon an order of individuative priority from the natures of such objects themselves to the natures of their perceptual appearances; but the indirect realist's appeal to *mind-dependent* direct objects of perception is committed throughout to the reverse and incompatible order of individuative priority.[15]

The indirect realist may reply at this point that my focus upon a conception of resemblance derived from reflection upon the order of individuation from mind-independent objects to their appearances that is characteristic of the standard model of primary qualities is entirely wrong-headed. A far more straightforward and familiar account is available. Our acquaintance with mind-dependent direct objects in perception provides us with a provisional conception of what mind-independent physical objects are because such direct objects resemble physical objects themselves in the simple sense of sharing their basic properties. The obvious counter to this reply echoes a well-known comment of Berkeley's, when he criticizes Locke's appeal to resemblance by insisting that 'an idea can be like nothing but an idea' (Berkeley, 1975b: §8). Here the point would be that a mind-independent physical object can (in the relevant sense) be like nothing but a mind-independent physical object.

The goal is to explain how perception provides us with a conception of *what* mind-independent physical objects are. The suggestion is that this is accomplished by the direct objects of perception instantiating the very properties characteristic of physical objects themselves, by such direct objects *being* what physical objects are. But this is possible only if the direct objects of perception *are* physical objects, which is inconsistent with the indirect realist's definitive rejection of (II).

Aiming to avoid this contradiction by postulating shared properties between mind-dependent direct objects and mind-independent physical

---

[15] See ch. 7 also for critical discussion of a purportedly 'no-priority' view concerning the individuation of the intrinsic properties of mind-independent physical objects in relation to the various appearances that show up in our perception of them.

objects themselves that are *not* characteristic of the nature of the latter as such clearly fails. For the whole point of the exercise is to explain how such resemblance grounds the fact that perceptual presentation provides us with our crucial conception of what mind-independent physical objects are. A historically significant variant of this failed approach is to invoke higher order, or structural, properties in common between the two kinds of objects. The proposal is that mind-independent physical objects have natures that in turn have certain properties; and the natures of the mind-dependent direct objects of our perception share these higher order properties too. The obvious counter is that if the common higher order structural properties are, as proposed, common to the first order natures of both mind-independent physical objects and the quite distinct mind-dependent direct objects of our perception, then they are neutral between the natures of these two kinds of objects, and indeed much else besides. So they are quite incapable of providing any substantive, even provisional, conception determinately of what mind-independent physical objects are. Thus, once again, the appeal to resemblance as shared properties fails.[16]

It is of course open to the indirect realist to offer another alternative construal of *resemblance* here that is compatible with the position and really does succeed in grounding an account of perceptual presentation that provides us with a substantive provisional conception of what mind-independent physical objects are. Nothing that I know of comes even close to doing so, though.

3.3 Conclusion

I conclude that indirect realism is inconsistent with the claim that perceptual presentation provides us with a conception of what mind-independent physical objects are. On the plausible assumption that any adequate account of perceptual presentation must do so, indirect realism is therefore inadequate as a theory of perception, and hence unsatisfactory as a response to the Inconsistent Triad set out in ch. 1. Even without this plausible assumption, it follows that indirect realism is unable to offer either of the two alternative

---

[16] For the basic idea of structural resemblance in defence of empirical realism, see Russell (1927). For the fundamental objection, see Newman (1928) and Demopoulos and Friedman (1985). There is a great deal more of interest and importance to be said about these ideas; but my discussion may be left here for present purposes.

responses that I set out above to the objection concerning its compatibility with the very idea of empirical content, with our capacity to grasp thoughts at all that are genuinely about the mind-independent world around us. Thus, either way, I contend, indirect realism as I understand it here is untenable.

Furthermore, notice that the indirect realist's attempt to resolve the Inconsistent Triad set out in ch. 1 by rejecting (II) faces precisely the difficulty that I raised against all six of the metaphysical views discussed in ch. 2 in connection with Berkeley's rejection of (I). It fails to sustain the empirical realist thesis that physical objects are both the objects genuinely presented to us in perception, and things that have a nature that is entirely independent of how they do or might appear to anyone. Chs. 5–7 develop in detail my own positive account of how exactly this empirical realism is to be sustained. In ch. 4 that follows I consider what I regard as the orthodox view in philosophy today of how empirical realism is to be maintained. Both current orthodoxy and my own position unsurprisingly involve rejecting (III); but, as always, the devil is in the detail.

4

The Content View

Recall the Inconsistent Triad of claims about the nature of perceptual experience and its objects that I set out in ch. 1.

(I) Physical objects are mind-independent.

(II) Physical objects are the direct objects of perception.

(III) The direct objects of perception are mind-dependent.

Chapters 2 and 3 highlighted difficulties in rejecting (I) and (II) respectively. This leaves what is without doubt the most common strategy today: to reject (III). Chapters 4 and 5 consider two quite different variants of this strategy. The first, which is the subject of the present chapter, is close to current orthodoxy in one form or another; but I argue that it is unsatisfactory. The second, to which I turn in the following chapter, is far less widely acknowledged. Yet it is in my view superior precisely in remaining significantly closer to some of the core insights of the early modern period that in so many ways initiate the debate as I present it in this book. These have been lost in the perfectly reasonable contemporary rush away from Berkeley's and Locke's own responses of rejecting (I) and (II) respectively. The primary purpose of my whole discussion is to elaborate, motivate, and defend this latter view. First, though, I consider the more familiar former variant of the strategy.

The leading idea is that perceptual experience is most fundamentally to be characterized by its *representational content*, roughly, by the way it represents things as being in the world around the perceiver. I call this the *Content View* (CV). This approach has no place for the technical early modern notion of a direct object of experience as I have been using it. According to that early modern idea, perception is most fundamentally to be construed as the subject's acquaintance with specific such direct objects. This is what provides the most basic characterization of which experiential condition is in question. According to (CV), on the other hand, the most fundamental account of our perceptual relation with the physical world is to be given in terms of the complete representational *contents* of perceptual experience rather than in terms of our relation with any kind of *object*. Thus, (CV) rejects (III). For there *are* no direct objects in the early modern sense.[1] Likewise (II) is strictly speaking false according to (CV), although it is absolutely standard to reinstate another sense in which physical objects are nevertheless genuine *objects* of perception. They are the very things that we see, touch, and so on, and not by seeing or touching anything else first either.[2] Correlatively, as we shall see in ch. 5, my own preferred alternative strategy for rejecting (III) certainly must and can provide an account of facts about a person's perceptual relation with the physical world that are expressed in terms of something very like representational content, that a particular object looks thus and so to her, for example. The essential difference is that this *Object View* (OV) insists, whereas (CV) denies, that such facts can only properly be understood on the basis of a more basic acquaintance relation between the subject and the objects of perception themselves very much in keeping with the early modern notion of a *direct object*.[3]

The obvious model of representational content for expounding (CV) is that of a person's *thought* about the world around him, as this is expressed in his linguistic communication with others, and registered by their everyday attitude ascriptions to him. Let us begin, then, with S's thought that *a* is *F*:

---

[1] I assume that it is a necessary condition on the truth of 'The *F*s are *G*' that there be *F*s.

[2] So proponents of (CV) may *say* that mind-independent physical objects are the 'direct objects' of perception according to their view. What they *mean* by this is that the account that they offer of the way in which we are presented with mind-independent physical objects has no need of any direct relation of acquaintance with mind-dependent entities of any kind. This is fine so far as it goes, although later in the present chapter I argue that their attempts to provide an adequate account of perceptual presentation in this context are unsuccessful. My point here is more straightforward. Throughout this book I use the expression 'direct object' to refer to those entities, if any, our direct acquaintance with which constitutes the most fundamental account of the nature of our perceptual experience. According to (CV) there are no such things. For the defining feature of their position is that the nature of perceptual experience is to be given directly in terms of its representational content instead.

[3] Representative proponents of (CV) include Anscombe (1962), Armstrong (1968: ch. 10), Dretske (1981: ch. 6), Searle (1983: ch. 2), Burge (1986), Peacocke (1989, 1992: ch. 3), McDowell (1986, 1994), Harman (1990), Tye (1992, 1995, 2000), and Byrne (2001). Although this is, as I say, close to current orthodoxy, there are other strong voices in opposition. These include Campbell (2002*a*, 2002*b*), Martin (2002), Travis (2004), Gupta (2006*a*, 2006*b*), and Johnston (2006).

a thought about a particular object in his environment, *a*, to the effect that it is *F*. Call this the *initial model* for content, (IM).[4]

The basic objection that I will be mounting over the course of this chapter is that, in assimilating perception to thought in this way, (CV) fails adequately to account for the fundamental *difference* between perception and thought: perception is an *experiential presentation* of the physical world around us that makes an essential contribution to our most basic conception of what mind-independent physical objects are that is in turn crucial to our capacity for any genuine thought about particular such things and to our growing empirical knowledge about them.

Recall to begin with that (CV) holds that the most fundamental account of our perceptual relation with the physical world is to be given in terms of the complete representational *contents* of perceptual experience rather than in terms of our acquaintance relation with any kind of *object*: (CV) gives no role to the early modern notion of a *direct object* that provides the most basic characterization of which experiential condition is in question. So it seems that there are just two directions for the development of (IM) in spelling out any particular variant of the position in such a way as to do justice to the difference between thought and perception.

First, it may be said that, although perception involves the very same *contents* as thought, the *attitude* is in this case different: perception is a matter of *perceiving*, as opposed to thinking, that *a* is *F*. At the present point in the dialectic, and in the absence of any further explication of the difference in attitudes involved, this is quite a weak move. For it consists in little more than a formal acknowledgement that perception is in certain respects like, and in other respects unlike, thought, without any substantive further theoretical illumination of the relevant similarities and differences. One possible strategy for developing the suggestion would be to appeal to the distinctive functional role of the perceptual propositional attitude, on the one hand, as against those of the other cognitive propositional attitudes. Still, the proposal faces an objection of principle when it comes to explaining the role of perception in grounding the possibility of empirical

---

[4] My suggestion is not that (CV) simply identifies perception with thought. Indeed I set out below a number of the dimensions along which its various proponents explain the differences between these two key mental phenomena. It is rather that (IM) provides the canonical context for the introduction of the key technical notion of representational content that plays the fundamental role in the (CV) account of the nature of perceptual experience.

thought. For perceiving that *a* is *F* either presupposes grasp of the content that *a* is *F* or it does not. If it does, then it is difficult to see what *explanatory* role perceiving that *a* is *F* might play in relation to the possibility of thinking that *a* is *F*, at least on the plausible assumption that grasping the content is at least a matter of already being able to think that thought. If perceiving that *a* is *F* does not presuppose grasp of the content that *a* is *F* then it is equally unclear how perceiving that *a* is *F* might be supposed to resolve any difficulty we may have in understanding how it is possible to think that *a* is *F*, since the latter clearly does require grasp of that very content. In the first case, any explanation presupposes what it is supposed to explain. In the second case, no explanation is obviously adequate; for grasp of the content that *a* is *F* is unnecessary for perceiving that *a* is *F*, so perceiving that *a* is *F* is clearly insufficient for grasp of that content.[5] It would be possible at this point to deny that perception has any special role in grounding our capacity for thought about the mind-independent physical world around us, and hence to reject the need for any kind of explanation of this purported role. This is obviously a substantive debate that I cannot resolve here other than by explicitly acknowledging my own commitment to the broadly empiricist idea that perception does play a fundamental role in making empirical thought possible. In any case, without further theoretical structure in the distinction between the attitudes of perceiving and thinking, and in particular without an account of the interaction between the natures of these attitudes and the contents that are 'available' to them, this move is at best a preliminary to further substantive work.

Positions along the second direction for the development of (IM) in giving a substantive (CV) account of our perceptual relation with the physical world focus directly on the *contents* of perception themselves.[6] The basic idea is that *perceptual* contents are distinct from the paradigm contents of *thought* in ways that illuminate and explain the crucial theoretical differences between the two modes of mind involved. Since this is the

---

[5] This objection is a central focus of John Campbell's case against (CV) (2002*a*, 2002*b*: ch. 6); and I read him as deploying it more generally also against variants of the view along my second direction for the development of (IM) that follows. A familiar reply insists that perceiving that *a* is *F* is a matter of being related to a non-conceptual content that plays a crucial necessary but insufficient role in the complete account of grasping the conceptual content that *a* is *F*. See n. 7 below for the notion of non-conceptual content. Peacocke (1992) offers the most developed version of this strategy.

[6] The two strategies may of course also be combined; but I cannot see how this possibility offers any further defence for (CV) against the objections given below.

primary focus of the vast majority of contemporary work in the area, I frame my own discussion below in these terms. Having said that, I believe that my objections to (CV) apply equally to variants along the first direction of development outlined above.

There are a number of dimensions along which differences between perceptual and thought contents may be marked. First, it is often said that, whereas the content of thought is essentially *conceptual*, the content of perception may be *non-conceptual* in nature.[7] Second, it is also remarked that the contents of *perception* are most aptly characterized or expressed in *demonstrative* terms, without invoking specific, more arbitrary, conventional *linguistic* terms and categories; and perhaps that such demonstrative characterization applies both in connection with the singular and the predicational components of the content in question. So, whereas one might *think*, for example, that John is 6 foot tall or that Elly's dress is teal, one might instead and more directly express the content of one's experience when faced with the relevant objects in *perception*, as that that (man) is that tall (indicating or attending to his height) or that that (dress) is coloured thus (similarly indicating or attending to its colour).[8] Third, philosophers sometimes note the *passivity* of perception in comparison with thought. Whereas one has a certain choice or freedom with respect to which contents occur in thought, one is in perception simply 'saddled' with determinate content.[9] Fourth, it is also pointed out that perception has a degree of *belief-independence* not generally present in thought. If I judge that *p*, or indeed, on one fairly standard use of the term, think that *p*, then I believe that *p* and am in that sense *committed* with respect to *p*.

---

[7] Although the precise characterization of this distinction is highly controversial, it has generated a huge literature. For pioneering discussions sympathetic to the idea, see Evans (1982: esp. ch. 6), Cussins (1990), Peacocke (1992: ch. 3), and Crane (1992). Critical discussion may be found in McDowell (1994) and Brewer (1999: ch. 5; 2005). See Heck (2000), Kelly (2001), Peacocke (2001), and Byrne (2005) for non-conceptualist rejoinders.

[8] See McDowell (1994: Lect. III, and Afterword, Part II; 1998: Lect. III) and Brewer (1999: chs. 5 and 6).

[9] Again this point needs handling with great care. One does have a certain amount of control over the content of perception through the direction and focus of one's concerns and attention. On the other hand, although I may choose to think about the distribution of primes as opposed to the Israeli atrocities in Gaza, for example, when I do so I cannot but arrive at the conclusion that there are infinitely many primes when that particular question arises, provided that I attend to the relevant considerations accordingly. Still, many argue that there is a degree of spontaneity or freedom in thought not present in perception. See McDowell (1994: Lectures I and II), Peacocke (2006, 2009), O'Brien (2007, 2009), and Soteriou (2009).

There are cases of perception, in contrast, that suggest that a parallel commitment at least need not hold. When I see the Müller-Lyer illusion, in full knowledge of its status as an illusion, the lines still *look* different in length even though I do not believe that they are different in length. Thus, many conclude that the content of perception is what it is in general quite independently of the subject's beliefs in connection with that content. We may very often go on to believe what we see, but we need not do so.[10]

These various ideas about the distinctive nature of perceptual content may of course also be combined and/or opposed in many ways. I do not myself endorse any of them, although they do all seem to me to be responses to genuine features of perception.[11] I mention them mainly to illustrate the range of theoretical options open to proponents of (CV) and then to set them aside with the comment that I intend my discussion in what follows to be conducted so far as possible at a level of abstraction sufficiently great not to depend upon any of these further commitments of various specific versions of the view.

The plan for the remainder of the chapter is as follows. First, at the start of §4.1, I explain the way in which phenomena of illusion and hallucination provide a primary motivation for (CV) in the current context. Indeed, it is often assumed that *only* a version of (CV) of some kind is equipped adequately to accommodate these undeniable phenomena. Second, in the main body of §4.1, I contend that (CV) accounts of illusion in particular are problematic on their own terms. Third, I argue that these difficulties are due to more fundamental defects in the whole (CV) approach: the inevitable involvement in perceptual contents of both the possibility of falsehood (§4.2) and the generality of predication (§4.3). I complete the picture by arguing in ch. 5 that my own alternative (OV) offers a superior account of illusion and hallucination. So the purported advantages of (CV) are themselves entirely illusory.

There are of course other motivations for (CV). I comment very briefly here on three of these before turning to illusion and hallucination.

First, it is sometimes said that only by thinking of perception in terms of its representational content is it possible adequately to account for the

---

[10] See Evans (1982: 123ff.), McDowell (1994: 60–3), Sellars (1997), Brewer (1999, esp. §5.3.3), and Smith (2001). For dissent, see Stroud (2001).

[11] See my discussion of the Müller-Lyer illusion and ch. 5 for a return to some of the underlying themes here.

epistemological role of perceptual experience in connection with our empirical beliefs; and this point may also be combined with the claim that some such epistemological role is in turn essential to the very possibility of empirical belief about how things are in the mind-independent physical world around us.[12] I explain in ch. 6 that (OV) is well placed simply to take over all that is correct in the positive (CV) account of the epistemological role of perceptual experience in connection with empirical belief; and indeed that it provides the indispensible foundation for that very account.

Second, arguments are given for (CV) from the phenomenon of perceptual *transparency*.[13] The premiss, very roughly, is that in attempting introspectively to scrutinize the nature of our perceptual experience we seem to alight directly upon the mind-independent physical world—at least as it appears to be—rather than any evident constituents or qualities of the experience itself. Hence it is supposed to follow that the nature of perceptual experience is to be given by how things appear in that experience to be in the mind-independent physical world, that is, by its representational content. The transparency premiss is in my view quite compelling, although hardly straightforward to state precisely. Again, though, I claim that (OV) is at least as well placed as (CV) to endorse it. For the whole point of (OV) is to insist that mind-independent physical objects themselves are the direct objects of perceptual experience in my early modern sense. Indeed, it would be fair to say that most proponents of (CV) who appeal to the transparency claim in this way do so themselves precisely in order to motivate their position over some form of *indirect* realism theory along the lines discussed in ch. 3, or perhaps over versions of (CV) that appeal to non-representational *qualia* as well as worldly representational contents in accounting for the nature of perceptual experience.[14] They may or may not assume that their position is the only possible alternative to such views. My point here is just that, regardless of the merits of the argument from transparency in that more limited context, it is not sufficient to motivate (CV) as against (OV).[15]

---

[12] See e.g. McDowell (1994) and Brewer (1999).

[13] See especially Tye (1995, 2000, 2002); and for helpful further discussion of the phenomenon of transparency itself, see Spener (in preparation (*b*)).

[14] For examples of the latter target see Peacocke (1983) and Block (1996, 1998, and 2003).

[15] I return briefly to transparency at the end of ch. 6.

Third, arguments have been appearing recently that purport to establish something quite like (CV) as a direct consequence of the very idea of (visual) perceptual experience of a mind-independent physical world.[16] There are important differences between these arguments and their various proponents explicitly acknowledge that the dialectic is complex. Still, I focus briefly on Schellenberg's (forthcoming) 'Master Argument' in the hope of clarifying further the nature and content of my own opposition to (CV) as I intend it here. In fact I consider only the first half of Schellenberg's Master Argument thus:

P1: If a subject is perceptually related to the world (and not suffering from blindsight etc.), then she is aware of the world.

P2: If a subject is aware of the world, then the world seems a certain way to her.

P3: If the world seems a certain way to her, then she has an experience with content C, where C corresponds to the way the world seems to her.

Conclusion 1: If a subject is perceptually related to the world (and not suffering from blindsight etc.), then she has an experience with content C, where C corresponds to the way the world seems to her.

Even this segment of the argument raises many complex issues of both interpretation and philosophical substance. I offer an interpretation of the argument on which its conclusion is in genuine tension with my own opposition to (CV), although there are others on which this is not obviously the case; and I explain how and why I object to the argument on that interpretation. Thus, I take it that the idea of a person having an experience *with content C*, as this figures in both P3 and Conclusion 1, is the idea of a person having an experience whose most fundamental nature is to be elucidated in terms of some kind of representational content C. Conclusion 1 is therefore very close indeed to the defining thesis of (CV) as articulated in the opening pages of this chapter, that the most fundamental account of our perceptual relation with the physical world is to be given in terms of the representational *contents* of perceptual experience.

---

[16] See especially Byrne (2009), Siegel (2010), and Schellenberg (forthcoming).

I assume an interpretation of what is involved in *being aware of the world* on which P1 is totally unproblematic. In order to focus my opposition as precisely as possible, I also offer an interpretation of P2 on which this is equally unobjectionable by my lights: if a subject is aware of the world, in vision, say, then there are truths of the form '*o* looks *F*' that qualify in a perfectly natural sense to capture how things seem to the subject. In ch. 5 I distinguish two importantly different varieties of such claims; and there is a substantive question about whether any conjunction of such claims deserves to be regarded as *the* way things look. I leave both these issues to one side for present purposes, though, in order to clarify my principle objection, which may now be targeted specifically at P3.

I simply deny that it follows from the fact that there are truths of the form '*o* looks *F*' that apply to a person *S* in virtue of her perceptual relation with *o*, that the most fundamental nature of that perceptual relation itself is to be characterized as having a perceptual experience with the representational content (of some kind) that *o* is *F*. On my interpretation of Schellenberg's Master Argument, this is the transition articulated explicitly by P3. The account of looks offered in ch. 5 proves that P3 is false on this interpretation. For I explain there precisely how various looks claims apply to *S* in virtue of her perceptual relation with the world around her without assuming that the very nature of that perceptual relation is itself to be characterized in terms of any corresponding worldly representational content. The perceptual relation between perceivers and the mind-independent physical objects in the world around them is on that account more basic than any such representational contents and grounds the truth of the looks claims that perfectly reasonably inspire talk of perceptual representation. For now, though, perhaps an analogy may be of some help in illustrating the tenor of my objection. If a mind-independent object *o* exists, then there are certainly (perhaps indefinitely) many true sentences of the form '*o* is *F*', but I would deny that *o*'s existence itself consists in the truth of those sentences or can be fruitfully illuminated by listing the facts that *o* is F_1, *o* is F_2, . . . , *o* is F_i, etc. *O*'s existence is more basic than any such facts and is what grounds the truth of all those sentences. Similarly, if *S* sees a mind-independent physical object *o*, then there are certainly (perhaps indefinitely) many true sentences of the form '*o* looks *F*', but I would similarly deny that *S*'s seeing *o* itself consists in the truth of those sentences or can be fruitfully illuminated by listing the facts that o looks F_1, o looks F_2, . . . , o looks F_i, etc., or the fact that it visually seems to S that o is F_1, o is F_2, . . . , o is F_i, etc. S's seeing o, her perceptual experiential relation with that particular mind-independent physical object is more basic than any such facts and is what grounds the truth of all those sentences as I attempt to explain in ch. 5.[17]

All three of these arguments for (CV) raise major issues that I cannot address fully here, although I do insist that none of them conclusively favours (CV) over (OV).[18] I focus primarily on illusion and hallucination in what follows for the following reason. *Some* version of (CV) may seem to be the only genuine option in the philosophy of perception if it is granted that the early modern conception of perception as conscious acquaintance with objects of some kind is bound to involve the postulation of mind-dependent such direct objects. For mind-dependent objects of experience or sense data of this kind are widely rejected today.[19] As I outlined in ch. 1, the arguments from illusion and hallucination are highly influential in supporting precisely this conviction that the early modern approach to perception is indeed committed to mind-dependent direct objects of experience. My overall aim in this book, though, is to explain how the early modern insight that perception is most fundamentally to be construed as a matter of the subject's conscious acquaintance with certain direct objects of experience is essential to any adequate defence of empirical realism; and I argue in ch. 5 that the identification of such direct objects with mind-independent physical objects themselves is perfectly compatible with the evident existence of illusion and hallucination. The point of the discussion to follow in §§4.1 and 4.2 is to demonstrate, somewhat ironically in this context, that (CV) has its own major difficulties in accounting for illusion that actually lead us back to precisely the early modern idea of perception as a relation of conscious acquaintance with mind-independent physical direct objects.

---

[17] I claim that similar considerations apply equally against related arguments offered by Byrne (2009) and Siegel (2010).

[18] At the same time I also acknowledge that some of the most sophisticated proponents regard the best case for (CV) as more like an inference to the best explanation of a whole range of disparate perceptual phenomena including those briefly discussed above and others besides. See especially Byrne (2001, 2009) and Pautz (2010) for development of this idea.

[19] Although I myself entirely endorse this rejection, it is certainly not universal. See, for example, Jackson (1977), Robinson (1994), Foster (2000), and O'Shaughnessy (2003).

4.1 Illusion, hallucination, and content

In an illusion a physical object, o, looks F, although o is not actually F.[20] Thus, according to (CV), an illusory perceptual experience is one with the false content that o is F. Similarly, in hallucination, it looks just as though there is a Φ-type physical object out there that is F, when there is no such thing at all, or at least no such thing causally responsible in the right way for the experience in question; and (CV) simply characterizes this as a perceptual experience with the false content that ϕ is F, for an appropriate empty name 'ϕ', or with the content that there is a Φ out there that is F.[21] Furthermore, given the arguments from illusion or hallucination as set out in ch. 1, it may seem as though the only alternative to this (CV) approach is to invoke mind-dependent direct objects of experience along the lines of Berkeley and Locke. This presents a choice between rejecting (I) and rejecting (II) from my opening Inconsistent Triad. I argue in chs. 2 and 3 that neither is satisfactory; and this scepticism about the theoretical adequacy of appeals to mind-dependent direct objects of perception is in any case widely shared today. So it can seem very much as though (CV) offers the only possible approach to understanding our perceptual relation with the physical world.

In the present section I express some doubts directly concerning the (CV) account of illusion. In the following two sections I develop more extended objections to (CV) based upon two of the most fundamental characteristics of any appeal to perceptual content: the possibility of falsehood and the generality of predication.

Consider the Müller-Lyer illusion (ML), for example, in which two lines that are actually identical in length are made to look different in length by the addition of misleading hashes. Rejecting any appeal to

---

[20] As noted in ch. 1, there are visual illusions that do not meet this provisional characterization. See also Johnston (2006) and ch. 6 below. The condition may also fail to be sufficient. See ch. 1 n. 8.

[21] In the case of *veridical hallucination*, this quantified content as it stands is true. The Φ out there is not *seen*, though, and the experience remains hallucinatory, since the Φ in question is not causally responsible in the right way for that very experience. Alternatively, following Searle (1983), it may be said that the relevant perceptual contents are causally self-referential: the Φ out there causally responsible (in the right way) for this experience is F. This will be false in cases of 'veridical hallucination'. Hallucination, like illusion, will in that case always involve false perceptual content.

mind-dependent direct objects that actually do differ in length, as we surely must, the proponent of (CV) insists that we describe this as a case in which the lines are falsely *represented* in visual experience as being unequal in length: A is longer than B, say.[22]

My concerns about this account revolve around the question of how exactly the world must be for the (ML)-experience to be veridical. (CV)'s insistence on characterizing perception by its content requires a specific answer to this question. Yet it is far from clear how one is non-arbitrarily supposed to be given, or even what the parameters are for making progress towards such an answer.

To begin with, is the line with inward hashes supposed to be represented as shorter than it actually is; or is the line with outward hashes supposed to be represented as longer than it actually is; or both; and by how much in each case? The most minimal answer here is that the content is simply, *and no more than*, that A is longer than B. This is McDowell's answer.

Suppose I say of two lines that are in fact the same length, that one, say A, is longer than the other, say B. In saying that, I am representing A as longer than B. It does not follow that I am saying that A is longer than it is, or saying that B is shorter than it is, or saying that both of these things are the case. One of those things would have to be so if what I say were true, but I am not saying of any one of them that it is so. A 'by how much?' question does not arise. Just so with an experience that represents one line as longer than the other. (2008a: 201)

It is fine so far as it goes; but this is surely not far enough. The idea, in the terms of (CV), that a normal perception of (ML) simply represents that A is longer than B, without offering any other information whatsoever about the distribution of the two lines in space, whether they are millimetres or miles long, whether they differ in length by very little or by a great deal,

---

[22] A possible (CV) alternative developed by Pautz (2009) is that both lines are truly represented as being of (equal) length, *l*, say; where the sense in which they nevertheless *look* different in length is that the perceiver has a strong inclination to believe that they are different in length. This seems to me quite an implausible approach. For the illusory look remains even for perceivers with no such inclination because they are fully aware of the illusory nature of the diagram. It is true that there may be perceivers with sufficiently unusual perceptual upbringing, as it were, for whom (ML) is not misleading: the lines do not look unequal in length. The current (CV) proposal that such lines are accurately represented as each of length *l* even by perceivers for whom they do misleadingly look unequal in length is absolutely not required to account for this possibility though. See §5.3 below for my own (OV) alternative account.

and so on, strikes me as wildly implausible.[23] For lines that we see before us just do look to be of certain specific lengths at least in standard conditions. Of course there are difficult questions for proponents of (CV) and everyone else about how best to capture the way in which their lengths are given in perception; but simply to deny it seems to me disingenuous. This is precisely a salient difference between saying and seeing. I may *say* that A is longer than B without saying anything at all about how long either A or B is, or by how much, whereas I normally *see* that A is longer than B by seeing the extent of A and the extent of B and noticing the former is greater than the latter by roughly such and such an amount. At least that is how it seems to me; and some such intuition figures as an important part of the motivation for various appeals to non-conceptual content or essentially demonstrative content in (CV) explanations of the distinction between the contents of perception and thought. The idea in both cases is that perceptual experience in general displays a far greater degree of determinacy and fineness of grain than is normally present in thought. McDowell's proposal that, so far as their lengths are concerned, the content of our perceptual experience of (ML) lines represents these merely *determinably* as one longer than the other, without assigning either any determinate length or giving any determinacy to the degree of difference in their lengths, is at odds with this whole way of thinking.

Matters are further complicated when we acknowledge that (CV) appears committed to some kind of conflict within the content of the (ML)-experience itself. For the endpoint of each line certainly looks to me to be exactly where it actually is, at its actual position on the (ML) diagram. (CV) presumably captures this fact with the claim that my perception has as part of its content that there are lines joining the relevant two pairs of endpoints: one joining a to a´ (A) and one joining b to b´ (B). At the same time, (CV) registers the illusory nature of my experience with the claim that it is also part of its representational content that A is longer than B. Such a conjoined content is not straightforwardly *contradictory*, as McDowell (2008a: 201) again points out.[24] For it does not

---

[23] McDowell (2008a: 201) does admit that there will be far more to the content of any actual (ML)-experience than simply that A is longer than B; but the example he gives is of the colours that lines and background are represented as having.

[24] There are those who regard even contradictory perceptual contents as perfectly unproblematic. See Crane (1988, 1992), who gives this as an argument for the non-conceptual nature of perceptual content. If the considerations that I offer below against impossible

follow from the fact that 'I say something that places four points deter-minately where they are in the objective world...and the distance between one pair of points is the same as the distance between the other pair' that 'I say that the distances are the same'. Still, (CV) is thereby committed to regarding the representational content of my (ML)-experi-ence as *impossible*: it cannot possibly be veridical. There is nothing obviously wrong with making or endorsing an impossible claim: 'Hes-perus is distinct from Phosphorus' is plausibly such. It does strike me as unattractive, though, to have to admit that this is what perception is bound to do whenever faced with the (ML) diagram. This would not be analogous to viewing an ambiguous figure, such as the necker cube, with respect to which observers may *switch* between mutually inconsistent aspects. The situation according to (CV) would be rather that (ML) compels us perceptually to represent reality as being a way that it could not possibly be, in a single take, as it were.

Perhaps proponents of (CV) may simply accept this result with equa-nimity. It does seem to be in serious tension, though, with relatively widely accepted views about the relation between conceivability and possibility.[25] Nobody thinks that distinct perceptions, even perceptions of a single subject over a short period of time, need *conjoin* consistently or possibly. But the idea that what we can conceive is a guide to what is possible plausibly rests, at least in connection with the perceptible macro-scopic physical world, on a combination of the following two principles. First, that what we can conceive in connection with the macroscopic physical world is constrained by what we may experience in a single perception: very crudely, perceptual experience provides the raw materials of genuine conception in this domain and also controls the ways in which these may legitimately be employed. Second, that what we may experi-ence in a single perception is at least a guide to what is possible: if we really are able to take something in in a single perception, then this must at least be a *possible* state of the world. Given these two principles, it follows that legitimate conception of this kind will be, as many believe that it is, a guide to what is possible with respect to the perceptible macroscopic physical world.

perceptual contents are sound, then this stronger commitment to the possibility of contradic-tion is also unacceptable. See §5.3 for more on this issue.

[25] See Gendler and Hawthorne (2002) for significant recent contributions to the debate.

This is clearly a major topic, and there are no doubt numerous qualifications and refinements to add; but I confine myself at this stage to two
salient points. First, this line of thought provides a prima facie obstacle to
the (CV) proposal that (ML) and other similar illusions automatically and
unavoidably produce impossible perceptual contents in a single experience. Second, the natural response in connection with (ML) to the idea
that what we may experience in a single perception must at least be a
possible state of the world is surely to distinguish in some way between our
awareness *of the lines themselves*, distributed in space as they are between two
pairs of equidistant points, on the one hand, and their misleading appearance as unequal in length, on the other. This is precisely the approach
taken by my own preferred (OV) in ch. 5. (CV) is restricted to accommodate all that there is to the nature of a single perceptual experience in its
representational content; and, as we have seen, this appears to undermine
the link between conceivability and possibility by being an impossible
content in the case of (ML) and other similar illusions.

A first response at this point on behalf of (CV) would be directly to
question the claim that what we may experience in a single perception is at
least a guide to what is possible. For we are familiar from the drawings of
Escher with numerous perceptions of 'impossible figures'.[26] We must be
careful here, though, about the distinction between the way in which the
lines of the drawing itself are perceptually represented as distributed on the
page, on the one hand, and the way in which a diagram as so represented
might in turn be taken to represent another state of affairs, on the other.
Only the latter and not the former is impossible in Escher cases. Yet the
perceptual representation that is held to be at least a guide to possibility is
the former and not the latter. The difficulty for (CV) is that our experience
of (ML) appears committed to impossibility in the former: in our most
basic representation of the lines of the diagram itself. For these are represented both as extending between two equidistant pairs of points and as
being unequal in length.

It may be replied instead, then, that (CV) is not absolutely committed to
the idea that illusions like (ML) produce impossible perceptual contents in
this way. One such move would be to claim that our perceptual content
conjoins a representation of one line as longer than the other with a

---

[26] See Hofstadter (1979) for many examples and interesting discussion.

placement of their endpoints as lying somewhere in a *region* around their actual position. This conjunction has possible instantiations, in which A is a little longer than it actually is, but with endpoints still within the relevant regions and B is similarly a little shorter than it actually is, for example. This is not true to my own experience of good (ML) diagrams, though. For I at least seem to experience the locations of the endpoints of the lines as closer to their actual positions than is compatible with the extent by which they simultaneously look to be different in length.

Another more promising move would be to insist upon the crucial role of attention in modulating our experience of (ML). Attending to the endpoints, these look to be just where they actually are, within a relatively small margin of error; attending instead to the relative lengths of the lines, these look to be significantly different. So there is no single experiential take in which the proponent of (CV) is committed to an impossible content. As I explain in ch. 5, there is something right in this idea that different, and possibly even incompatible, looks, or appearances, may be produced by shifts in attention to a single unchanging object. The difficulty for proponents of (CV) at this point in the argument, though, is to accommodate the fact that the constancy in length of the two (ML) lines is also absolutely evident in our experience of shifting attention from their endpoints to their relative lengths and back. Thus, the lines that are represented as unequal in length are represented there and then as those that extend between the pairs of end points a–a′ and b–b′, and similarly vice versa: the lines that are represented as extending between endpoints a–a′ and b–b′ are represented there and then as those that are unequal in length. Since this whole combination is not possible, (CV) is indeed committed to impossible overall representational contents. The lesson I draw in my own (OV) is that there is a fundamental level of perceptual experience whose nature is not to be captured in terms of any representational content, but rather in terms of a conscious relation of acquaintance between the subject and the particular mind-independent objects in question. This grounds and explains all the various ways that those things may look. But this is precisely what (CV) cannot admit. For the defining feature of (CV) is commitment to the idea that the most fundamental account of our perceptual relation with the physical world is to be given in terms of the complete representational *contents* of perceptual experience rather than in terms of our relation with any kind of *object*. This is what leads to the problematic endorsement of impossible overall contents in certain cases of illusion.

The attempt on behalf of (CV) to invoke shifts in attention in order to avoid the postulation of impossible contents that are in tension with the role of perception-based imagination in the epistemology of possibility suggests to me at least both the fundamental source of the difficulty for (CV) and the direction in which to pursue a more satisfactory alternative. The proposal was that shifting attention between the locations of the endpoints of the main lines of the (ML) diagram, on the one hand, and their relative lengths, on the other, produces *successive* contents accurately representing the endpoint locations and illusorily representing the relative lengths. The *conjunction* may be impossible, but each on its own is perfectly possible. The latter representation of A as longer than B is simply false: hence the (ML) illusion. My response was that the constant extent of the two main lines is surely evident throughout our experience of the (ML) diagram, even whilst we are attending to their relative lengths and thus misrepresenting one as longer than the other. The only way that (CV) can register the experiential presence of that constant extent is by appeal to a content that represents those lines as extending between the accurately represented endpoints. Thus, the impossible conjunction shows up in a single experiential take. The obvious alternative that I develop at length in ch. 5 is that the evident presence in experience throughout of the unchanging lines is to be captured, not in terms of representational *content* at all, but in terms of a conscious relation of acquaintance between the subject and the mind-independent *object* in question: the (ML) diagram itself. In this way, I contend, the phenomenon of the presentation of mind-independent physical objects in perceptual experience is not a matter of a level of representational content that gets something about the object *right*, and which therefore opens the door to impossible contents in various cases of illusion in which the very same features of the object are according to (CV) also *mis*represented. It is a direct experiential relation between the subject and the particular mind-independent object in question itself, that is the fundamental ground of the possibility of getting anything right or wrong in perception at all. The postulation of impossible contents in some illusions is therefore just a symptom of more fundamental problems at the heart of (CV). I turn now to a more direct discussion of what I take these to be: the possibility of falsehood (§4.2) and the generality of predication (§4.3).

4.2 The possibility of falsehood

According to (CV), the most fundamental account of our perceptual relation with the physical world is to be given in terms of the representational content of perceptual experience. Such contents are determined as true or false by the way things actually are in the world around the perceiver. Various ways in which they may turn out to be false appear well suited to accommodate the evident possibilities of illusion and hallucination. In particular, in the case of illusion, a particular mind-independent physical object *o* looks *F* although it is not actually *F*. Thus, according to (CV), it is *o* that looks *F* because *o* is presented in perception; and this is presumably due to the fact that the content of the perception in question in some way *concerns o*. Yet *o* is not the way that that content represents it as being, namely *F*. This combination is perfectly unproblematic in *thought*; but when the errors become very significant it seems to me to put serious pressure upon the (CV) account of experiential presentation in *perception*. For this involves actually *seeing* or otherwise consciously perceiving *that very object*.

I begin with a toy example to illustrate the point. I can certainly *think*, of a figure that you hide behind a screen, that it is square when actually it is circular; but, if we insist on characterizing my perceptual *experience* as a representation of something as square directly before me, then how can we claim that it is actually a circle that is thereby *perceptually presented*, even if there actually is a circle out there, where I represent a square as being, which is somehow causally relevant to my purported perceptual representation? Crudely, if all that (CV) has to go on in accounting for the phenomenon of perceptual presentation is the representational content of the experience in question, then this central notion of perceptual content seems to come under serious tension from demands that pull in opposite directions. On the one hand, the phenomenology of genuine perceptual presentation surely places certain limits on the nature and extent of any errors involved. On the other hand, the basic notion of false content, which is crucial to the (CV) account of illusion, appears subject to far less demanding, if any, such limits. I now attempt to spell out this line of argument against (CV) in more detail.

We have been agreed from the outset that physical objects are *presented* to us in perception. This is intended to capture the utterly uncontroversial sense in which we *see* and otherwise consciously perceive physical objects without commitment to any specific theoretical elucidation of what such

perceptual presentation consists in. According to (CV), the most fundamental account of our perceptual relation with the physical world is to be
given in terms of the representational content of perceptual experience.
(CV) has no place for any more basic or independent notion of a direct
object of acquaintance in perception. Hence the account of perceptual
presentation must be given entirely in terms of content. Presumably the
basic form of the account is that a mind-independent physical object o is
presented in perception just if the content of the experience in question
concerns o. I use the technical term 'concerns' here in order to remain
neutral on the precise account of this relation to be given. For there are
many different approaches taken to account for presentation along these
lines.[27] One important question is whether the contents of perception are
general or singular. In the former case a range of illustrative accounts
would be as follows. A perceptual content of the form $<\Phi x, Fx>$ *concerns*
o just if o is (a) the unique Φ in some appropriately demarcated domain of
the physical world around the perceiver, or (b) the unique closest approx-
imator in some sense to be specified to a Φ in some appropriately demarcated domain of the physical world around the perceiver, or (c) the Φ in
the relevant region of the physical world that is appropriately involved in
the production of the experience in question, or (d) the closest approx-
imator in some sense to be specified to a Φ in the relevant region of the
physical world that is appropriately involved in the production of the
experience in question, or...[28] In any case, the idea would be that the
content is veridical just if the relevant o is F. In the latter case of singular
perceptual contents the idea would be that a content of the form $<Fa>$
concerns o just if o is the reference of the singular content component 'a',
and once again the content as a whole is veridical just if the relevant o is F.
No doubt there are many other possibilities besides. The basic proposal,
though, is that a physical object o is presented in a perceptual experience
just if its content concerns o.

---

[27]   The literature here is immense. For some of the most important discussions of the way in
which perceptual contents may concern particular mind-independent physical objects, in my
sense, see Grice (1962), Lewis (1980), Dretske (1981), Searle (1983, 1991), Armstrong (1991),
Burge (1991), McDowell (1991), Davies (1992), Owens (1992), and Soteriou (2000).

[28]   There will surely be some causal requirement here. The difference between (a) and (b),
on the one hand, and (c) and (d), on the other, is that the former build this into the content of
Φ itself, whereas the latter do not.

For present purposes, we may characterize a visual illusion as a perceptual experience in which a physical object, o, looks F, although o is not actually F.[29] It is an absolutely essential feature of illusion, as opposed to hallucination, that some object, o, is indeed presented in the illusory experience. Thus, according to (CV), a visual illusion is a perceptual experience with a content that concerns o, and represents it as F although it is not in fact F.

Now, it seems to me that there are limits on the nature and extent of any errors involved in illusion, as opposed to hallucination, due to the fact that this involves genuine perceptual presentation of the object o that illusorily looks F. These are not hard and fast, there may be wildly abnormal circumstances in which the illusions I reject are in fact possible, and I certainly don't propose strict principles governing which are and which are not possible, or even suppose that there are any such general principles. Still, although a pair of lines of equal length about a metre away directly in front of me may look unequal in length, or may look unparallel when they are parallel,[30] those very lines could not normally look like a single perfect circle, or two perfect circles, for example. Similarly, although a rabbit curled up on the chair next to me may look like a cat or a cushion, that very animal could not normally look like the Eiffel Tower. This is due to the fact that genuine perceptual presentation is in general incompatible with extreme error. I suggest that this in turn is a consequence of the fact that, just as perceptual presentation is the source of a rough and provisional conception at least of what physical objects are, it is likewise the source of a rough and provisional conception at least of what the particular presented physical objects in question are. This explanatory proposal is not crucial to the argument, though. The datum, I claim, is that there are limits on the nature and extent of any errors involved in illusion, as opposed to hallucination, due to the fact that the former, but not the latter, involves the *presentation* of particular physical objects in perceptual experience. The challenge to (CV) is to account for these limits, given that they are not obviously entailed by the structure of the position so far.

It may be objected right away that any such limits as there may be on the nature and extent of the perceptual errors that are compatible with *illusion*, in which a mind-independent physical object is genuinely presented in

---

[29] See above and ch. 6 for caveats to this provisional characterization.
[30] For a classic illusion involving the latter, see Zöllner (1860).

perception, as opposed to hallucination, in which no such object is presented, are merely contingent upon the nature of the environment and the workings of subjects' perceptual systems. They are not a consequence of the very nature of perceptual presentation itself and so cannot be exploited in arguing in general against (CV) as I propose. In reply I accept that there is a certain degree of contingency in the limits that I contend govern the kind of perceptual error that is compatible with genuine presentation. The range of ways that an object of a given nature may look, for example, certainly depends to an extent upon the peculiarities of the environment and perhaps also upon the match between this and the context in which subjects' perceptual systems evolved. Still, I claim, given a fixed environment and evolutionary context, there are limits beyond which an object fails to be genuinely presented in perception regardless of its causal involvement in the production of a representation with the relevant false content. To anticipate a little, I argue in ch. 5 that the ways that an object looks are a function of its de facto visually relevant similarities, in the circumstances and from the point of view in question, with paradigms of various perceptible kinds. Which similarities are visually relevant may depend upon evolutionary and experiential history; and which such similarities an object actually has in given circumstances from a particular point of view clearly depends upon the relevant environment. Still, as I say, there *are* limits beyond which an object fails to be presented in perception regardless of its role in causing an experience in which there looks to be something thus and so out there. Thus, although variation in the environment or evolutionary context may modify these limits to some extent, some such limits remain in any setting. It is these that I contend (CV) struggles to accommodate. If the objector's claim is that anything may illusorily look any way in any context, then I simply disagree.

So the situation is this. (CV) accounts for the *presentation* of a mind-independent physical object *o* in experience in terms of the fact that the subject's perceptual content *concerns o* in one of the various ways outlined above. The (CV) account of illusion entails that such presentation must be compatible with error in the predicational component of the perceptual content in question. Given a certain environmental and evolutionary setting, there are limits on the nature and extent of such error compatible with genuine presentation, beyond which the subject's experience must be regarded as a hallucination of some kind in which *o* is not subjectively presented at all, regardless of the fact that it may be involved in the causal production of the perceptual representation in question. The challenge for (CV) is adequately to acknowledge, incorporate, and account for such limits. For they are not an obvious consequence of the basic notion of a representational content simply concerning a mind-independent physical object as elucidated so far. I consider general and singular perceptual contents in turn to illustrate the point and the problem for (CV).[31]

On the side of general perceptual contents, there is no restriction whatsoever, so far as I can see, on the nature or extent of any error involved in a content of the form $<\Phi x, Fx>$, unless this is accomplished by stealth, as it were, by Φ already imposing a condition that the object concerned, o, is not sufficiently different from an F to prohibit illusory *presentation* as such. And I can see no reason to expect such stealth always and everywhere to obtain. To give a concrete example, there is no obvious bar, for all that has been said so far, to each of the following contents *concerning* an (ML) diagram: $<$x is directly in front of me (and causing this experience), x consists of two lines, the upper longer than the lower$>$; $<$x is directly in front of me (and causing this experience), x is a perfect circle$>$. Yet the right result here is surely that, although the first may well be an illusory experience in which the (ML) lines look unequal in length, the second is at best a hallucination that may in some way be caused by the presence of the (ML) diagram. Only the former, and not the latter, involves the perceptual presentation of the very (ML) diagram itself before the subject. The generalist proponent of (CV) may mimic this result by revising the account of perceptual presentation along the following lines. A content of the form $<\Phi x, Fx>$ presents o just if it concerns o, as above, *and o is not beyond the pale* in difference from paradigm exemplars of F, given the subject's point

---

[31] An important (CV) response here would be to deny the need for an *explanatory account* of the kind that I am asking for of the limits on the nature and extent of the predicational errors that are compatible with genuine perceptual presentation. According to (CV), presentation depends upon a *degree* of matching between the representational content of perceptual experience and the nature of the objects that cause it; but it is no part of the position that any complete specification may be given of the details of this matching condition. Perhaps there are even reasons for thinking that it is in principle uncodifiable. This is certainly often said to be the case in connection with other structurally similar supervenience claims. Why might it not also be the case here? This protest clearly raises a number of major issues about the point and purpose of the theoretical project here and the basic assumptions on which it is based. The substance of my response is given in §4.3 below in the course of a critical consideration of the proposal that being presented in perception with a particular mind-independent physical object might be a *composite condition*, with an internal experiential matching component, I, and an external environmental-cum-causal component, E.

of view and other relevant circumstances of perception. Of course this would secure the right result, but only by brute force and without any kind of explanation of the limits on the nature and extent of any errors involved in perceptual presentation. The notion of being 'beyond the pale' is simply manufactured to respond to these limits without giving any account of them or why they obtain.

What this suggests to me at least, and what I endorse wholeheartedly in my own (OV) in ch. 5, is that the question of which mind-independent physical objects are presented in perceptual experience is prior to and more fundamental than any question of how those things may look from the relevant point of view and in the circumstances in question. Perceptual presentation is absolutely not to be reduced to or manufactured out of supposedly fundamental perceptual contents of this kind. Given that a particular object is indeed presented in perception, limits on the ways it may look intelligibly follow from its nature and the subject's point of view and various other relevant circumstances of perception.

I turn now to singular perceptual contents, where my conclusion is exactly the same. Once again, there is no restriction whatsoever of the kind we are interested in, so far as I can see, on the nature or extent of any error involved in a content of the form $<Fa>$, at least in so far as this is conceived as the content of thought.[32] Suppose we name the figure on a diagram you have in your pocket that happens to be of the (ML) lines 'Al'. 'Al consists of two lines of unequal length' and 'Al consists of a perfect circle' are perfectly coherent thought contents. You may even present me with two pieces of paper each inscribed with one of the sentences expressing these two contents, and ask me to choose between them. I will be wrong whichever I choose. For the lines are in fact equal in length. Indeed I can see no significant difference between them that is adequate as things stand to account for the fact that only the former is a candidate content for a genuine perceptual illusion that *presents* the (ML) lines in experience. Now, recall the account of perceptual presentation given above for singular contents of this kind: $<Fa>$ presents o just if o is the reference of the singular content component 'a'. So the singularist proponent of (CV) may attempt to

---

[32] Perhaps there are categorical constraints. See Magidor (2009) for very helpful sceptical discussion. In any case, such categorical constraints would clearly not suffice to secure the relevant data concerning perceptual presentation.

replicate the fact that only <a consists of two lines of unequal length> is a candidate content for a genuine illusion presenting the (ML) lines in experience by insisting that the singular components of *perceptual* contents, unlike some thought contents at least, are demonstratives whose successful reference to particular mind-independent physical objects places limits upon the nature and extent of any errors involved. Of course this would secure the right result, but it depends entirely upon the claim that the relevant demonstratives refer only in the absence of errors beyond the limits in question. This seems to me absolutely right; but it is a consequence of two further facts: first, that the relevant demonstratives are *perceptual* demonstratives that refer to the objects presented in perception; and second, that there are limits on the nature and extent of any errors involved in cases of genuine perceptual presentation. Thus, far from explaining the phenomenon in question, of limits on any error in perceptual presentation, this account simply presupposes and recycles it.[33]

Once again then, it seems to me that the presentation of mind-independent physical objects in perception is a more fundamental phenomenon than the specific ways such things may look on any particular occasion, and is not itself to be explained, as (CV) is compelled to explain it, in terms of the representational contents of perceptual experience. The ways physical objects look is a consequence of, and thereby constrained by, the more basic phenomenon of the presentation of particular physical objects in perception. Perceptual presentation provides the ground for the very possibility of particular mind-independent physical objects *looking* any way at all. This is the source of the limits on the nature and extent of any errors involved in genuine perceptual illusion. Hallucination is to be given a quite different account. These are all topics for ch. 5. In §4.3 I discuss a second problematic feature of (CV): the essential generality involved in its commitment to predication at the most fundamental level of our perceptual relation with the physical world.

---

[33] The same point applies equally in response to the related proposal that the genuine presentation of particular mind independent objects is accompanied by the possibility of at least some direct non-inferential knowledge about those very objects. This may indeed entail limits on the nature and extent of the perceptual errors involved, but these are in my view a consequence of more basic such limits integral to perceptual presentation itself along with the fact that the appropriate non-inferential knowledge in turn depends upon such presentation.

4.3   The generality of predication

(CV) characterizes perceptual experience by its *representational content*. In doing so, it retains even at the level of our most basic perceptual encounter with the physical world around us a key feature of (IM), namely, that content admits the possibility of falsity: the world might not actually be the way that a given content *represents* it as being; and the scope for such error may in certain cases be quite drastic. It is often assumed to be a major benefit of (CV) that this feature may be put to use in its explanation of perceptual illusion and hallucination. I argued in §4.2 above, though, that this assumption is mistaken, and that the possibility of falsity at the most fundamental level of our perceptual relation with the physical world is a net cost, not a benefit, to (CV): it stands in the way of an adequate account of the genuine presentation of physical objects in perception and illusion, as against hallucination.

The current section proceeds as follows. First, I explain the way in which (CV) is committed to a certain *generality* in its most fundamental account of our perceptual relation with the physical world. Second, I argue that this generality is in tension with the datum that particular mind-independent physical objects themselves are presented to us in perception.

According to (CV), the most fundamental material for understanding our perceptual relation with the physical world comes from the worldly representational content of perceptual experience: the way such experience represents things as being in the world around the subject. The generality of the predication involved in perceptual content is most obvious in connection with (IM): the thought content that *a* is *F*. Here a particular object, *a*, is thought to be *a specific general way*, *F*, that such objects may be, and that infinitely many qualitatively distinct possible objects are. '*F*' is associated with a specific general condition; and the particular object, *a*, is thought to meet that very condition. I claim that this generality of predication that is explicitly present in the simple thought content that constitutes (IM) is essential to the truth-evaluability of content in general, which provides the key motivation for the (CV) account of illusion and hallucination. The 'particulars' involved need not necessarily be persisting material objects, or, indeed, 'objects' of any kind. Even the most abstract formulation of a truth-evaluable content as that things (or the relevant realm of reality) are (is) thus and so (as opposed to some other way), displays the particular/general combination.[34] Thus, I claim that the representation of some item or items as being some more or less specific general way is a crucial characteristic of the contents that are fundamental to (CV). Furthermore, the key feature of such contents for my purposes is the generality of their predicational component: this places a demand upon items of the relevant kind that may be satisfied *equally* by a whole range of numerically and qualitatively distinct individuals of that kind. Of course, if 'x is F' is the predicate in question, then there is *a* way in which the items meeting the associated demand may not qualitatively differ, namely in all being F; but there are (possibly indefinitely) many other ways in which they may be qualitatively distinct. I claim that this generality of predication, which is crucial to (CV) perceptual contents, precludes an adequate account of the presentation of particular mind-independent physical objects in perception.

Suppose that you see a particular red ball—call it 'Ball'. According to (CV), your perceptual experience of Ball is to be characterized by its representational content. Let us assume that this content makes singular reference to Ball.[35] Your experience therefore represents that Ball is a specific general way, F, that such objects may be. Whichever way this is supposed to be, its identification requires making a determinate specification of one among indefinitely many possible generalizations from Ball itself. Ball has colour, shape, size, weight, age, cost, and so on. So perception must begin by making a selection amongst all of these, according to (CV). Furthermore, and far more importantly for my present purposes, on any given such dimension—colour, or shape, say—the specification in experience of a determinate general way that your perception supposedly represents Ball as being requires further crucial abstraction. Supposing that your experience is veridical, it must be determinate to what extent, and in which ways, Ball's actual colour or shape might vary consistent with the truth of the relevant perceptual content. This is really just to highlight the fact that (CV) is committed to the idea that your perceptual experience has

---

[34] Even this very general claim has its opponents. For a helpful and historically informed survey of the debate beginning with Ramsey (1990*b*), see MacBride (2005).

[35] So far as I can see this assumption may be made without loss of generality, since the argument would be unaffected if the content in question were quantificational instead, instantiated in some way by Ball.

specific truth *conditions*, which go beyond anything fixed uniquely by the actual nature of the particular red football—Ball—that you see.

According to (CV), then, perception—even perfectly veridical perception, whatever exactly this may be—does not consist in the simple presentation to a subject of various constituents of the physical world themselves. Instead, it offers a determinate specification of the general ways such constituents are represented as being in experience: ways that other numerically distinct such constituents, *qualitatively distinct from those actually perceived by any arbitrary extent within the given specified ranges*, might equally correctly—that is, truly—be represented as being. Any and all such possible alternatives are entirely on a par in this respect with the object supposedly perceived, so far as the way things are presented in experience according to (CV) is concerned. In regimenting our most fundamental perceptual relation with the physical world by appeal to an abstract act of predicational classification or categorization in this way, (CV) therefore fails to provide any adequate account of the direct perceptual presentation of particular mind-independent physical objects themselves in perceptual experience. For there is no genuine substance to the idea that it is the actual physical objects before her that are *presented* in a person's perception, rather than any of the equally *truth-conducive* alternative possible surrogates. She may supposedly be referring to a privileged such entity *in thought*, but it is hard to see how it is evidently that thing, rather than any other, that is truly presented to her in experience. The generality of the predication that essentially occurs in the complete contents central to the (CV) account of our fundamental perceptual relation with the physical world bars any adequate account of the way in which perception presents particular mind-independent physical objects to us in experience.

An initial reply to this line of objection would be to protest that (CV) is perfectly consistent with the idea that the actual constituents of the mind-independent physical world are presented to us in experience. For the constituents in question are the very properties of physical objects that are ascribed to them by the predicational components of complete perceptual contents.[36] I have two points to make in response. First, this reply as it stands is an explicit admission of the failure of (CV) to account for the fundamental phenomenon that was agreed on all sides from the outset of

---

[36] Thanks to Tim Crane for this suggestion.

the presentation in perceptual experience of particular mind-independent physical *objects*. Second, my own nominalist view is that the general properties of physical objects are not genuine constituents of the mind-independent world itself. Of course physical objects have all the properties that they have; and their having them is in many cases a perfectly mind-independent truth, in no way constituted by whether or not they seem to have them to us or to anyone else. Still, it is a mistake to postulate constituents of reality corresponding to the predicates used in expressing such truths on a par with the objects themselves corresponding to the relevant singular terms and of which the predications in question are truly made.[37] Hence the current reply to my objection in my view threatens even the more general idea that perception involves the experiential presentation of genuine constituents of the mind-independent physical world itself.

A second reply on behalf of (CV) seeks to undermine the particular conception of the generality of predication upon which my objection is based.[38] I claim that this imposes a demand upon the object perceived that might equally be satisfied by any number of numerically and qualitatively distinct alternatives, and that this obstructs a satisfactory account of the sense in which that very object itself is presented in experience: that thing and nothing else is actually seen. Suppose for simplicity of presentation again that the content in question is that a is F, and that a is in fact F. The objection depends upon the fact that 'x is F' may equally be satisfied by a whole range of alternatives to a that differ from a not only numerically but also, and in (indefinitely) many ways, qualitatively too. The reply is that the range of alternatives to a do not differ from a qualitatively at least, since the relevant way that they all are is F: they are all precisely 'the way . . . [that a] visibly is' (McDowell, 2008a: 204). This is just the point I made above, though, that there is indeed one respect in which all and only the objects satisfying 'x is F' may not qualitatively differ: they are F; but this is perfectly consistent with the equally evident fact that there are

---

[37] For an excellent overview of the issues here and very helpful bibliographical references, see Rodriguez-Pereyra (2008). Nominalism is of course a massive issue and I cannot possibly engage with it adequately here. I mention my own commitments for completeness; the dialectical weight at this point is adequately borne by my first response.

[38] This objection is due to McDowell (2008a: §4).

(indefinitely) many other ways in which the items satisfying any such predicate may be qualitatively distinct; and this is all that my objection requires.

A third reply to the current objection to (CV) is that the idea that it is the actual physical objects before her that are *presented* in a person's perception, rather than any of the equally *truth-conducive* alternative possible surrogates, is to be substantiated by the fact that it is those very things, rather than any alternative such surrogates, that play an appropriate role in causing the perceptual experiences in question. I argued in §4.2 above that it is a necessary condition upon the subjective presentation of a particular mind-independent physical object, *o*, in perceptual experience that there should be some degree of match between the way things look in such experience and that very object, *o*, itself, although this must of course also be compatible with the possibility of various kinds of illusion. The current proposal is that this must be supplemented with a *causal* condition according to which *o* itself is suitably implicated in the production of an appropriately matching experiential representation if that very thing is genuinely to be *presented* in perception. This is what it *is* for *o* to be so presented. The result is perhaps the most natural development of the (CV) approach to perception.

An initial counter would be to query whether this is the right kind of response to address the objection raised. The worry was that, according to (CV), perceptual experience itself appears to be subjectively silent on whether *o* itself is determinately presented in experience in the face of the equal claim of a whole range of appropriately matching qualitatively distinct alternatives. The current response simply acknowledges this subjective silence and hopes to make up for it by appeal to the causal history of the actual experience involved. The intuition motivating the objector, though, is that perceptual presentation of a particular mind-independent physical object is precisely a *subjective* matter: it is as central to the way things are experientially for the subject of perception as anything could be that he is presented with a particular object before him. This initial counter is relatively inconclusive as it stands, though. For the whole point of the present (CV) response is explicitly to insist that the phenomenon of perceptual presentation should on reflection be reconstrued as a composite of relatively independent subjective-experiential and causal components. At this stage, then, there is danger of a static stand-off between opponent and proponent of the (CV) approach.

I wish to argue further that the proposed decomposition is in itself seriously problematic. Hence the initial intuition that perceptual presentation is absolutely essential to the intrinsic subjective nature of perceptual experience is absolutely sound and the current objection to (CV) therefore stands. Appeal to the causal role of various mind-independent physical objects in the production of perceptual representations is incapable of saving the core phenomenon of the experiential presentation of particular such things in perception in the context of (CV). The argument is a direct application of a very powerful general strategy to undermine the decomposition or 'factorization' of cognitive phenomena that is due to Timothy Williamson (1998, 2000, forthcoming).

Suppose that being presented in perception with a particular mind-independent physical object, o, a large white cube, say, is a composite condition, with an internal experiential matching component, I, and an external environmental-cum-causal component, E.[39] Thus, being presented with o is equivalent to I&E. Now, on the present version of (CV), a person may certainly be presented with o by having an experience in which there looks to be a large white cube immediately to her right that is caused by o being immediately to her right in ideal viewing conditions. So having an experience caused by o being immediately to one's right in ideal viewing conditions is compatible with I&E and hence with E. Call this environmental-cum-causal condition—having an experience caused by o being immediately to one's right in ideal viewing conditions—E′. Similarly, a person may also be presented with o according to the present version of (CV) by having an experience in which there looks to be a small grey dot a long way off to her left that is caused by o being a long way off to her left in poor lighting conditions. So having an experience in which there looks to be a small grey dot a long way off to one's left is also compatible with I&E and hence with I. Call this internal subjective experiential condition—having an experience in which there looks to be a small grey dot a long way off to one's left—I′. Next, assume that any possible internal experiential condition is compatible with any possible

---

[39] The purported independence of these two components is essential to the argument. In particular, the proposal is that I is the quite general subjective-experiential condition of sufficiently matching o at least to be a candidate, given appropriately cooperating external-cum-causal considerations, to constitute a perceptual presentation of that very object. This is supposed to be a descriptive identification of a purely internal condition, independent of its environmental cause.

environmental-cum-causal condition.[40] It follows that I&I′ is compatible with E&E′. Since this is a condition in which I&E, it is a condition in which o is presented in perception. Yet it is a condition in which a person has an experience in which there looks to be a small grey dot a long way off to her left that is caused by o (a large white cube) being immediately to her right in ideal viewing conditions; and this I claim is *not* compatible with being genuinely subjectively presented with that very cube, o, in experience, even given the acknowledgement above of a certain degree of contingency in the limits upon the nature and extent of the errors in perceptual appearance that are compatible with genuine presentation in experience. It therefore follows that being presented with o itself in perception cannot be decomposed into any pair of logically independent internal, experiential, and environmental-cum-causal components.[41]

Thus, the strategy of giving substance to the idea that it is the actual physical objects before her that are *presented* in a person's perception, rather than any of the equally *truth-conducive* alternative possible surrogates by appeal to the fact that it is those very things, rather than any alternative such surrogates, that play a role in causing the perceptual experiences in question, cannot be sustained. The present objection to (CV) stands. In regimenting our most fundamental perceptual relation with the physical world by appeal to an abstract act of predicational classification or categorization, (CV) fails to provide any adequate account of the direct perceptual presentation of particular mind-independent physical objects themselves in perceptual experience.

However automatic or natural the general classification essentially involved in the perceptual predication central to (CV) may be, it still constitutes an intrusion of conceptual thought about the world presented in perception into the account of our fundamental perceptual relation with the physical world. According to my own positive position (OV) as I develop this in ch. 5, the selective categorization of particular constituents of physical reality enters the picture of a person's relation with the world

---

[40] This assumption may be questioned. It is a very natural assumption to make on the present version of (CV), according to which the phenomenon of being perceptually presented with a particular mind-independent physical object is to be construed as a composite of relatively independent subjective-experiential and causal components. I leave it as an explicit assumption of my argument here against this (CV) proposal.

[41] See Williamson (1998, 2006) for detailed discussion and application of the anti-decomposition strategy also implemented here.

around her only when questions of their various similarities with, and differences from, other such things somehow become salient. This categorization depends upon a more fundamental level of the presentation to her of particular mind-independent physical objects in perceptual experience rather than constituting an essential part of that very perceptual presentation. Perceptual presentation itself constitutes the fundamental ground for the very possibility of any such general classification of the constituents of the physical world that are in this way made available in perceptual experience. This most fundamental perceptual phenomenon is not to be characterized in terms of any kind of predicative generality, as it is according to (CV). It is in itself wholly particular in my view.

Proponents of (CV) may hope to soften the impression that their characterization of perceptual experience by its representational content in this way constitutes a mistaken importation of selective abstraction and categorization into the most fundamental account of our perceptual relation with the physical world, along the following lines. Genuine—that is veridical—perception presents a person with various constituents of the physical world themselves: particular mind-independent physical objects. Still, it must be acknowledged that this always involves less than perfect acuity. There is a determinate range of respects in which those very things might have been different without any relevant difference in the impact made by them upon the subject in question. Thus, her perception is bound to involve a degree of generality. The general way that her experience represents such things as being is precisely the way that would determine the resultant perceptual content as true if and only if the relevant worldly constituents were as they actually are in every respect, or were instead different in any of the specific respects within this range.[42]

---

[42] I think that McDowell's (2008a: §4) objection to this disjunctive formulation rests on a confusion. Of course, if it is already given that my experience represents *a* as *F*, then the second disjunct of a disjunctive statement of its truth conditions is clearly otiose: either *a* is *F* or it is any way that would be indiscriminable from being *F* by the question of whether or not it is *F*. The point of the current proposal on behalf of (CV), though, is supposed to be to motivate, or at least defend, the position by offering an approach to determining truth conditions for perceptual contents, or by providing a constitutive account of what the truth conditions of a given perceptual experience are. The basic idea is that in any case in which a person has a particular object successfully in view, then the predicational component of the content of the relevant experience imposes a determinate demand upon objects in the world in general that they be qualitatively exactly like the particular object in question, or sufficiently similar not to make a relevant difference to the experience along the property dimension in question, such as colour or shape. This fixes the 'band-width', as it were, of

Such hope is in my view misguided. For this proposal faces a number of serious difficulties.[43]

First, and most importantly, it has more than a whiff of circularity. The suggestion is that perceptual experience is to be characterized by its representational content, which is in turn to be identified by a certain procedure that takes as its starting point a worldly situation in which that very content is supposed to be determined as true. That is, the truth conditions definitive of the experiential content in question are to be specified by a kind of generalization from a paradigm instance of its actual truth. Yet how is it supposed to be determined what is to count as such an instance of its truth, for the purposes of generalizing to these truth conditions, in advance of any specification of those very conditions? This proposed procedure for the characterization of perceptual experience cannot even get started unless it has already been completed. It is therefore either useless or unnecessary.

Second, suppose that we have somehow determined that the case before us is one of genuine—that is, veridical—perception, rather than illusion or hallucination; and suppose, further, that we have some way of fixing the actual constituents of the subject's environment that are experientially accessible to her. The proposed specification of the representational content of her experience then proceeds as follows. Its truth conditions are satisfied if and only if things are precisely as they actually are, or they are different in any of the various respects in which they might have been different *without making any relevant difference to their impact upon her*. This immediately raises the question *which differences are relevant*, in the impact made upon the subject. Any change in the worldly constituents in question makes a difference *of some kind*, even if this is only characterized in terms of her relational embedding in a different environment in which that change obtains. *Relevant* changes of the environment, though, are those that transform the world from a condition in which the initial target

---

the perceptual experiential predication along that dimension. As I argue below, the proposal *is* unacceptable, and for reasons along the lines McDowell suggests; but this is not to the benefit of (CV), but entirely to its detriment.

[43] These are not simply technical or empirical issues of detail that may be regarded by proponents of (CV) as either relatively independent of the argument sketched above from imperfect perceptual acuity or pertaining to a challenge that need not be taken on to specify *exactly* what the content of any given perceptual experience is. They are intended rather as objections in principle to the proposed theoretical regimentation of genuine phenomena of imperfect acuity in terms of the generality of perceptual representational content.

content of her perceptual experience is to be regarded as true, to one in which it is to be regarded as false. So the question of which worldly differences are relevant is clearly crucial. I cannot establish here that *no* satisfactory account of what makes such differences relevant can possibly be given. So this line of argument is bound to remain a challenge to the present defence of the way in which (CV) imports generality into the characterization of our most fundamental perceptual relation with the physical world, rather than a conclusive refutation. Still, the following four proposals are clearly problematic.

1. A worldly change is relevant iff it makes an *intrinsic* physical difference to the subject's perceptual system. This is plausibly neither necessary nor sufficient for the world to change its condition from one in which the subject's initial perceptual content is true to one in which it is false, according to (CV). Any trace of that form of externalism in the contents countenanced for perceptual experiences on which these fail to supervene upon a subject's intrinsic physical condition simply consists in the denial of its necessity; and some such externalism is widely endorsed by proponents of (CV) (see e.g. Pettit and McDowell, 1986; Burge, 1986; Peacocke, 1992: ch. 3; and Davies, 1997). On the other hand, the idea that an effect on the intrinsic physical condition of the subject's eyes, say, is sufficient to transform any worldly condition in which a given experiential content is veridical, into one in which it is not, surely individuates perceptual contents far too finely. For we are notoriously capable, from a very early age, of representing crucial environmental constancies, such as shape and colour, *as such*, across variations often far more significant than these; and there is a vast amount of information that is picked up by the visual system, for example in unconscious perceptual priming, that we are not conscious of at the time, but that may be brought to light by appropriate later testing.[44] The required (CV) response that the overall perceptual content changes in some way in *every* such case strikes me as rather desperate.

2. A worldly change is relevant iff it actually makes a difference to the way the subject believes things are out there. Again, this is arguably neither necessary nor sufficient for a worldly change to be relevant in the required sense. If she is suitably preoccupied with the colour of an object before her, for example, variation in its shape, say, to an extent that would render her

---

[44] See Forster and Davis (1984) for representative examples and discussion.

current perceptual representation of this shape false, may nevertheless make no impact whatsoever on her actual beliefs about it. On the other hand, (CV) must presumably allow for the possibility, at least, that a change in the way things are in the world around her makes a difference to the subject's beliefs about the world entirely independently of the way things are actually represented as being *in her experience*. Indeed, proponents of the present version of (CV) have no alternative that I can see but to appeal to this very idea, of worldly changes affecting a person's beliefs otherwise than by influencing the content of her experiential representations, in explanation of the systematic effects of various masked stimuli, for example.[45]

3. A worldly change is relevant iff it actually does make, or might, without modifying its intrinsic physical effects upon the subject, have made, a difference to the way she believes things are out there. Perhaps a possible effect upon the subject's worldly beliefs of this kind is a necessary condition of any worldly change which renders a previously veridical experiential content false, although any such possibility is intuitively causally explanatorily grounded in experiential change rather than constitutively explanatory of it. Still, since the current condition upon the relevance of a world difference is strictly weaker than the previous one that I argued is insufficient, it must be insufficient too: rapidly masked stimuli may actually (hence actually-or-possibly) affect a subject's beliefs about the world without showing up in any way in experience.

4. The nature of this insufficiency suggests a fourth approach that is surely in the vicinity of what (CV) *needs* here, although I shall argue that it is either circular or independently objectionable in the current context for reasons that we have already seen. The proposal is that a worldly change is relevant, in the required sense, iff it makes a difference to the subject's *experience* of the world. This immediately raises the question, though, how such differences in experience are to be characterized. I can see just two possibilities, neither of which is acceptable.

First, they are differences in its representational content. The idea would presumably be something like this. A person has a perceptual experience, and we are presuming for the sake of the argument both that it is veridical

---

[45] These are cases in which very briefly exposed items systematically affect the beliefs of subjects who deny any conscious perception of them. See Breitmayer and Ogmen (2006: esp. ch. 8) for a comprehensive survey and bibliography.

and that we have identified the worldly objects and their features that it concerns. In order to determine its specific representational content, we are to consider the various ways in which these very objects might have been different with respect to such features. The content of the experience will be true in all of those cases in which such variation does not change its content. In other words, in order to carry out this procedure for the determination of perceptual content, we have already to have fixed that very content. So the procedure is clearly unacceptably circular. One might insist in reply to this simple objection of circularity that there are distinct *levels* of content in perception. Thus, 'higher' levels may be determined in the way outlined above by appeal to the various worldly changes that leave the 'lower' levels unaffected. This hierarchy of levels presumably has a lowest member in every case, though, and the objection of circularity applies directly at that level, and therefore applies indirectly throughout. So, again, this first implementation of the idea that worldly changes are relevant in the required sense iff they make a difference to the subject's experience of the world is unacceptable.

Second, the differences in experience, by reference to which the required notion of relevant worldly variation is to be characterized, are differences in its intrinsic character, where this is to be elucidated prior to and independently of any question of its representational content. This is explicitly inconsistent with (CV) as I define it, though. For the whole point of the current proposal is to avoid the circularity of the previous suggestion by appeal to a characterization of perceptual experience more fundamental than its representational content, and on the basis of which such content may be understood. Yet the definitive commitment of (CV) is the claim that the most fundamental account of our perceptual relation with the physical world is to be given directly in terms of the complete representational *contents* of perceptual experience. So this second implementation of the idea that worldly changes are relevant in the required sense iff they make a difference to the subject's experience of the world is equally unacceptable in the current context.

The basic idea here is much more conducive to the indirect realist setting in which perceptual experience consists most fundamentally in acquaintance with certain mind-dependent direct objects. Such experience nevertheless represents the way things are in the mind-independent physical world around the perceiver. In order to determine its characteristic representational content in any given case, we begin with a situation in which the perceiver has an experience with the direct objects in question and everything is operating *normally*, however exactly normal operation is initially to be identified. We then consider gradual changes in the world around the perceiver along various property dimensions up to the point at which the relevant direct objects of experience themselves change as a result. The truth-conditions of the perceptual content in question are that the world be within that range around its initial condition along each of the property dimensions in question. The result is a form of indirect realism according to which the mind-dependent direct objects of experience are *natural signs* of various mind-independent worldly states of affairs (Ayers, 1993: i. ch. 7). The extent of the generality introduced into perceptual content corresponds to the degree of acuity in the signing system. We saw in ch. 3 that any such position is not only inconsistent with (CV) but also untenable in its own terms.

Still, there may be something important and right about the basic idea here that the fundamental nature of our perceptual experience of mind-independent physical objects is the prior and independent ground of the way that such objects actually do and possibly might look to us in perception. My aim in chs. 5–7 is to elucidate an account along precisely these lines in some detail.

Unfortunately for proponents of (CV), though, the basic insight is circular if it attempts to combine this with a characterization of experience itself exclusively in terms of its representational content; and it collapses into an untenable indirect realism if it attempts to supplement this content-characterization with any appeal to more basic, mind-dependent direct objects of experience. The right response to this impasse, in my view, is to reject (CV) altogether. The fundamental nature of perceptual experience does indeed provide the explanatory ground of the ways things do and might look to subjects from various points of view and in various circumstances of perception. It does so, though, not by serving up fully formed representational *contents*, but, rather, by presenting her directly with the actual constituents of the physical world: persisting mind-independent physical *objects* themselves.

Of course there are many more possible proposals than the four that I have considered here for the way in which the most basic representational contents of perceptual experience are supposed to be determined according to (CV). Still, I do think that one might perfectly reasonably conclude from this representative sample of failures that the current attempt to defend (CV)'s commitment to predicational generality faces a very serious challenge. The presence of predicational components is essential to the representational contents that are definitive of the (CV) account of the fundamental nature of our perceptual relation with the physical world. The challenge that I offer to its proponents is to explain at least in principle how to arrive at a specification of the various worldly changes that are relevant to the transition from truth to falsity in any given perceptual experience. For these are crucial to determining the significance of the general predicational components involved in its content.

In any case, all these problems for giving a specific account of how the most basic representational contents of perception are supposed to be determined according to (CV) combine with the objection of principle that I set out earlier in the present section. The generality of predication that is crucial to the representational contents that (CV) regards as funda- mental to our perceptual relation with the physical world around us is in fact incompatible with any adequate account of the presentation of partic- ular mind-independent physical objects to us in perceptual experience. I argued in §4.2 that the possibility of falsehood in perceptual contents that many regard as a primary motivation for (CV) also stands in the way of any proper acknowledgement of fact that mind-independent physical objects are presented to us in perception. These tensions came out further in my discussion in §4.1 of the particular difficulties faced by any attempt on behalf of (CV) to exploit the possibility of false perceptual contents in accounting for illusion and hallucination. I therefore conclude that (CV) has to be rejected. In the three remaining chapters and in the light of all that has gone before, I offer, elucidate, and defend my own positive account of our most fundamental perceptual relation with the physical world.

5

The Object View

Recall once again the Inconsistent Triad of claims about the nature of perceptual experience and its objects that I set out in ch. 1.

   (I) Physical objects are mind-independent.
  (II) Physical objects are the direct objects of perception.
 (III) The direct objects of perception are mind-dependent.

Physical objects are such things as stones, tables, trees, and animals: the persisting macroscopic constituents of the world that we live in. The entities of a given kind are *mind-independent* if and only if their nature is entirely independent of their appearance: it is not in any way a matter of how they do or might appear to anyone. More precisely, the mind-independence of physical objects consists in the individuative priority of their nature over the various appearance properties that show up in our perception of them. So an account of our perceptual experience of physical objects preserves realism if and only if it offers a characterization of the natures of physical objects themselves as the prior and independent basis on which it goes on to give a characterization of the relevant appearances that such objects may present in perception. According to the early modern approach to perception that I began with, the nature of perceptual experience is to be elucidated by reference to certain direct objects that are set before the mind in such experience. Thus, the most fundamental characterization of a specific perceptual experience is to be given by citing, and/or describing, specific such entities: the experience in question is one of acquaintance with just those things, which identify any given perceptual experience as the specific modification of consciousness that it is. Thus, the *direct objects* of perception are those objects, if any, that provide the most fundamental characterization of our perceptual experience in this way.

The arguments from illusion and hallucination seem to establish that any such direct objects of perception must be mind-dependent. Hence philosophers sympathetic to the early modern approach appear committed to (III) above and therefore obliged to choose between rejecting (I) and rejecting (II). In chs. 2 and 3 I considered these two options, taking off from the historical views of Berkeley and Locke respectively. I found in complete generality that neither option is acceptable. So I turned in ch. 4 to the current orthodox response of rejecting (III) *by rejecting the early modern approach altogether*. This Content View (CV), according to which the most fundamental account of our perceptual relation with the physical world is to be given in terms of the representational content of perceptual experience, I also found unacceptable. I propose in chs. 5–7 to rehabilitate the early modern insight, as I see it, that the most fundamental characterization of perceptual experience is to be given in terms of a relation of conscious acquaintance with certain direct objects of perception. I argue that this insight is perfectly consistent with the thesis that the direct objects of perception are the persisting mind-independent physical objects that we all know and love.[1] I therefore reject (III) whilst remaining faithful to the early modern insight. This in my view provides the only fully adequate elucidation and defence of the *empirical realist* conviction that physical objects are both presented to us in perceptual experience and have a nature that is entirely independent

---

[1] The other opponents of (CV) that I mentioned in ch. 4 above are sympathetic to these ideas too; but there are also significant differences between our views. See Campbell (2002*a*, 2002*b*), Martin (2002, 2010, forthcoming), Smith (2002), Travis (2004), Gupta (2006*a*, 2006*b*, forthcoming), and Johnston (2006). One major difference deserves mention right away. According to (OV) as developed in detail below, the only *objects* that are ever direct objects of perception in my early modern sense are mind-independent physical objects themselves, along perhaps with certain events involving them, parts or collections of physical objects, and possibly other related phenomena such as shadows too (see ch. 1). Smith (2002) and Gupta (forthcoming) introduce intentional or non-real objects as the objects of awareness or of presence in their senses respectively to accommodate cases of illusion and hallucination. The basic idea is that perception consists in a conscious relation with mind-independent physical objects in perfect cases when everything is as it seems, and in the same relation with something else in the various misleading cases in which things are not entirely as they seem. A major part of the point of (OV) is to avoid appeal to such shady entities and yet accommodate illusion and hallucination entirely satisfactorily anyway. Gupta's position is under construction. So I reserve any explicit assessment for another occasion. For critical discussion with which I am broadly sympathetic of Smith's appeal to intentional objects in cases where these are not simply identical with mind-independent physical objects themselves, see Siegel (2006: esp. §7).

of how they do or might appear to anyone: the very objects that are presented to us in perceptual experience are themselves mind-independent in nature.

I believe that the simple conjunction of (I) and (II) above provides the most stable and satisfactory framework for sustaining empirical realism. This is the core of my own positive position in the area: the *Object View* (OV). Accordingly, the most fundamental characterization of our perceptual relation with the physical world is to be given in terms of a relation of conscious acquaintance between perceiving subjects and the particular mind-independent physical objects that are presented to them in perception as genuine direct objects in the early modern sense. As I acknowledged from the opening pages of ch. 1, I take it to be agreed on all sides that we are presented with physical objects in perception; and it is without doubt our commonsense starting point that such physical objects are mind-independent. So the characterization of our perceptual relation with the physical world as a presentation of mind-independent physical objects should be common ground between all the participants in the debate I have been conducting throughout except for the various anti-realists discussed in ch. 2. The (OV) thesis that the most fundamental characterization of our perceptual relation with the physical world is as a matter of conscious acquaintance between perceiving subjects and particular mind-independent physical objects is far stronger than this relatively uncontroversial claim in the following two respects. First, the point is that perceptual presentation irreducibly consists in conscious acquaintance with mind-independent physical objects. It is not to be elucidated or further understood, either in terms of a relation of direct acquaintance with mind-dependent entities that are suitably related to mind-independent things, or in terms of a relation with some kind of representational content that 'concerns' such things in the sense in which I introduced this term in ch. 4. Second, (OV) insists that this characterization of perceptual presentation as conscious acquaintance with mind-independent physical objects provides the most fundamental elucidation of which modification of consciousness any specific such experience is: the fundamental nature of perceptual experience is to be given precisely by citing and/or describing those very mind-independent physical objects of acquaintance. Such objects really are direct objects in something very close to the early modern sense that I have been working with throughout. Every aspect of the position is clearly in need of further elucidation; but a central claim of the current chapter in developing (OV) in connection specifically with vision is as follows. From various points of view, and in various circumstances of perception, these mind-independent physical direct objects of acquaintance have certain evident similarities with paradigm exemplars of various *kinds* of such things, in virtue of which they *look*, very roughly, to be of those kinds. This is the basic form of the (OV) account of the ways that mind-independent physical objects look in perception.

This outline sketch of (OV) is obviously in need of major elaboration and defence at every point. I aim to provide this below in what remains of the present chapter. First (§5.1), I consider an immediate objection to (OV) along with a closely related source of concern and a kind of converse objection too. Second (§5.2), I explain the (OV) accounts of illusion and hallucination. Third (§5.3), I develop the (OV) account of the way in which particular mind-independent physical objects look certain ways to us in perception. In ch. 6 below I address the epistemological commitments and ambitions of (OV) as I intend them; and ch. 7 considers the question to what extent the truth of (OV) is evident from the perceiver's own perspective.

5.1 Presentation

According to the early modern approach, the direct objects of perception provide the most basic categorization of an experience of acquaintance with those objects as the specific modification of consciousness that it is. The identity and nature of such entities serve to elucidate what it is to be in that very conscious experiential condition. An immediate objection to the (OV) proposal that the mind-independent physical objects that are presented in perception themselves constitute its direct objects in this early modern sense is that there can be quite different perceptual experiences—had by the same subject or by different subjects—with identical such physical direct objects. For example, I may view a coin head on and then from a wide angle and have significantly different experiences as a result; experiences of its head side are different from those of its tail side; I may view the coin on the day it is minted and then again a few years later when it is tarnished and battered; I may view it in bright light and in dim light; I may see it and then feel it, again with quite different experiences as a result.

The key to my reply on behalf of (OV) is that perceptual experience is a matter of a person's conscious acquaintance with various mind-independent physical objects *from a given spatiotemporal point of view, in a particular sense modality, and in certain specific circumstances of perception (such as lighting conditions in the case of vision)*. These factors effectively conjoin to constitute a third relatum of the relation of conscious acquaintance that holds between perceivers and the mind-independent physical direct objects of their perceptual experience. Thus, the experiential variations noted above, and any others along similar lines, may all perfectly adequately be accounted for by variations within this third relatum.[2] For example, head-on v. wide-angle experiences, and those of the head side v. the tail side involve different spatial points of view. Experiences of the newly minted v. tarnished and battered coin involve different temporal points of view. Seeing v. feeling it clearly involve different sense modalities; and bright light v. dim light viewings involve different circumstances of perception. Still these are all cases of conscious acquaintance with the very same mind-independent physical coin—with variations in the third term of the perceptual relation. The basic idea of (OV) is that these complex specifications of my overall perceptual relation with the particular coin in question constitute the most fundamental characterization of my experiential condition in each case.

Appeal to this third relatum is also crucial to understanding another feature of perceptual experience that may initially appear in tension with (OV). According to (OV) the most fundamental characterization of our perceptual relation with the physical world is to be given in terms of a relation of conscious acquaintance between perceiving subjects and the particular mind-independent physical objects that are presented to them in perception as genuine direct objects in the early modern sense. There is a certain symmetry with respect to the objects themselves between their shape, their colour, and their mass, say, at least to the extent that these are all equally *properties of those objects*.[3] Our perceptual experience is not

---

[2] See Campbell (2009) for related discussion of this idea of consciousness as a three-place relation. Notice, though, that the control on Campbell's third relatum—'standpoint'—comes from the requirements upon Fregean sense (Frege, 1993) rather than any more basic notion of perceptual presentation.

[3] Of course there are numerous controversies surrounding various distinctions sometimes made between such properties: primary v. secondary, intrinsic v. extrinsic, and so on. These may all be ignored for the purposes of the issue currently under discussion.

likewise symmetric with respect to these properties. Although we can sometimes tell how massive objects are by sight, there are many cases in which this is simply not possible even though their colour and shape clearly do show up somehow in the nature of our experience of them. No satisfactory account can possibly be given of the nature of our perceptual experience of physical objects that fails to respect this asymmetry at least on those occasions. Yet (OV) may seem designed precisely so as to be incapable of giving it any respect whatsoever. Experience is acquaintance with the object, and the object has shape, colour, and mass equally, not to mention the atomic number of its constituent material that plausibly never shows up in perception at all. Indeed it is surely part of the point of (CV) precisely to respect this kind of distinction, between the ways that objects are actually *represented* as being in perception and ways that they may *be* all right but that they are not represented as being in perception.

Of course I agree that on any specific occasion physical objects look some ways and not others; and perhaps there are ways that physical objects may be that they never, or at least very rarely, look. I give a detailed and extended account of how these phenomena arise within (OV) in §§5.2 and 5.3. For the moment I simply mention some of the materials that this account employs in order to move forward in developing the position. The key to the (OV) account of the ways things look is the notion of certain *relevant similarities* between the direct objects of perception them-selves and the paradigms of various kinds of physical objects that play a central role in our understanding of what those kinds are. (OV) construes the most fundamental perceptual condition as a relation of conscious acquaintance between a subject and certain mind-independent physical objects from a given spatiotemporal point of view, in a particular modality, and in certain specific circumstances of perception. The similarities that are relevant to the ways that such things *look* are specific to the visual modality and also to the spatiotemporal point of view and other circumstances in question. The same goes for the other modalities. Thus, for example, although the similarities that a coin has with a paradigm circle may be relevant from head on, these similarities are not relevant when viewed from edge on—rotated by 90°. Again, its similarities with our paradigms of silver colour are relevant in vision in good lighting conditions, but less so in dim lighting conditions, and not at all in touch. Finally, its similarities with paradigms of a certain mass are rarely relevant in vision at all. Thus, I claim, and will go on to explain further below, the uncontroversial data concerning how physical objects do and do not, can and cannot, look in perception do not constitute an insurmountable obstacle to (OV).

Before moving on to consider illusion and hallucination in §5.2, it is worth addressing a kind of converse of the initial immediate objection set out at the start of this section. There the difficulty was supposed to be that perceptual experiences with the same direct objects may nevertheless be quite different; and the response was to stress the importance of a third relatum consisting of spatiotemporal point of view, sense modality, and relevant circumstances of perception. Here the challenge to (OV) is to explain the manifest similarity between experiences with distinct direct objects. For the most obvious and straightforward kind of example, consider visual experiences of two numerically distinct but qualitatively identical apples from corresponding points of view and in the same perceptual circumstances. (OV) characterizes these as relations of conscious acquaintance with distinct objects, yet surely the experiences are identical? Absolutely not! Just as the apples cannot possibly be distinguished by looking, so the visual experiences cannot possibly be distinguished by introspection either; and just as their visual indistinguishability does not entail that the apples are one and the same, so it does not follow from their introspective indistinguishability either that the experiences are one and the same. Just because a person may be unable to distinguish two experiential conditions it absolutely does not follow that these have to be characterized as one and the same experiential condition. Indeed, the introspective indistinguishability of the two visual experiences *follows*, according to (OV), from the qualitative identity of their numerically distinct direct objects. So this can hardly be an objection to the view.

There are really two points here. First, the proponent of (OV) simply denies that introspective indistinguishability *entails* identity in the fundamental theoretical characterization of perceptual experiences. A full account of introspection is governed by many and various constraints and requirements. Any assumption from the outset that it must deliver the result that introspection is infallible concerning experiential identity in this way, though, is certainly not axiomatic, and arguably leads to very serious epistemological and metaphysical problems.[4]

---

[4] See McDowell (1982) and Williamson (1996) for epistemological and metaphysical objections to this principle that have been very influential; and see Evans (1982: ch. 7) for the outlines of a far more promising and plausible approach to introspection.

The second point is that identity in the fundamental characterization of experiences is not even the best, and certainly not the only, *explanation* of their introspective indistinguishability in the cases in question. (OV) offers a perfectly adequate alternative. Experiences are most fundamentally to be construed as relations of conscious acquaintance with particular mind-independent physical objects, from a given point of view, in a particular sense modality and in certain specific circumstances of perception. Those objects look various ways, in the visual case, in virtue of the visually relevant similarities that they have relative to the point of view and perceptual circumstances in question with various paradigms of certain physical kinds. As a direct and perfectly explicable consequence of this, numerically and qualitatively distinct objects may look the same in various respects from appropriate points of view in appropriate circumstances. For such objects may have the same visually relevant similarities with the same paradigms from the points of view and in the circumstances in question. The resultant experiences may indeed therefore be introspectively *indistinguishable*; but that is no reason to regard them as one and the same experiential condition. They are cases of conscious visual acquaintance with particular distinct mind-independent physical objects from various points of view in various circumstances of perception. As will become clear in what follow in §5.3, similar points may be made in relation to other kinds of case, for example, in which a circular coin viewed from an angle looks in certain respects similar to an elliptical disc viewed from head on, or a white piece of chalk in red lighting conditions looks like a red piece of chalk in white lighting conditions.

The whole point of (OV) is to insist that, with the exception of hallucination, which is addressed directly in §5.2, we can only properly understand the ways things look in perception as the product of a fundamental relation of conscious acquaintance between subjects and the particular mind-independent physical direct objects that are presented in their experience from a given point of view and in certain circumstances. In a slogan, the ways things *look* are the ways (perceptually presented) *things* look from that point of view in those circumstances. The ways things are for the subject in perception are certain of the ways that the objects of perception are from the subject's point of view. This approach, I claim, has a relatively straightforward and compelling explanation of the various experiential similarity data raised in objection to it.[5] In contrast to the (OV) approach, (CV) effectively attempts to provide the most fundamental characterization of our perceptual relation with the physical world simply in terms of the looks of things themselves, the various ways that things are represented as being in perceptual experience. We saw in ch. 4, though, that this has the fatal consequence that it is impossible subsequently to reclaim the crucial basic datum of a conscious experiential presentation of particular mind-independent physical objects themselves in perception.

I end the present section by addressing explicitly a final closely related line of objection.[6] I hope that this serves further to clarify the content, aims, and ambitions of (OV). Consider visual experiences of two qualitatively identical but numerically distinct objects from corresponding points of view in relevantly similar circumstances. The objector may grant that these are not exactly the same in *all* respects—not least because they have distinct worldly objects. Still, they have identical *phenomenal characters*: what it is like for a subject to have the two experiences may be exactly the same. Yet according to (OV), the fundamental nature of an experience is a relation between a perceiving subject and a particular mind-independent physical direct object from a given spatiotemporal point of view, in a particular sense modality and in certain specific circumstances of perception. This supposedly provides the most basic characterization of the conscious condition that having that experience is. So the two experiences in question are distinct conscious conditions, and this fails to capture their identical phenomenal character.

Although put in different terms, I regard this objection as a close variant of one that I addressed above. (OV) is perfectly compatible with, and indeed *explains*, the significant similarities between many different pairs of experiences that it characterizes as distinct at the most fundamental level of relations between subjects and objects from points of view in modalities

---

[5] The key idea here is to highlight the importance to (OV) of a third component in its account of perceptual experience as a relation of conscious acquaintance between a person and the particular mind-independent physical objects around him that consists of the point of view, modality, and perceptual circumstances involved. This has the effect of integrating what may often be regarded as factors to be cited in *explanation* of why a person has the specific perceptual experience that he does on certain occasions into the constitutive account of the nature of his perceptual experience itself. This deliberate and motivated integration of the explanatory and the constitutive is a feature of the position that recurs in ch. 6 and especially ch. 7.

[6] This formulation of the objection is due to an anonymous reader for Oxford University Press.

and circumstances. Some such pairs have very striking similarities indeed: crudely, things look F to the subject in each of them for all and only the same relevant predicates 'F'. Still, the experiences themselves are the subjects' relations with the numerically distinct but qualitatively identical particular objects that look F for all these various 'F's in the two cases. This qualitative identity of their direct objects *explains* the correlation in the ways things look between the two experiences. According to (OV), though, we cannot make proper theoretical sense of the facts about the ways things look in either case, and so cannot even begin to understand the correlation between the two cases, without regarding such looks as the way *those particular presented mind-independent objects* themselves look, given their natures and the specific points of view and circumstances in question. So we absolutely have to register the numerical distinctness of the two direct objects in giving the most fundamental theoretical characterization of the experiences of them. Still, that insight is perfectly consistent with, and indeed explanatory of, the possibility that experiential relations with numerically distinct objects have the same phenomenal character *in this sense*: for all relevant predicates 'F', o_1 looks F iff o_2 looks F.

Once again, then, I claim that (OV) is perfectly compatible with the genuine data concerning the various similarities and differences between perceptual experiences.

5.2 Illusion and hallucination

(OV) construes empirical realism as the simple conjunction of (I) and (II) above. It rejects (III) within the context of the early modern approach to the characterization of perceptual experience in terms of its direct objects: perception consists most fundamentally in a relation of conscious acquaintance *with mind-independent physical objects themselves*, from a given spatio-temporal point of view, in a particular sense modality, and in specific circumstances of perception. In ch. 1 I set out the arguments from illusion and hallucination as objections to precisely this combination of claims. The evident existence of illusions and hallucinations appears to establish that the direct objects of perception in the early modern sense must be mind-dependent items distinct from any mind-independent physical objects. This appearance is in my view mistaken; and in the present section I begin to explain how (OV) may perfectly adequately account for the existence of illusion and hallucination. The explanation is completed in the course of my general elucidation of the (OV) account of the ways physical objects look in perception in §5.3 below. In keeping with my discussion throughout, I focus on the case of vision, and I begin with the characterization that I gave in ch. 1 of a visual illusion as an experience in which a physical object, o, looks F, although o is not actually F.

As I sketched above, the (OV) strategy exploits the fact that the mind-independent physical objects that are the direct objects of our perceptual experience have, relative to a given spatiotemporal point of view, a particular sense modality, specific circumstances of perception, and various similarities with our paradigms of general kinds of such things. Very crudely, illusions come about in cases in which the direct objects of experience have such similarities with paradigm exemplars of kinds of which they are not in fact instances.[7]

Consider once again the Müller-Lyer illusion (ML), in which two lines that are actually identical in length are made to look different in length by the addition of misleading hashes. The (ML) diagram, in normal viewing conditions in which the illusion is evident, has relevant similarities with a pair of lines, one longer and more distant than the plane of the diagram, one shorter and less distant; and those lines in themselves are a paradigm of inequality in length. In this sense the two lines look unequal in length: it is perfectly intelligible how someone seeing it might therefore take that very diagram as consisting of unequal lines, regardless of whether or not she actually does so.

Which similarities are *relevant* in this sense, though? For anything has unrestricted similarities with everything. The first thing that has to be specified in determining relevance is the sense modality involved; and in line with my general policy here I focus in what follows on vision. The spatiotemporal point of view of the subject and various other circumstances of perception also make certain similarities relevant and not others; but which, why, and how? There are no simple answers, and the determinants of relevance are many, varied, and largely empirical. All I can offer here and in §5.3 is a series of pointers and examples.

An important preliminary point, though, is that the *relevant similarities*, in our case, *visually relevant similarities*, cannot simply be defined as identities

---

[7] See below for clarification concerning 'similarities' and 'paradigms'.

in the ways that the relevantly similar relata are visually *represented* as being, or else (OV) clearly collapses into a version of (CV). That is to say, we cannot simply say that two objects have visually relevant similarities, from a given point of view and in specific circumstances just when there are sufficiently many common properties amongst those that each is visually represented as having from that point of view and in those circumstances. For the purpose of introducing the notion of visually relevant similarities is to provide an explanation, within the context of the (OV) conception of perception as most fundamentally a matter of conscious acquaintance with mind-independent physical objects, of what grounds the truth of claims to the effect that a particular such object, *o*, looks *F* (to a subject, *S*, on a particular occasion). Yet the elucidation of visually relevant similarity just given in terms of the way that such objects are represented as being in experience simply presupposes the (CV) account.

The (OV) alternative, then, is that visually relevant similarities are those that ground and explain the ways that the particular physical objects that we are acquainted with in perception look. That is to say, visually relevant similarities are similarities by the lights of visual processing of various kinds. Objects have visually relevant similarities when they share sufficiently many common properties amongst those that have a significant involvement in the various processes underlying vision. Thus, and very crudely, visually relevant similarities are identities in such things as the way in which light is reflected and transmitted from the objects in question, and the way in which stimuli are handled by the visual system, given its evolutionary history and our shared training during development.[8]

---

[8] This is absolutely not intended as a complete explicit definition of the notion as it figures in the (OV) account of looks. See §5.3 below for further extended elucidation and clarification concerning visually relevant similarities. It is worth emphasizing right away, though, the occurrence of 'sufficiently many' in the formulation given in the text. This is not simply a numerical matter, but rather concerns the *appropriateness* of the visually relevant similarities involved in the concepts occurring in the looks ascription in question. For example, suppose that I am looking at a rectangular figure directly in front of me in good viewing conditions. It has *some* visually relevant similarities with paradigm squares; but it does not look square. According to the proponent of (OV), this is because it does not have *sufficiently many*, or, better, all the *appropriate* such similarities. Thanks to Marcus Giaquinto for the problem example and its solution. A similar point goes *some* way towards explaining the differences in the ways that a regular square and a regular diamond normally look according to (OV) (see Peacocke, 1992: ch. 3 for seminal discussion; I was urged to consider this contrast by Chris Peacocke in discussion). For the paradigms here have distinct canonical *orientations* that have implications for which visually relevant similarities are the appropriate ones in direct objects of

(OV) also appeals here to our *paradigms* of various physical kinds: what are these supposed to be? Again very roughly, they are instances of the kinds in question, whose association with the terms for those kinds partially constitutes our understanding of those terms, given our training in the acquisition of the relevant concepts. They are paradigm exemplars of the kinds in question relative to our grasp of the concepts for those kinds.[9]

This suggestion opens up a major philosophical topic that I cannot possibly engage with satisfactorily here: the nature of concept possession. I confine myself to a brief presentation of the key issue and an acknowledgement of my own commitments. Berkeley (1975*a*, 1975*b*) read in Locke (1975) the claim that our grasp of general terms consists in our association with them of a peculiar kind of *abstract idea* that somehow *determines* the extension of the term in question. He argues within the shared assumption of an imagistic conception of ideas that no such idea is possible; and the same arguments in my opinion also demonstrate that no finite collection of determinate imagistic ideas could possibly succeed in any such unique determination of the extension of a general term. Closely related arguments are also developed and articulated powerfully and influentially by Kripke (1982) on behalf of Wittgenstein (1958).

Many philosophers take these arguments to establish that conscious awareness of particular exemplars plays *no role whatsoever* in our grasp of general terms; and they adopt a theory on which such understanding consists simply in our appropriate *use* of the terms in question, perhaps in the context of the similar use of others in our linguistic community.[10] I believe that this is an overreaction that misses the point of Berkeley's own insistence as I read him that a particular imagistic idea is still crucial to our grasp of general terms in constraining and guiding the use that we make of such terms on particular occasions. Particular ideas do not, and cannot, serve this purpose by uniquely determining in advance for every possible

---

perception that look square and diamond-shaped respectively. Further important differences between the ways that these two figures look also enter at the level of their *thick* looks, that is to say, in the subject's recognition or registration of such visually relevant similarities with the paradigms in question. See §5.3 for introduction and discussion of the distinction between thin and thick looks.

[9] Pictures or images (perhaps based on description) may play the role of paradigm exemplars in certain cases, specifically, for example, in connection with non-existents or kinds with respect to which we have no experience of actual instances.

[10] For significant early examples see Wright (1981) and Kripke (1982).

object whether or not the term applies. Their role is rather one of grounding and prompting our natural inclinations to apply or withhold the term on the basis of what strikes us in the context of our experience and education as relevant similarities and differences with the paradigms that such ideas offer, and of providing retrospective confirmation of the appropriateness of our use of the terms in question.

My own favoured account of concept possession likewise insists upon an essential role for our conscious confrontation with paradigm instances in our acquisition and application *with genuine understanding* of our most basic empirical concepts. Only in the light of this do we have the crucial appreciation of what we are up to in deploying them as we do in connection with the particular mind-independent physical objects in the world around us. Paradigms, as I invoke them above and in what follows below in explaining the ways that such objects *look* in perception, are precisely the instances of various kinds that do, or are apt to, play this crucial role in our possession of the relevant concepts for such kinds. Of course this immediately raises a number of pressing questions: which concepts, exactly, are to be handled in this way; might these same concepts also be acquired and properly deployed otherwise than on the basis of consciousness apprehension of paradigms, more theoretically perhaps; what precisely is the role of our awareness of paradigms in guiding and constraining application of the concepts in question; and so on? I cannot answer these questions here. The fact is that I commit myself without defence to a controversial account of concept possession, on which concept possession normally involves, at least in the case of concepts for the most basic kinds of mind-independent physical objects, some conscious association with the term for the concept in question of various paradigm exemplars, or of images derived from experience thereof.[11]

Thus, according to (OV), in a case of visual illusion in which a mind-independent physical object, o, looks F, although o is not actually F, o is the direct object of visual perception from a spatiotemporal point of view and in circumstances of perception relative to which o has visually relevant similarities with paradigm exemplars of F although it is not itself actually an instance of F. This is perfectly possible, as we have already seen in the case

---

[11] See Fodor (1998: esp. ch. 5) for a helpful bibliography of proponents of this kind of approach to concept possession and strong opposition on his own behalf. See Brewer (1995) for more on the rule-following context for this issue.

of (ML). So the existence of illusion is entirely compatible with (OV). Indeed, I claim that this account covers many of the most standard cases of visual illusion. Here are two further examples for illustration.

First, a half-submerged straight stick looks bent. Here the direct object of perception is that very (straight) stick itself. Nevertheless, it looks bent in virtue of its visually relevant similarities with an unsubmerged bent stick that has its top half coincident with the unsubmerged half of the stick seen and its bottom half in the position of the relevant virtual image of the bottom half of the latter from the subject's point of view and given the refractive index of the liquid in question. In what sense are these two things similar? In the region of space in the vicinity of the eye—that is to say in the region above the refracting surface of the liquid as things actually are—light from corresponding parts of the two sticks travels, or would travel, along the same paths. Given the way that the liquid actually refracts light from the submerged portion of the stick seen, the visually relevantly similar stick described is a paradigm bent stick. Thus, the partially submerged stick *looks bent*. This is a direct result of the (OV) characterization of experience as conscious acquaintance with the relevant mind-independent physical object—the half-submerged straight stick—along with its visually relevant similarities with a paradigm bent stick. So it can hardly be an objection to (OV) that it is unable to accommodate the illusion in question.

Second, a white piece of chalk illuminated with red light looks red. Again, the (OV) proposal is that the perceptual experience in question is most fundamentally a matter of the subject's conscious acquaintance with that very piece of chalk itself: a particular persisting mind-independent physical object. From the viewpoint in question, and, most importantly in this case, given the relevant perceptual circumstances—especially, of course, the abnormally red illumination—it has visually relevant similarities with a paradigm red piece of chalk, of just that size and shape. Their visually relevant similarity consists in the similarity of the light reflected from both. Thus, the white chalk looks red; and again (OV) provides a perfectly adequate explanatory account of the illusion in question rather than being in any way in tension or incompatible with it.

It may be objected at this point that similarity is symmetrical. So (OV) has the unacceptable consequence, in connection with the (ML), for example, that the relevant paradigm pair of lines of unequal lengths at different depths look equal in length, for the very same reason. Similarly

(OV) may seem to be committed to the claim that a bent unsubmerged stick looks straight and that a red piece of chalk in normal lighting conditions looks white.[12]

I would make two points in reply to this line of objection. First, o looks F, according to (OV), in virtue of its visually relevant similarities relative to the spatiotemporal point of view and other circumstances of perception with *paradigm* exemplars of F. The (ML) diagram does not constitute a paradigm case of lines that are equal in length. Given the misleading hashes, it would certainly be an inappropriate exemplar to use in manifesting or acquiring the concept of equality in length. So, although plain similarity is symmetrical, the relevant condition of similarity to a paradigm is not. Similarly, a half-submerged straight stick is not a paradigm straight object; and a white piece of chalk illuminated with red light is not a paradigm white object. It may be questioned, though, in the case of the (OV) account of (ML), whether the pair of lines of different lengths at different distances from the perceiver with which the diagram is said to have visually relevant similarities are themselves a paradigm of inequality in length as the account requires. Provided that their difference in depth is absolutely clear and not masked or obscured in any way, then I would say that they are. They constitute a perfectly appropriate exemplar for the acquisition of that concept and for guidance in its subsequent application. This connects directly with my second point: that misleading cues *could* no doubt be added to unequal lines at different depths to bring about an inverse to the (ML) illusion from a suitably chosen point of view. Notice, though, that *which* such cues should be added, and from which point of view the illusory construct should be viewed, would be ascertained precisely on the basis of knowledge of the physical processes involved in vision: the combination of cues and point of view should be precisely that relative to which the resultant figure has visually relevant similarities with an appropriate paradigm of lines of equal length.

Recall my presentation of the argument from illusion in ch. 1. This is supposed to establish that the early modern approach to perceptual experience as our conscious acquaintance with certain direct objects is forced to admit that such direct objects are always mind-dependent. Hence claim (III) of the Inconsistent Triad that forms the framework for

---

[12] Thanks to Tim Williamson for this objection.

my whole discussion. The argument has two phases. The first is intended to establish that the direct object of an *illusion* is bound to be mind-dependent. The second is supposed to generalize this result to all perceptual experience, including that involved in veridical perception. The sub-argument of the first phase is as follows. A *visual illusion* may be characterized as a perceptual experience in which a physical object, *o*, looks *F*, although *o* is not actually *F*. According to the early modern empiricist approach, the way to account quite generally for the fact that something looks *F* in an experience is to construe that experience as the subject's acquaintance with a *direct object* that provides the most fundamental characterization of that very conscious condition and *that must therefore, presumably, itself be F*. In cases of illusion, then, any such direct object is bound to be distinct from the physical object, *o*, which is not *F*, although it looks to be so. For one is *F* and the other is not. The occurrence and nature of such an illusion is manifestly independent of the accidental presence of any mind-independent object in the vicinity that happens to be *F*. So its direct object must be mind-dependent.

The (OV) response is quite clear. It does not follow from the fact that perceptual experience involves conscious acquaintance with certain direct objects, that the direct object of any such experience in which something looks *F* must itself actually *be F*. For I have just explained how a perceptual experience with a mind-independent physical object, *o*, as its direct object that is not itself *F*—not actually constituted by two lines of unequal length, not actually bent, or not actually red, in my three examples so far—may nevertheless be an experience in which *that very object, o*, looks *F*. The argument from illusion therefore fails to establish, even in the case of illusion itself, that the direct objects of perception are mind-dependent. So, even though I also find serious problems with any version of phase two of the argument that I know, that point is dialectically unnecessary. The evident existence of illusions of the kinds that I have been discussing is perfectly compatible with the (OV) rejection of (III) as outlined above.

Of course there are very many quite different kinds of visual illusion. I cannot possibly consider representatives of all such kinds here. I turn next instead to consider how (OV) accounts for hallucination. This generates a related explanation for cases of illusion of a rather different kind that may initially appear more problematic for (OV) than those that I have considered so far. Further materials to fill out the overall (OV) account of illusion, and, indeed, of 'veridical' looks too, also emerge in §5.3. First of all though, how is (OV) supposed to acknowledge the evident existence of hallucination? The intuitive category that I have in mind consists of *purely inner phenomena*, in the following sense. Nothing in the mind-independent world is *presented* in hallucinatory experiences. They have no mind-independent direct object. (OV) also rejects any attempt to characterize hallucination in terms of purportedly *mind-dependent* direct objects. Rather, according to the version of (OV) that I myself endorse, hallucinatory experiences have to be characterized by giving a qualitative description of a more or less specific mind-independent scene, and saying that the subject is having an experience that is not distinguishable by introspection alone from one in which the constituents of such a scene are the direct objects. No more positive characterization of the experience may be given.[13] Thus, for example, I once had an experience that was not distinguishable by introspection alone from one in which a large pink elephant in a desert was the direct object of my perception.

This approach to the theoretical characterization of hallucination raises many issues and has become quite controversial in recent philosophy of perception.[14] I hope that what follows gives a fair impression of the main lines of objection and at least indicates the ideas that I would pursue in order to defend it. I do not claim exhaustive completeness, though. Furthermore, the positive core of (OV) itself is plausibly compatible with alternative approaches to the incorporation of hallucination, and my own concern is certainly primarily with non-hallucinatory cases. So, although I personally prefer the introspective indistinguishability approach to hallucination (IIH), described above, those who find this unsatisfactory and yet see the broader merits of (OV) may be free to take another tack. In any case, my subsequent discussion of (IIH) proceeds thus. First, I consider potential counterexamples that lead to a refinement and clarification of the embedded notion of introspective indistinguishability. Second, I respond to an objection from the potential role of hallucinatory experience in explaining our acquisition of empirical concepts. Third, I outline the responses made available by (IIH) to the argument from

---

[13] I rely heavily here upon Martin (2004).
[14] For important representative debate see: Martin (2004, 2006), Johnston (2004), Siegel (2004, 2008), Kennedy (2010), and Pautz (2010).

hallucination as presented in ch. 1. Fourth, I derive further useful materials for accounting for illusion.

The basic idea of (IIH) is set out above: hallucinatory experiences have to be characterized by giving a qualitative description of a more or less specific mind-independent scene, and saying that the subject is having an experience that is not distinguishable by introspection alone from one in which the constituents of such a scene are the direct objects. Thus, in characterizing a specific hallucinatory experiential condition, we first specify a type of *perceptual* experience, such as seeing a mind-independent physical object that is F_1, F_2, . . . and F_n, say, in good lighting conditions directly before us; and then we characterize the hallucination in question as one of being in a condition that is not distinguishable by introspection alone from that perceptual condition, where condition A is not distinguishable by introspection alone from condition B iff in condition A nothing is knowable by introspection alone that rules out being in condition B. (In what follows I assume the qualification 'by introspection alone' unless otherwise indicated.)[15]

An obvious source for potential counterexamples arises from the experience of subjects incapable of any introspective knowledge at all, either because they are entirely unconscious or because they lack the required conceptual or other cognitive resources. Such subjects are in a condition in which *they* know nothing by introspection that rules out their seeing a mind-independent physical object that is F_1, F_2, . . . and F_n in good lighting conditions directly before them—because they know nothing or nothing of the relevant kind at all. But they are not, or may well not be, in the target hallucinatory condition. Martin (2006) offers what seems to me to be the correct response here. This is to invoke an *impersonal* notion of introspective indistinguishability. The idea is that specific hallucinatory experiences are those that are not introspectively distinguish*able* from specified perceptual conditions: nothing is know*able* in them that rules out the corresponding perceptual condition. This is not a matter of what would or could be known *by the subject in question*, or by any other *specific*

---

[15] I also assume throughout the idea of introspective knowledge. I do not pretend to have an adequate account of introspection. All I mean by this is the means that we all have of coming to know the nature of our own mental and especially experiential states directly, without drawing on any extraneous information. I certainly intend the notion to be used sufficiently liberally to include various ascent routines derived from Evans's (1982: ch. 7, esp. 7.4) 'outer judgement model' of self-knowledge to qualify as accounts of introspection.

subject, if only things were different in such and such specific ways, for example, in the presence of superior conceptual and/or other cognitive capacities and appropriate attention to the task at hand etc. It is a more basic, unanalysable, and genuinely impersonal notion, grounded in what is knowable by introspection alone in the condition in question *simpliciter*.

No doubt this is a contentious notion; but I make two points by way of preliminary clarification.[16] First, a similar impersonal epistemic notion is common currency in mathematics. When it is asserted that in a certain context it is unknowable whether the continuum hypothesis is true, this is not based upon a view about what a particular mathematician, George, could or would know in that context under such and such specific intellectual idealizations. It is a matter of what is knowable *simpliciter* in that context. Similarly, I claim, we have a fairly clear conception of what introspection can and cannot bring to light in various conditions, and therefore of what it is for two experiential conditions to be introspectively distinguish*able* or indistinguish*able*, in the required sense, without having to get hold of any specific subject to try to distinguish them for us, or to list specific conditions in which that or some other subject could or could not do so. Indeed, and this is my second point, this impersonal notion of introspective indistinguishability is at the heart of discussions of scepticism throughout the history of epistemology. The whole point of Descartes's dreaming and malicious demon scenarios (1986: Med. I), for example, and indeed their modern 'brain-in-a-vat' counterparts, is that the experiences of their unfortunate subjects are impersonally introspectively indistin-guishable from our normal perceptual experiences. Of course there is controversy over whether it follows from the fact that experiences in such scenarios are indistinguishable from normal perceptual experiences that our normal perceptual experiences are likewise indistinguishable from them—and this is what the sceptical arguments standardly turn on. I myself believe that it does not follow.[17] But my point in the current context stands unaffected. Such familiar epistemological discussions are driven by a perfectly clear, comprehensible sense of impersonal introspective indistin-guishability; and this is all that (IIH) requires.

---

[16] I acknowledge that a great deal more could be said in giving a full treatment.

[17] See Williams (1978: ch. 7 and esp. app. 3) and Williamson (2000: esp. chs. 8 and 9) for very helpful discussion and elaboration. I would similarly endorse an asymmetry in distin-guishability between normal perception and corresponding hallucination.

My second clarification of (IIH) concerns a rather different line of objection.[18] For certain more or less 'observable' empirical concepts at least, e.g. *F*, say, perception of particular instances plausibly plays a role in explaining our capacity for beliefs whose content contains those concepts. Similarly, it may be said, hallucination as of an *F* equally explains the subject's capacity for beliefs whose content contains the concept *F*. Simply being in a condition that is indistinguishable by introspection alone from seeing an *F*, though, cannot plausibly explain anyone's capacity for beliefs whose content contains the concept *F*. So (IIH) is incorrect as an account of the nature of hallucination.

The obvious immediate reply would simply be to deny that (IIH) is incapable of meeting the explanatory requirement in the case of hallucination. In so far as it is intelligible how seeing *F*s explains the capacity for beliefs whose content contains *F*, then what is the obstacle *in principle* to the same being true of conditions in which nothing is knowable by introspection alone that rules out that *F*s are being seen? Perhaps the difficulty is in seeing how a 'negative condition' such as failing to know anything incompatible with seeing an *F* could explain anything. I think that this would be a mistake. First, 'negative conditions' are often perfectly explanatory, as, for example, when an accident is explained by a driver failing to spot a cyclist. Making out a genuine necessary condition on an explanation that is clearly failed by (IIH) here would be a serious undertaking to say the least. Second, hallucinatory conditions are not *blank* according to (IIH). Having a hallucination as of an *F* is being in some condition or other, the only unifying theoretical characterization of which is that it is indistinguish*able* from seeing an *F*. *If* it is perfectly clear how, had the subject's condition been one of actually seeing an *F* instead, this *would* have explained her capacity for beliefs whose content contains *F*, then why would a condition indistinguishable from this not have served equally well? After all, this just *is* the intuition behind the current objection to (IIH) that hallucination as of an *F* is equal to perception of an *F* in explaining the capacity for beliefs whose content contains *F*.

A familiar and powerful source of resistance at this point comes from the insight that our capacity for beliefs whose content contains determinate

---

[18] Again this is due to Adam Pautz (2010, and written comments on draft MS), although he may still doubt the success of my response to it. There are many substantive further issues raised by these considerations that I cannot address fully here.

concepts of specific mind-independent properties depends on far more than mere experience up to introspective indistinguishability, as it were. That is to say, the explanation that seeing Fs plausibly provides of our capacity for beliefs whose content contains F is far from simple or straightforward. It may well be that, in so far as F really is a concept of a way mind-independent things objectively are, the relevant explanation crucially involves the role of seeing Fs in attentional tracking of actual mind-independent Fs in the world, as unchanging in the relevant respects—in being Fs, that is—across variations in viewing conditions, and thus the role of seeing Fs in successful demonstrative reference to that very way that such things may be. So it may well turn out that hallucinations do not equally explain our capacity for such beliefs at all. In that case the motivating claim behind the current objection to (IIH), that hallucination as of an F is equal to perception of an F in explaining the capacity for beliefs whose content contains F, is simply false.

This certainly suggests a refinement to (IIH). Great care is required with the notion of a hallucination as of an F, correlative with the cognitive sophistication of the corresponding perceptual condition relative to which it is introspectively indistinguishable. On the one hand, hallucination as of an F may be a hallucinatory correlate of simply being faced in perception with what happens to be an F, in the absence of any capacity to make any sense of the idea of variations in viewing conditions upon a single unified worldly condition. This is plausibly insufficient on its own to explain the capacity for beliefs whose content contains the concept of mind-independent F-ness itself. So the current line of objection to (IIH) does not get started. On the other hand, hallucination as of an F may be a hallucinatory correlate of explicit perceptual categorization of something *as* an F, which involves actualization of that very concept—in the hallucinatory case of course only in some judgement to the effect that it looks as though there is an F present, rather than any objectual predication of F-ness. This presupposes possession of the concept and so provides at best a degenerate explanation of the capacity for beliefs whose content contains it: anyone capable of such hallucinations is capable of such beliefs. Once again, though, the objection to (IIH) fails.

Although this is a massive topic for another occasion, I claim that what *substantively* explains the capacity for beliefs whose content contains the empirical concept F, in the relevant cases, is the role of actually seeing Fs in tracking that determinate condition of mind-independent things—being

F—across variations in other conditions, along with a great deal more besides. Just as a hallucination cannot possibly provide anyone with a determinate demonstrative conception of any particular dagger, so a hallucination introspectively indistinguishable from being presented with an *F* from a given point of view *P* in such and such circumstances *C*, that is also therefore introspectively indistinguishable from seeing an *F′* from *P′* in *C′* or an *F″* from *P″* in *C″* and so on, cannot on its own explain anyone's capacity for beliefs whose contents determinately contain the concept of mind-independent *F*s.

Recall now my brief presentation of the argument from hallucination in ch. 1. Like the argument from illusion, this is supposed to establish that the early modern approach to perceptual experience as our conscious acquaintance with certain direct objects is forced to admit that such direct objects are always mind-dependent. Hence claim (III) of the Inconsistent Triad that frames my discussion throughout. In cases of hallucination, there is no plausible candidate mind-independent direct object of perception, so this must be a mind-dependent thing. Then, since every perceptual experience is subjectively indistinguishable from one in a possible case of hallucination, the same goes across the board. The direct objects of any perception are bound to be mind-dependent. Again there are two phases to the argument. The first is intended to establish that hallucinatory experience must be construed as a relation to a mind-dependent direct object. The second is supposed to generalize this result to all perceptual experience, including that in veridical perception.

Once again (OV) rejects entirely the first phase of the argument. In the case of pure hallucination, unlike that of illusion, though, it is indeed true that there is no mind-independent physical direct object of perception. But this is absolutely not to be addressed by the provision of a mind-dependent direct object instead. The apparatus of direct objects of experience is simply not applicable in this case according to (OV). Hallucinations have no positive characterization in those terms. They are rather to be characterized in the derivative manner outlined above, as indistinguishable by introspection alone from 'corresponding' cases of genuine conscious acquaintance with mind-independent physical direct objects of various kinds.

Notice that (OV) is therefore committed to the invalidity of the inference from the fact that an experience is indistinguishable by introspection alone from one with such and such direct objects to the conclusion that the former experience also has direct objects of those same kinds.

For hallucinations are indeed indistinguishable by introspection alone from perceptions with various mind-independent direct objects; but the former have no direct objects at all. So hallucination constitutes a counterexample to the inference in question. This in turn blocks the second phase of the arguments from illusion and hallucination as they would normally be formulated in this current context of the early modern approach to perception. For those phases both attempt to establish that the direct objects of all perceptual experience are mind-dependent from the premiss that any veridical perception has a corresponding possible illusion or hallucination from which it is indistinguishable by introspection alone, along with the purported conclusion of the arguments' first phases that the direct objects of such illusions and hallucinations are bound to be mind-dependent.

Now, hallucinations may be caused in many and varied ways, such as by taking certain drugs or getting a firm knock to the head. Other ways of bringing about hallucination may also involve distal external objects, sometimes relatively systematically. Indeed, this may even occur in cases in which the relevant mind-independent objects are also presented as direct objects of vision, supplemented, as it were, by their hallucinatory products. An example here might be seeing a blue afterimage on a white screen after staring at a bright red stimulus. The white screen may be presented as a mind-independent direct object of perception, supplemented by a hallucination introspectively indistinguishable from seeing a blue stimulus corresponding to the original red one. This possibility of mixed perceptual-cum-hallucinatory experiences provides (OV) with the resources to account for some cases that may pre-theoretically be classified as illusions. Hermann's Grid, in which pale grey patches appear at the intersections of the white channels formed by a grid of closely spaced black squares, is plausibly a case in point. We see the grid of black squares as a mind-independent direct object of perception supplemented by a systematic hallucination introspectively indistinguishable from seeing light grey patches at the intersections of the white channels between these black squares.

Two further related phenomena remain to be considered. Both concern 'illusions' due to some degree of abnormality or malfunction of the visual system, or of the perceptual system in another sensory modality; and I must confess that I am struggling clearly to formulate principles to determine which of the two (OV) strategies offered here should be adopted in which cases. Still, these certainly offer additional materials for the characterization of various perceptual phenomena within the context of (OV).

First, very much along the lines suggested above in connection with Hermann's Grid, there are cases in which physiological abnormality or some kind of overload to the system may also lead to a systematic *superimposition* upon perception of the physical world of an additional layer of hallucinatory experience as elucidated above. I would be inclined to treat the supposed general yellowing of the jaundiced person's perception in this way. Their experience, at least according to the standard philosophical description of the case, consists in visual acquaintance with the objects before them partially obscured by a general hallucinatory superimposition introspectively indistinguishable from the presence of a wash of yellow light.

Second, there are cases in which perceptual system malfunction results in an impediment of some kind to normal conscious visual acquaintance with the relevant mind-independent physical objects. According to (OV), the ways that such objects normally look is the result of our acquaintance with them together with their visually relevant similarities from the point of view and in the perceptual circumstances in question with paradigms of various kinds. Obviously, there are significant and highly complex physiological enabling conditions on our being so acquainted with them in vision, and indeed also in the other sensory modalities; and these may on occasion fail partly or fully in all sorts of ways. In certain cases, experiences are therefore to be construed most fundamentally as merely *degraded acquaintance* with the physical objects in question. Thus, (OV) may account for a red/green colour-blind subject's visual experience of an apple, say, as a case of degraded conscious visual acquaintance with that very object from a given point of view in specific circumstances of perception, or, equivalently, as conscious acquaintance with that very thing, from a given point of view, *in a degraded visual modality* and in such and such specific circumstances of perception.

There may well be other experiences indistinguishable by introspection alone from those of the jaundiced and colour-blind perceiver respectively, as just characterized: that of being visually acquainted with a physical scene bathed in a wash of yellow light, for example; and *perhaps* that of a normal subject visually acquainted from an equivalent point of view with a greyish apple. But these are fundamentally quite different perceptual experiences according to (OV), regardless of their introspective indistinguishability.

As I say, it is not absolutely clear to me how most neatly to decide between these two strategies—hallucinatory superimposition or degraded acquaintance—in connection with various similar and related cases. I simply offer the conviction on behalf of (OV) that one of the strategies provides an adequate and correct account of every case of this general kind that may arise. Further cases to consider in an exhaustive treatment here would include at least the following.[19] In each, I provide a sketch indication of what strikes me at present as the most fruitful (OV) approach.

First, an object in the periphery of the visual field may look red but no specific shade of red. This seems to me to be a relatively straightforward case of degraded visual acquaintance. The object would look red$_{13}$, let us say, and of course red *simpliciter* too, in a focal presentation, but peripheral presentation leads merely to degraded acquaintance. Second, how might (OV) handle cases in which objects look blurred? Perhaps there are different cases here. If the blurred vision is due to a malfunction in the visual system, then this would again be a case of systematically degraded acquaintance. If the blurring is due instead to the reflection of excessive bright light, say, then perhaps it is a case in which visual acquaintance is conjoined with systematic hallucinatory superimposition as in Hermann's Grid. Third, consider the motion after-effect known as the Waterfall Illusion (e.g. Mather, Verstraten, and Anstis, 1998). Here a stationary stimulus appears to move when viewed immediately after staring at a moving object. For example, a rock appears to move upwards after one stares at the waterfall in the river beside it. The illusion is complicated by the fact that the rock also appears to be stationary. This latter fact is easy to explain on (OV), since the rock is stationary and has visually relevant similarities with paradigm stationary objects. I would propose explaining the illusory motion after-effect again as a systematic conjoined hallucination. No doubt there is a great deal more to be said about each of these cases and many more besides. But I hope at least to have indicated how these two phenomena of degraded acquaintance and hallucinatory superimposition extend the explanatory resources of (OV) significantly in connection with a wide range of further perceptual peculiarities.

Thus, I conclude quite generally that the evident existence of illusions and hallucinations is absolutely no obstacle to (OV).

---

[19] Thanks to Adam Pautz for these suggestions. See also Pautz (2010).

5.3 Looks

The goal of the present section is to elaborate further and defend the (OV) account of the ways mind-independent physical objects look in perception. Perceptual experience consists at its most fundamental level in a person's conscious acquaintance with particular mind-independent physical objects from a given point of view, in a particular sensory modality and in specific circumstances of perception. Those objects look various ways to her in virtue of their visually relevant similarities with paradigms of various kinds of such things, relative to the point of view and other circumstances of perception in question. Although the following proposal will be subject to significant development and qualification here, the basic idea is that a mind-independent physical object, *o*, looks *F* to a subject, *S*, in virtue of the fact that *S* is consciously visually acquainted with *o* from a point of view and in circumstances of perception relative to which *o* has visually relevant similarities with paradigm exemplars of *F*, where *visually relevant similarities* are similarities of the various kinds to which the physical processes enabling visual perception respond similarly, as a result of both their evolutionary design and their development over the course of our lives. I work towards greater elucidation and defence of the proposal through a consideration of a series of objections and concerns.

It might be helpful right away, though, to put the whole discussion here in dialectical context *vis-à-vis* a potentially powerful general line of objection.[20] (OV) construes our most fundamental visual perceptual relation with the physical world in terms or our conscious acquaintance, from a given point of view and in certain specific circumstances, with particular mind-independent objects. It goes on to offer an account of the ways that such physical objects look in terms of their *visually relevant similarities*, from the point of view and in the circumstances in question, with certain *paradigm exemplars* of various kinds. The objection takes the form of a dilemma. Either the key notions of *visually relevant similarities* and *paradigms* are given complete explicit definition or they are not. If they are, then there will inevitably be counterexamples. If they are not, then no specific position has adequately been identified under the title of '(OV)'. Either way, (OV) fails. My response is to insist that these two options are absolutely not exhaustive. The key notions are indeed theoretical to an extent, in that they go beyond

---

[20] This is due to Adam Pautz.

our commonsense understanding of the terms expressing them. It is certainly also true that I have nowhere given a complete explicit specification of every respect in which they do so from which the whole of the (OV) account of looks may be derived in every possible situation. Still, I have given a rich and detailed combination of theoretical-definitional pointers and well-worked examples and illustrations of how I intend these terms to be used in elaborating (OV) that provide specific guidance in many cases and indicate how to go on in developing the (OV) account in many more. What follows is significantly more in the same vein. I contend that this is precisely what is possible and desirable by way of proper elucidation of any illuminating philosophical position in the area.

To begin with, then, it might be objected that, in rejecting (CV) and insisting that our fundamental perceptual relation with the physical world is to be characterized in terms of the mind-independent physical direct objects of our conscious acquaintance, from a given spatiotemporal point of view, in a particular sense modality, and in specific circumstances of perception, rather than directly in terms of any representational *content* of perceptual experience, (OV) misses entirely the crucial point: the more or less determinate ways that things *look* to us in perception, for example, are an *experiential* matter, a matter of how things are for the subject there and then in that very experience; and similarly, illusions such as (ML) are *experiential* illusions. The ways that things look are therefore not a matter of abstract similarities between those and other things—various paradigms or anything else—but rather a matter of the phenomenology of perceptual experience *itself*; similarly, the (ML) lines look, *phenomenologically*, unequal in length![21] I agree with the data, but I disagree that only (CV), and not (OV), may accommodate them.

This objection raises a number of very interesting issues directly concerning the nature of perceptual experience and it also connects with a range of further major philosophical questions in other areas. So my reply will inevitably be incomplete or somewhat dogmatic in certain respects. I begin with a general analogy that reappears in more detail in ch. 6 below; and I pursue the point more fully in reply to the current objection also by way of particular examples. Suppose that *o* is *F*. According to one kind of resemblance nominalism, *o* satisfies the predicate 'x is *F*' in virtue

---

[21] Thanks to Ian Phillips for pressing this objection very forcefully in his paper at the 2005 Warwick University Mindgrad conference. See his (2005).

of the fact that *o* sufficiently and appropriately resembles the paradigms whose association with that predicate plays a significant role in determining its meaning.[22] Thus, *o*'s being *F* is a matter of its resemblance to other things. Still, it is *o* itself that *is F*. Similarly, I claim, if *o* has certain visually relevant similarities with paradigm exemplars of *F* relative to a given spatiotemporal point of view and specific circumstances of perception, then *o* itself *looks F* in a perceptual experience of conscious visual acquaintance with that very object from that point of view in those circumstances; and I see no good reason to worry that this is anything other than a fully phenomenological fact about the experience itself in which *o* is visually presented.

Indeed, it seems to me that (CV) is, if anything, *less* well placed than (OV) in connection with this concern. For (CV) construes facts about the ways things look as facts about the representational contents of perceptual experience; and almost all theories of content involve a significant degree of externalism, according to which the contents of mental states are extrinsically or relationally determined, perhaps on the basis of the normal cause or biological-evolutionary function of states of that (more intrinsic) kind. So it is a feature of both views that a complete account of looks involves a certain amount of relationality somewhere. Furthermore, as the analogy with resemblance nominalism brings out, the visually relevant similarities that are central to the (OV) account of looks are at least similarities of the very kind that grounds facts about *o* itself, from the point of view and in the circumstances in question; and the core claim of the position is that the most fundamental account of our perceptual relation with the mind-independent physical world is to be given precisely in terms of conscious acquaintance, from that point of view and in those circumstances, with that very object.

To illustrate, elucidate, and expand upon these basic ideas concerning the (OV) account of the phenomenology of looks, consider a series of examples.

First, suppose that I see a duck. According to (OV) my experience consists in my conscious visual acquaintance with that very animal out there from a particular point of view and in specific circumstances of perception. Provided conditions are relatively normal, then the direct

---

[22] Nominalism is obviously a major topic. See Rodriguez-Pereyra (2002) for an overview and defence of a related version of the position.

object of my experience has visually relevant similarities, relative to that point of view and those circumstances, with paradigm ducks. In this sense it looks ducklike. Being an experience in which that very animal looks ducklike in this way, this is an appropriate context for the teaching and learning of the concept of being a duck—although of course much more must also be done. Such an experience is also an intelligible ground for the application of that concept by those who already have it.[23] Still, given the actual direct object involved, and its visually relevant similarities with paradigm ducks from the point of view and in the circumstances in question, we may also say that it looks ducklike even to a child without that concept. All that is involved in her having the experience, though, is that that very animal is presented from a point of view and in circumstances relative to which it has visually relevant similarities with various paradigms *of ours*. Reference to that object, given her viewpoint and the relevant circumstances, along with a shared currency of paradigms central to *our* grasp of the concept, entirely captures and serves to convey her phenomenology. *We* may further register the relevant similarities with such paradigms when presented with a duck in perception in this way. Most importantly, we may note the intelligible applicability of the *concept* of a duck and thereby come to see it *as* a duck. This is a further genuinely *phenomenological* affair associated with our conceptual classificatory engagement with what is directly presented to us in experience: that very *duck*, as we would now say.[24]

Thus, (OV) has an appropriately rich and nuanced account of the various ways that mind-independent physical objects look to us in perception. At its foundation is the simple idea that *o* looks *F* iff *o* is the direct object of a visual experience from a point of view and in circumstances relative to which *o* has visually relevant similarities with paradigm exemplars of *F*. I will say in such cases that *o thinly* looks *F*. *O thickly* looks *F* iff *o* thinly looks *F* and the subject recognizes it *as an F*, or registers its visually relevant

---

[23] See ch. 6 below for further development of this idea in a more explicitly epistemological context.

[24] There *may* also be other less demanding modes of *registration* of visually relevant similarities in perception that do not explicitly draw upon fully conceptual categorization. Something along these lines is plausibly involved in simple systematic sorting behaviour or other robust differential responses, for example. Registration may also consist in noticing various organizational, orientational, or other gestalt phenomena. For clarity of exposition I leave these possibilities largely to one side in what follows. See ch. 6 for further discussion of conceptual registration.

similarities with paradigm exemplars of *F* in an active application of that very concept.[25]

Conceptual phenomenology of this latter kind is not simply a matter of being caused to make a judgement employing the concept in question. It is a matter of actively and intelligibly subsuming the particular presented as the direct object of experience under that concept, in virtue of its evident similarities with the paradigms central to our understanding of that concept. We may simply find ourselves with that concept in mind, but, in cases of seeing *o* as *F*, in which it thickly looks *F*, the concept is evidently appropriate—to us—to that particular in virtue of the de facto existence and attentional salience of such visually relevant similarities. Note also, and importantly, that the concept *F* may be evidently appropriate *in this way*, in virtue of our conceptual registration of the visually relevant similarities, even if we know that we are subject to some kind of illusion and that *o* is not in fact *F*, and so, for that reason or any other, do not actually make any *judgement* to the effect that *o* is *F*—although we may in such a case judge that *o* looks *F*.[26]

The mind-independent physical objects that are presented to us in perception de facto *have* visually relevant similarities with very many paradigms relative to our points of view and circumstances of perception. So, for example, my study carpet thinly looks blue, navy blue, and maximally determinate navy blue shade N, say, and many other ways too. In registering some and not others of these similarities I explicitly recognize and categorize it, for example, *as* navy, although, as I say, I may for some reason withhold an all-out judgement to the effect that it actually is navy. This makes a significant difference to the nature of my perceptual relation with the carpet; but it is absolutely not a matter of *perceiving that a similarity relation obtains between the carpet and something else*—not least because I do not perceive the relevant something else itself, that is, the paradigm of navy that plays a central role in my grasp of that colour concept. Still, I claim in reply to the present objection, thick looks as well as thin looks are a genuinely phenomenological matter.

It might be objected to this last claim that recognizing the carpet as falling under the concept 'navy' cannot possibly make a phenomenological difference of any kind. For if it did, then it would not be possible to

---

[25] As I say, there may also be intermediate levels of such registration and categorization.

[26] See my discussion of belief-independence below for further clarification of this point.

have two phenomenologically identical experiences of seeing the same carpet from the same viewpoint in the same circumstances, in one and not the other of which it is conceptually registered as navy in colour. But this surely is possible. Indeed it would apparently follow from denying its possibility that when it is recognized as navy it somehow looks different in colour; and surely that cannot be right.[27] The reply is straightforward. Both before and after any categorization using the colour concept 'navy' the carpet thinly looks navy; and this is a matter of *constant* visual phenomenology. After conceptual registration of its visually relevant similarities with paradigms of navy blue it also thickly looks navy; and this is a phenomenological *change*. Any problem arises only on the assumption that there is a *single* uncontroversial notion of visual phenomenology on which it makes perfectly good sense to ask, and it is always possible determinately to answer, whether two experiential conditions are phenomenologically identical *tout court*. The whole point of the thin v. thick looks distinction is precisely to deny that assumption. All that is involved is acknowledgement of a familiar phenomenon. Recognition—of a cloud as shaped like a bull, or of a doodle as a distorted name, say—is *both* classificatory and phenomenological. In one sense it changes the way the thing in question looks; in another sense the shape it looks is unchanged. It is surely a virtue rather than a vice of (OV) that it has easily to hand the materials to make this simple acknowledgement.

Consider as a closely related second example Jastrow's (1900) Duck Rabbit (see also Wittgenstein, 1958: II. ii). Suppose that I am simply presented with the diagram head on in normal lighting conditions. According to (OV), my fundamental perceptual condition is one of conscious visual acquaintance with that diagram. Relative to my point of view and circumstances of perception, it has visually relevant similarities with paradigms of both a duck and a rabbit. It therefore thinly looks both ducklike and rabbitlike regardless of whether I notice either resemblance: perhaps I am preoccupied with other things.[28] Suppose that I register it as ducklike: I notice its visually relevant similarities with the paradigms

---

[27] This line of objection came up in correspondence with Susanna Siegel.

[28] It has these visually relevant similarities with paradigms of both a duck and a rabbit even if I do not have either concept myself. Still it thinly looks like both: either characterization by others with the relevant concepts of how things look in my experience would be (thinly) correct.

central to my grasp of that concept. It thickly looks ducklike and I see it as ducklike. This is a phenomenological fact, according to (OV), although one of conceptual classificatory engagement with the very diagram presented to me in perception, which continues thinly to look both ducklike and rabbitlike. Similarly, when I shift aspects and see it as rabbitlike, there is an alteration in this phenomenology of the categorization of what is presented.[29]

Consider third the case of (ML). Suppose that I have the diagram presented to me, head on and in good lighting conditions, with my eyes open and a normally functioning visual system. According to (OV), my experience is most fundamentally one of conscious visual acquaintance with that very diagram as its mind-independent physical direct object, from that point of view in those circumstances. Relative to the viewpoint and circumstances in question the (ML) diagram presented has visually relevant similarities with a paradigm pair of unequal lines at different depths. Thus, its two main lines thinly look unequal in length; and again we can perfectly correctly mark the de facto existence of these visually relevant similarities in this way in connection with children without the relevant concepts. This is genuine phenomenology consequent upon the identity and nature of the direct object of experience, given the viewpoint and relevant circumstances involved. It is fully captured by (OV) without any need for (CV). Possessing the concept of inequality in length as I do, I may notice the visually relevant similarities in question with my paradigms, either because the question of the relative length of its main lines becomes relevant in some way and I attend accordingly, or simply because they jump out at me or *capture* my attention. As a result of this conceptual registration, the lines thickly look unequal in length, regardless of whether I actually judge them to be so, as most likely in this case I do not because I am well aware of the illusion. In any case, this is a perfectly genuinely phenomenological matter; but one which is again captured entirely by (OV), along with my deployment of attention and active conceptual endowment.

---

[29] As I mentioned above, there may be more primitive phenomenological differences possible in such cases too, where the subject registers a figure as oriented that way (left) and then shifts to register its orientation as that way (right). Here registration perhaps involves a kind of active demonstrative categorization of orientation.

Return as a fourth example to the case of a white piece of chalk illuminated with red light. I explained the way in which (OV) accounts for the fact that this illusorily looks red. (OV) appears equally committed to the claim that it looks white-in-red-light. For everything presumably has visually relevant similarities with itself however exactly these are to be defined; and this may well be a paradigm case of something that is white-in-red-light. This plausibly entails that the chalk looks white *simpliciter*, which is suspect at best in the envisaged circumstances. Furthermore, parity of reasoning suggests that (OV) is committed to the idea that a red piece of chalk in normal lighting conditions similarly looks white-in-red-light, and therefore looks white *simpliciter* too. This is surely completely unacceptable.[30]

Again, the key to making sense of all of this in the context of (OV) lies in the distinction between thin and thick looks. A suitable squiggle, for example, thinly looks quarter-note-rest-shaped to all of us; it thickly looks quarter-note-rest-shaped only to some of us—those who recognize it as (at least an attempt at) such. The duck-rabbit diagram thinly looks both ducklike and rabbitlike; it thickly looks at most one of these to a given subject at any one time. The looks locution is I think standardly interpreted thickly, although the thin reading can certainly be and often is made appropriate. When we see a white piece of chalk in red light, it thinly looks white-in-red-light, as well as red; it is very unlikely thickly to look white-in-red-light without considerable stage setting; but *then* it may well be right to say that it does: for example, when trying to pick out the white piece from a collection of differently coloured chalks in a setting in which we all know that the light is abnormally red. The correct target looks white (in-red-light). A red piece of chalk in normal lighting also thinly looks white-in-red-light, as well as red. It would not normally thickly look white-in-red-light; but again, given sufficient stage-setting, it may be brought to do so. Notice, though, that the sense in which the white chalk in red light, and the red chalk in normal light, thickly look white, if and when they do so with sufficient stage-setting, is essentially *indirect*, involving an explicit conjunction elimination by the subject from the evident similarities that the direct object in question has in the

---

[30] Many thanks to Anil Gupta, who raised this line of objection in his excellent comments at the Pacific APA, 2006, in Portland.

circumstances with a complex paradigm of something white-in-red-light.[31] Still, it seems to me that all this serves to confirm, rather than in any way undermine, the (OV) contention that the rich and various looks that particular mind-independent physical objects have in perception are the product of a fundamental relation of conscious visual acquaintance with particular such things from a given point of view and in specific circumstances of perception and the visually relevant similarities that those objects have with various paradigms relative to the point of view and circumstances involved, along with sometimes quite sophisticated attentional and classificatory phenomena.

It may be objected here that (OV) now appears committed to the possibility of perceptual experiences in which things have impossible combinations of looks in just the way that I argued was unacceptable in the case of (CV). For I claim that there are senses in which the white chalk in red light looks red and in which it looks white, for example; but nothing is or could be red (all over) and white (all over). Similarly, and more simply, a round coin seen from an angle both looks elliptical and looks round; yet nothing could be round and (eccentrically) elliptical. The situation is quite different though, and is not so far as I can see in any tension with the genuine role of perception and conceivability in the epistemology of modality. First, the direct objects of these experiences are particular mind-independent physical objects. These actually exist and so they are clearly possible. Their looks are a product of direct acquaintance with that very thing, and so there is no need whatsoever to characterize perception by reference to anything impossible at all. The problem for (CV) was that it is committed to impossibility at the most fundamental level of the characterization of perceptual experience. Furthermore, according to (OV), the thin looks of the mind-independent physical direct objects of perception are a product of the various visually relevant similarities that they have from the point of view and in the circumstances in question with certain paradigms. All of this is a matter of what is also actual and hence perfectly possible. Their thick looks conceptually register some but not others of these similarities, in each particular case,

---

[31] Such conjunction elimination is not appropriate in the case simply of thin looks. It seems to me wrong to say that the white chalk in red light or the red chalk in normal light thinly look white *simpliciter*. For they do not have visually relevant similarities in the envisaged circumstances with *paradigm* white objects.

corresponding to a way that the object in question might be whether or not it actually is so. Thus, suppose that the white chalk in red light thickly looks red; it might have been red; but it actually is not. In so far as it can be brought thickly to look white, this is also of course a way that it might have been because it actually is. Just as with the duck-rabbit, though, it does not thickly look both ways for a given subject at the same time. Similarly, the coin may thickly look elliptical, which it might have been but is not; or it may thickly look round, which it might have been because it is. It is a notable datum that we cannot focus on impossible combinations of such aspects together. The closest we get, for example, as subject of the experience itself, is to register on the basis of perception that the coin *is* round even though there's a sense in which it looks elliptical; and again there is nothing impossible in that.[32]

There are of course many more cases to consider in clarifying the (OV) account of looks completely. I confine myself to three that illustrate what are hopefully helpful points of principle about the position.[33]

First, how does (OV) handle variation in colour vision: for example, a case in which Janet and John are both looking at a colour chip in good lighting conditions that looks pure blue to Janet and green-blue to John? This case raises issues about the nature of the colours of mind-independent physical objects themselves that are beyond the scope of the present discussion. I confine myself to a relatively dogmatic statement of my own (OV) account. The pertinent issue is: whose paradigms of specific colour shades are in question in the characterization of the way the chip looks to Janet and John? Given fixed paradigm exemplars of pure blue, either the chip has visually relevant similarities with them or it does not.[34] If so, and provided that Janet and John are both in optimal viewing conditions, then *in that sense* it looks pure blue to both of them. (Envisage this report in the voice of someone for whom the fixed paradigms in question are precisely those that play a central role in his understanding of the colour term 'pure blue'.) If not, then in the same sense it looks pure blue to neither of them. The sense in which the chip looks pure blue to

---

[32] See my discussion below of the purported belief-independence of perception for a little more that is relevant to this kind of situation.

[33] Once again these are due to Adam Pautz. See Pautz (2010) for further discussion.

[34] See n. 8 above for the condition that *visually relevant similarity* in the sense invoked in the (OV) account of looks requires sufficiently many similarities of visually relevant sort with paradigm exemplars of the kind in question.

Janet is that it has visually relevant similarities with *her* paradigm exemplars of pure blue: those that play a central role in her understanding of 'pure blue'. Similarly, it looks green-blue to John because it has visually relevant similarities with *his* paradigm exemplars of green-blue: those that play a central role in his understanding of 'green-blue'. They just have slightly different such paradigms, and so understand the specific colour terms slightly differently. This is all perfectly consistent so far as I can see and no threat to (OV). It clearly raises further issues about the nature of shared language understanding in the domain of colours and indeed more widely. There is a delicate balance to be drawn between the fundamental genuinely public nature of a shared language and the datum that we *can* sometimes talk past each other. Although it would be ludicrous to deny it could ever happen, there are also I believe strong forces massively limiting the range and significance of any such idiolectical deviation. Again though, I must leave these issues aside for present purposes.

Second, suppose that all the actual exemplars of *red* are round. That is, everything that is actually red happens also to be round. Presumably this entails that all the *paradigm* exemplars of *red* are round. So if a person is visually acquainted with a blue round object, then this has visually relevant similarities with paradigm exemplars of *red*. Thus, according to the (OV) account of looks, it looks red, at least thinly. This is surely false: except in abnormal illusory circumstances, a blue round object would not look red in this situation.

Supporters of (OV) should in my view deny the move from the hypothesis that all the actual exemplars of *red* are round to the claim that all *paradigm* exemplars of *red* are therefore also round. Paradigms are not simply a subset of actual exemplars. They are actual exemplars, or images derived from perception or description of them, as representatives of *all possible exemplars*, or as *indicative* of the set of all possible exemplars. As Hume (1978: I. 1. vii) points out in connection with the ideas associated with general terms of predication, 'The word raises up an individual idea, along with a certain custom; and that custom produces any other individual one, for which we may have occasion'. Hence, although a blue round direct object of perception has visually relevant similarities with every actual exemplar of red, it does not have visually relevant similarities with *paradigm* exemplars of red, for these also include, at least potentially as it were, possible but non-actual *non-round* red things. (OV) is therefore not committed absurdly to the idea that the blue round object looks red in any sense in the objector's envisaged scenario.

An extension of the broadly Humean idea also accounts for the fact that a white wall illuminated with red light in a world in which there are no genuinely red objects nevertheless looks red. For, although there are no actual exemplars of *red*, the redly illuminated wall nevertheless has visually relevant similarities with possible but non-actual exemplars of red: the paradigm exemplars, our imagination of which plays a central role in our understanding of the predicate 'is red'.[35]

Third, suppose that there were sentient creatures but no concept users. Red objects may still look red to such creatures, even though there are presumably no paradigm exemplars of *red*, in this case because there are no subjects for whom any such exemplars play any role in their possession of the concept *red*: nobody has that concept or any other. Here once again it is crucial to note the distinction between thin and thick looks, and indeed to recall a point I made briefly earlier in elucidating this distinction. An object, *o*, thinly looks *F* if *o* is the direct object of a visual experience from a point of view and in circumstances relative to which it has visually relevant similarities with paradigm exemplars of *F*. These are the exemplars that

---

[35] See my discussion in §5.2 of hallucination and the explanatory role of perception in connection with our capacity for beliefs whose content contains various empirical concepts for more on the complex stage-setting that is required for our acquisition of uninstantiated such concepts. This is clearly a historically familiar problem for empiricist-minded philosophers that I cannot solve in complete generality here. See Rodriguez-Pereyra (2002: ch. 5) for extended discussion of a parallel appeal to non-actual instances in defence of a resemblance nominalist account of the difference between distinct but contingently coextensive properties. Rodriguez-Pereyra's view about necessarily coextensive properties is that any apparent example of distinct such properties is 'in fact just a case of semantically different predicates applying in virtue of one and the same property or relation' (ibid. 100). I remain neutral on the correct individuation of properties. But I do think that a parallel proposal applies in some cases at least in connection with the (OV) account of looks. Suppose that *F* and *G* are necessarily coextensive. Then, given the comments on paradigms offered in the main text above, *F* and *G* *may* have identical paradigm exemplars, although see n. 8 above for an important qualification concerning the orientation-sensitivity of certain paradigms. In such cases, according to (OV), an object thinly looks *F* iff it thinly looks *G*. This seems to me absolutely right in certain cases at least (again modulo n. 8 above). Just as an appropriate squiggle *thinly* looks quarter-note-rest-shaped even to the musically uninitiated, a triangle thinly looks both three-sided and three-vertexed, as well as triangular, as it were, to all of us, reading these in the senses in which they are indeed necessarily coextensive. Things become far more complicated with respect to thick looks, of course, because a great deal more is involved in conceptually registering visually relevant similarities with various paradigm exemplars than simply being presented with an object that has them.

play a central role in our possession of the concept *F* in terms of which the look in question is to be characterized. Provided that the appropriate visually relevant similarities obtain for the subject, from the point of view and in the circumstances in question, the thin look ascription holds even if she does not have the concept *F* itself in terms of which this is to be expressed. The creature whose experience is to be characterized here may be in precisely the same situation. We may truly say that objects look red in its experience even though *nobody* in the world in question is capable of making or understanding that very ascription. The case is clearly controversial and raises many disputed issues. I simply contend that (OV) has the resources to account for the idea that red objects may still look red to such creatures in such circumstances. Of course nothing thickly looks red to anyone in the world in question. For this additionally involves recognition of the objects as red, or conceptual registration of the pertinent visually relevant similarities.

I conclude from my consideration of all these examples and everything that has gone before that (OV) is amply able to capture the rich, varied, and nuanced *phenomenology* of the ways mind-independent physical objects look in perception.

I turn now to address the question of the extent to which my own final position really is an *Object* View on the model of the early modern empiricists, or whether it might not better be characterized simply as a variant of the currently orthodox *Content* View. Unsurprisingly I contend that the distinction remains firm and (OV) has all the virtues of (CV) without its vices.

To begin with, given the rich (OV) account of looks and the illusions that they give rise to, one might wonder what the force is supposed to be of the claim that a relation of conscious visual acquaintance with the particular mind-independent physical direct objects themselves that are presented in perception constitutes the most fundamental characterization of perceptual experience.[36] I clearly reject the early modern empiricist biconditional that something looks *F* in perceptual experience iff the direct object of that experience is *F*. The direct objects of perception are certainly not basic to our understanding of perceptual experience in this very simple sense. Nevertheless, I have explained the way in which the

[36] Thanks again to Anil Gupta for pushing this question in discussion at the 2006 Pacific APA.

nature of the mind-independent physical direct objects of perception is still the source of the most perspicuous account of the way that those very things look in perception, given the point of view from which and specific circumstances of perception in which we are visually acquainted with them on any particular occasion. Those very objects are therefore what explanatorily ground and unify the various ways that they do and might look in perception from any point of view and in any circumstances. Thus, every such perception most fundamentally consists in our conscious acquaintance with particular such things. The relation between the direct objects of perception and their looks is more complex according to (OV) than according to the early modern empiricists; but the underlying insight is just the same: only by thinking of our perceptual relation with the physical world most fundamentally in terms of our conscious relation of acquaintance with certain direct *objects* of experience can we properly understand the various ways that physical objects look to us in perception at all.

It may help to clarify this (OV) approach to the ways that mind-independent physical objects look in perception to probe further the particular relation between the look of inequality in length and our conscious visual acquaintance with the (ML) diagram as the direct object of our perception.[37] Since the main lines making up that diagram are not themselves unequal in length it may appear difficult for (OV) adequately to capture the robustness of the illusory appearance. On the other hand, if the look of inequality in length is held to be essential to the fundamental characterization of our experience of (ML), then the (OV) insistence that our fundamental perceptual relation is one to objects and not contents may sound rather hollow. The objection has the form of a dilemma. Is the fact that the main lines look unequal in length essential to the characterization of our fundamental perceptual relation with (ML) or not? If not, then (OV) fails to capture the robustness of the illusion: someone may stand in just that perceptual relation and yet the lines not look unequal in length. That seems wrong. If the fact that the lines look unequal in length is essential to the characterization of our fundamental perceptual relation with (ML), on the other hand, then, since the main lines of the diagram are not themselves unequal in length, representational properties must be

---

[37] My discussion here is motivated by questions from Matt Soteriou.

essential to the characterization of our fundamental perceptual relation in order to secure that look of inequality in length. (OV) therefore appears to have given way to a version of (CV).

This is a very helpful challenge, for it enables us to appreciate the interesting and subtle division of labour between ourselves and the world in accounting for the (ML) illusion; and, indeed, in making sense of the way that mind-independent physical objects look to us in perception generally. According to (OV), the main lines of the (ML) diagram thinly look unequal in length in virtue of the fact that we are visually acquainted with that very diagram from a point of view from which and in circumstances of perception in which it has visually relevant similarities with certain paradigm cases of lines of unequal length. Already this depends upon certain contingencies about ourselves, our evolutionary development and our experience in life. Of course we have to have a visual system; but this also has to have evolved a sensitivity to certain stimuli and a propensity to group them and to identify and distinguish them in various ways. Only so is there a relatively settled notion of visually relevant similarity in order to determine the thin looks of the objects that we see. This dependency upon contingency deepens with respect to thick looks. The main lines of (ML) thickly look unequal in length in virtue of our further *registration* of these visual similarities with the paradigms that play a central role in our own grasp of the concept of inequality in length as it applies to such things. Here there is a further role for the particular nature of our own particular experience in acquiring and deploying that concept. Were these factors sufficiently different, then the (ML) lines would not look unequal in length in the relevant thin or thick sense and our experience of them would not in this way be misleading. This is right in my view: the illusion is not unrestrictedly robust.[38] Still, given these deep contingencies about our evolution and development, the fact that the main lines look unequal in length follows from the fact that we are visually acquainted with that very diagram from a particular point of view and in specific circumstances without any need for appeal to independent representational properties.

---

[38] See McCauley and Henrich (2006) for empirical confirmation from results that suggest that susceptibility to the (ML) illusion is dependent upon being in a carpentered world, whose orthogonal joints invest the diagram's hashes with their misleading association with depth.

These points apply to the (OV) account of looks quite generally. The ways things look depend upon the identity and nature of the objects themselves that are consciously presented in perception and the range of visually relevant similarities that they have from the points of view and in the circumstances in question with paradigms of various kinds. Which such similarities are *visually relevant* and what constitute the various *paradigms* each depends in complex ways upon numerous more or less deep contingencies about us and our nature, evolution, education, perceptual experience to date, and so forth. Taken together these factors determine the robustness of the looks in question, and so of any illusions to which these may give rise. This certainly raises many interesting questions: to what extent, and how, might it have been possible to *see* the objects in question, from those points of view and in those circumstances, and yet for them not to look those ways? Perhaps their having some, but not others, of the looks that they actually have is more central to the fact that the sensitivity that we have to them is a case of *seeing* rather than something else. Perhaps we might have picked up on them in radically different ways that were less, or more, susceptible to various forms of illusion. However things might have been, and whichever alternative scenarios are held to be genuinely possible, and, indeed, however one thinks that it is to be determined which such scenarios *are* genuinely possible, I claim that (OV) is absolutely right in discerning a complex cooperation in determining the ways things look between the contributions of the worldly objects themselves that we see and the external and internal, historical and contemporary, physical, psychological, educational, and other processes that are involved in our seeing them as we do.

Still, it may be objected further, this just brings out the fact that my own characterization of illusions involves *categorization*: they are experiences in which o looks F although o is not F; and I certainly accept in general that when S sees o there are numerous truths of the form o looks F to S. Yet this surely entails an immediate assimilation of (OV) to (CV)?[39] It is certainly true that looks phenomena as explained and elaborated above are precisely the aspect of my development of (OV) that is intended to accommodate the features of perceptual experiences that are central to (CV); but this absolutely does not collapse (OV) into a version of (CV). For (CV)

---

[39] Thanks to Nicolas Bullot for pressing the issue in this way in his helpful comments on my presentation of (OV) to the 2006 Pacific APA in Portland.

134 THE OBJECT VIEW

attempts to capture our most fundamental perceptual relation with the
physical world directly and wholly in contentful terms, whereas (OV)
explains the truth of looks claims, involving the categorization that they
clearly do, as the product of a more basic subjective presentation of a
particular object, along with its salient visually relevant similarities with
various paradigms in the circumstances.

Consider analogously Grice's (1989*a*, 1989*b*) discussion of conversation-
al implicature. It is a datum that we communicate a highly complex
message in speaking a language that our audience understands. Grice's
opponents regard every aspect of this message as part of an undifferentiated
notion of meaning. Grice insists, on the contrary, upon a partition into
core semantic truth-conditional meaning, on the one hand, and any
pragmatic implicature that may be conveyed by choosing to say something
with just those truth-conditions in the circumstances, given the conven-
tions governing good communication, on the other. Similarly, I claim
that, although 'unequal in length', for example, really is part of how the
(ML) lines look, it is right to regard this as the product of a more basic
relation of conscious visual acquaintance with those very lines themselves,
along with their visually relevant similarities with certain paradigms of
inequality in length from our point of view and in the circumstances, and
the ways that we may or may not register these similarities, given our
evolution, training, conceptual endowment, attention, and interests at the
time. Looks in general flow from the core early modern empiricist insight
at the heart of (OV), given independently motivated additional theoretical
materials. They are not to be accommodated by any direct and undifferentiated appeal to a barrage of perceptual contents that are simply served
up to us in experience. Acquaintance with the mind-independent physical
direct objects of perception is the fundamental basis only in terms of which
we can properly and in turn understand the rich and varied superstructure
of the ways that such things look and otherwise appear to us in perceptual
experience. Thus, I claim that the (OV)/(CV) contrast remains entirely
robust and stable.[40]

---

[40] Not wishing to labour the analogy beyond its useful limits, the partition illustrated above
in connection with the conditional robustness of the (ML) illusion, between the contribution
of the object and that of the perceiver in accounting for the way things look in perception,
provides an analogue of the *cancellability* of Gricean implicature (see again his 1989*a* and
especially 1989*b*). For looks are conditional not only upon visual acquaintance with the object
in question, from the right point of view and in the right circumstances, but also upon the

Before turning to explicitly epistemological issues in ch. 6, I would like to make a few comments about the various proposals that I mentioned in ch. 4 as to how (CV) might draw the distinction between the representational contents of perception on the one hand, and of thought on the other.

According to (OV) *o* thinly looks *F* iff it is the direct object of conscious visual acquaintance from a point of view from which and in circumstances in which it has visually relevant similarities with certain general paradigms of mind-independent *F*-ness. This may be the case and so we may correctly describe another subject in this way even if she does not have the concept of an *F*. Thus, in this sense, *o* may non-conceptually look *F*. O thickly looks *F* to *S* iff it thinly looks *F* and *S* registers the visually relevant similarities in question. In the most important case this is a matter of recognizing it as an *F* and thereby taking it to be one, although she may simply note that it looks like an *F* instead if she has reason to believe that it is not actually one. In this sense *o* conceptually looks *F*.[41] This distinction between non-conceptual and conceptual looks is quite different from that normally invoked within the context of (CV), although it remains true that non-conceptual thin looks as elucidated here are a feature of perception and all thought content is conceptual.

Demonstrative registration exploits the presented particular itself as a paradigm for the subject's grasp of the conceptual category in question. Her experience is most fundamentally a matter of her conscious visual acquaintance with that very mind-independent physical object. So truths of the form 'that looks thus', for the appropriate range of demonstrative predications, certainly capture a peculiarly basic feature of her perceptual condition. Proponents of (CV) appealing to this phenomenon are certainly onto something, although they deploy it in my view to mistaken

---

various contingencies that determine visual relevance, paradigm exemplars, and conceptual registration. Specific such looks may therefore be 'cancelled' by envisaging a similar visual acquaintance with that object from the same point of view and in the same circumstances in the absence of the relevant additional factors actually involved.

[41] I do not here rule out the possibility of non-conceptual modes of something like this registration of visually relevant similarities that may be involved in simple systematic sorting behaviour or other robust differential responses, for example. I stand by my earlier arguments (1999) that only conceptual registration of the kind outlined in the text is suitable to ground the fully epistemic reason-giving role of perceptual experience.

ends in forcing their account of perception into the fundamentally contentful mould.

In connection with the proposed passivity of perception, (OV)'s commitments are as follows. Suppose that S is visually acquainted with o from a given point of view and in specific circumstances of perception. That this is the case is normally of course a matter of some freedom for the subject: she may choose where to look and whether to open her eyes and so on. In any case, the ways that o thinly looks are simply a matter of its visually relevant similarities relative to that point of view and those circumstances with paradigms of various kinds of mind-independent physical objects. Although, as noted earlier, the question of which similarities are visually relevant depends upon S's visual system, and the paradigms involved are also dependent upon the conceptual schemes of the subject and attributor, these ways that o thinly looks are not in any way within S's control. It just looks the ways it looks. Further freedom enters in connection with the question of which such visually relevant similarities she registers conceptually. Although these may on occasion capture her attention automatically, she may also direct her attention according to certain specific concerns, focusing on questions of colour as opposed to shape, for example, or on comparisons with one set of paradigms as opposed to another. Still, the visually relevant similarities that are there to be registered in this way are again simply a matter of the nature of the mind-independent physical direct object presented itself and not at all up to her. Thus, the balance of passivity and activity is a subtle one; and what I said here is clearly incomplete. The main point is that (OV) is in an excellent position fully and adequately to account for its complexity.

Finally, what of the proposed belief-independence of perceptual content? Again there is a great deal that could be said here. For present purposes two points suffice. First, thin looks are clearly belief-independent in the sense outlined in ch. 4. O may thinly look F to S even though S does not believe that o is F, or perhaps even cannot do so because she does not have the concept 'F'. With respect to thick looks things are less straightforward. In the normal case in which S registers the visually relevant similarities between an object, o, that is presented to her in perception and the paradigms that play a central role in her grasp of the concept 'F', she does so by recognizing o as an F in an active application of that concept with the genuine force of a judgement. In cases in which she has reason to believe that o is not actually F she may still register its visually relevant similarities with paradigm exemplars of F conceptually, but in the judgement that it *looks* F instead. So there is a good deal that is correct in the various (CV) claims of belief-independence; but these miss the fact, according to (OV) as developed here, that the normal case of conceptual registration is one of judgement actively subsuming the presented particular under the general concept in question.[42]

[42] I recall suggestions along these lines, for which I am grateful here, from unpublished work by Johannes Roessler.

6

Epistemology

There is a sense in which it is right to say that mind-independent physical objects are *given* to a person in perception according to (OV): the fundamental fact of perception is our conscious acquaintance with such things from a given spatiotemporal point of view, in a particular sensory modality and in specific circumstances of perception; and this is intended to play a crucial role in the explanation of how empirical knowledge is possible. Yet at least since Sellars (1997), this whole idea of an empirical given in perception has been viewed with great suspicion. So I begin my discussion of the epistemological commitments and ambitions of (OV) by indicating (in §6.1) how Sellars' initial objection is to be avoided. I then give an extended sketch (in §6.2) of how the positive epistemology of empirical knowledge might proceed in the context of (OV), illustrating at various points (in §6.3) how further objections motivated at least in part by Sellars' discussion may be handled. I move on (in §6.4) to a brief comparison between this (OV)-based epistemological outlook and my own earlier views (Brewer, 1999). The section ends with a return to the topic of transparency that I raised briefly in the introduction to ch. 4. The epistemology of perception is of course a major topic and I acknowledge explicitly that what follows really is a sketch of the direction in which I believe that it should be pursued according to (OV) rather than any kind of comprehensive treatment of the issues raised.

6.1 The myth of the given

Like early modern empiricists, and indeed the sense-datum theorists of the first half of the twentieth century that are Sellars' own more direct target,[1]

---

[1] See e.g. Broad (1925), Price (1950), Ayer (1956, 1963), Moore (1953), and Russell (2001), although not all these authors endorsed the position without qualification themselves. For

(OV) construes perceptual experience most fundamentally as a relation to *particulars*. In contrast with those earlier views, the particulars in the case of (OV) are mind-independent physical objects themselves. Again, like the early modern empiricists and sense-datum theorists, though, (OV) regards this basic experiential relation of acquaintance with certain particulars as of significance in explaining our possession of empirical *knowledge*.[2]

One way to secure this epistemic result, or at least to make a move towards it, is to analyse acquaintance in explicitly epistemic terms. It may be said, for example, that a person is acquainted with an object *o* just if there is some property '*F*' (perhaps from an appropriately circumscribed range) such that she non-inferentially knows that *o* is *F*. Indeed, the weaker claim that acquaintance entails such knowledge would suffice to get the epistemic story going. The remainder of the explanation then of course depends upon the proposed relations between such direct objects of acquaintance and the physical objects of empirical knowledge themselves, and upon the way in which knowledge of the former is supposed to provide a *basis* for knowledge of the latter; and this is all itself notoriously problematic (Brewer, 1999: 4.2, esp. 4.2.4–4.2.6). In any case, this whole approach is in tension with another feature of the positions that constitute Sellars' target.

For they have taken givenness [acquaintance with a given direct object in my terms] to be a fact which presupposes no learning, no forming of associations, no setting up of stimulus-response connections. In short, they have tended to equate sensing sense contents with being conscious, as a person who has been hit on the head is not conscious whereas a new born babe, alive and kicking, is conscious. (Sellars, 1997: 20)

Only so, the thought must be, could givenness possibly constitute the unproblematic *start* of the epistemological explanation.

In a somewhat similar spirit, the whole point of (OV) is to insist upon conscious acquaintance as a fundamental perceptual relation between

---

important modern variants of the sense-datum view see Jackson (1977), Robinson (1994), Foster (2000), and O'Shaughnessy (2003).

[2] For continuity within my own discussion I use 'acquaintance' and its cognates for our basic experiential relation with the direct objects of perception, although I mean it to apply quite generally here in connection with all the views considered. Sellars chooses to use the terminology of 'sensing' and 'sense content' for its relatum. I adopt his own terminology in the extended quotation to follow.

subjects and mind-independent physical objects from a given point of view, in a particular sensory modality, and in specific circumstances of perception, that is more basic than any relation with facts, propositions, or contents concerning the particular physical objects in question, and that is therefore more basic than any *epistemic* relation with such things.

In the light of these reflections, Sellars (1997: 20–1) suggests that all such views are

confronted by an inconsistent triad made up of the following three propositions:

A. *x senses red sense content s* entails *x non-inferentially knows that s is red.*
B. The ability to sense sense contents is unacquired.
C. The ability to know facts of the form *x is φ* is acquired.

A and B together entail not-C; B and C entail not-A; A and C entail not-B.

Once the classical sense-datum theorist [or indeed the proponent of (OV)] faces up to the fact that A, B, and C do form an inconsistent triad, which of them will he choose to abandon?

1) He can abandon A, in which case the sensing of sense contents becomes a noncognitive fact—a noncognitive fact, to be sure which may be a necessary condition, even a logically necessary condition, of non-inferential knowledge, but a fact, nevertheless, which cannot *constitute* this knowledge.

2) He can abandon B, in which case he must pay the price of cutting off the concept of a sense datum from its connection with our ordinary talk about sensations, feelings, afterimages, tickles and itches, etc., which are usually thought by sense-datum theorists to be its common sense counterparts.

3) But to abandon C is to do violence to the predominantly nominalistic proclivities of the empiricist tradition.

The proponent of (OV) clearly rejects A. Conscious acquaintance with mind-independent physical objects is more fundamental than perceptual knowledge in precisely this sense. For, as I explain below, visually based perceptual knowledge that *o* is *F* depends upon *o thickly* looking *F*; and it is possible as we have seen repeatedly in ch. 5 to be consciously acquainted with a mind-independent physical object *o* that is *F* and yet it not thickly look F for a variety of different reasons.[3] Hence, for any property 'F' of a mind-independent physical object, o, it is possible to be visually acquainted with o and yet not have visually based perceptual knowledge that o is F. This is part of the point of the (OV) mantra that conscious acquaintance is the fundamental perceptual relation between subjects and mind-independent physical objects from a given point of view, in a particular sensory modality and in specific circumstances of perception, that is more basic than any relation with facts, propositions, or contents concerning the physical objects in question, and that is therefore more basic than any *epistemic* relation with such things.

Of course this rejection of A constrains the kind of explanation that is available to (OV) of perceptual *knowledge*. It cannot be assumed that our perceptual acquaintance with mind-independent physical objects in and of itself constitutes a foundational level of knowledge about such things. The account that I offer makes no such assumption. Its purpose is to explicate the commonsense commitment that perception of the physical objects in the world around us is, in the context of further additional conditions, a *source* of knowledge about those very things.

I argue in ch. 7 that there is an important sense in which B is also contentious according to my own development of (OV). The core idea at the heart of (OV) is that mind-independent physical objects themselves are the *direct objects* of perception in the early modern sense that I have been adopting throughout. Perceptual experience is most fundamentally to be characterized, *as the specific conscious condition that it is*, as conscious acquaintance, from a point of view, in a particular sense modality, and in certain circumstances, with specific mind-independent physical objects. The nature of the experience itself is to be elucidated by reference to those very things that are presented in perception. I argue in ch. 7 that the mind-independence of the physical objects that constitute the direct objects of perception in this way according to (OV), shows up from our own perspective *as perceivers* in our commitment to certain commonsense-physical explanations of the actual and counterfactual order and nature of our perceptual experience on the basis of the perceptible natures of the very mind-independent physical objects that we perceive. And this is an essential part of what holds in place the (OV) identification of those very

---

[3] See also §6.3 below for a fuller treatment of the various possibilities here.

mind-independent physical objects themselves as the direct objects of our perception in the first place. Thus, our acquaintance determinately with precisely *those direct objects* in perceptual experience is in part secured by patterns of explanation that are acquired in the course of our developing engagement with the mind-independent physical world around us. In this sense, then, my own elaboration of (OV) questions B above.

At the same time, there is something right in B too. For (OV) insists that a person's acquaintance with a particular mind-independent physical object, *o*, in a given perceptual experience on any specific occasion, is not dependent upon his *actual categorization of that very thing* in any acquired manner whatsoever. I explain below how the (OV) account of the role of perceptual experience in our possession of empirical knowledge squares with these commitments concerning B.

(OV) straightforwardly endorses C. Factual knowledge depends upon possession of the concepts employed in the propositional articulation of that knowledge; and we *acquire* such concepts again precisely through our developing cognitive engagement with the physical world in which we live.

(OV) is therefore entirely immune to the accusation of inconsistency that Sellars levels at proponents of a given in perception on the basis of various theorists' apparent commitment to A, B, and C above.

6.2 Empirical knowledge

The next and most important task is to outline the positive explanation that I propose on behalf of (OV) as to how perceptual experience conceived as acquaintance with mind-independent physical objects constitutes a source of empirical knowledge.

Suppose that *o* is *F*, for an appropriate '*F*' that can be known on the basis of vision, say. Thus, given what '*F*' means, *o* makes application of '*F*' correct: *o* itself is what makes '*o* is *F*' true and in this sense constitutes a reason to apply the predicate.[4] The crux of the epistemological account

---

[4] I would say myself that this truth consists in the fact that *o* resembles the *F* things; and this is how *o* makes '*o* is *F*' true. See Rodriguez-Pereyra (2002, 2008) for elaboration of the form of resemblance nominalism that I personally favour. I am uncertain, and I think that this is a very interesting and delicate issue, of the extent to which such nominalism provides further motivation for my development of (OV), or whether my overall case for (OV) instead provides support for resemblance nominalism as a metaphysical account of the physical world that we perceive. I would certainly say that the two are made for each other.

that I propose on behalf of (OV) is that conscious acquaintance with o in vision, say, therefore normally makes application of 'F' in judgement *evidently* correct for a subject who grasps the concept 'F' and is viewing o from a point of view and in circumstances that enable her registration of the appropriate visually relevant similarities between o and the paradigm exemplars of F that are central to her understanding of that concept.[5] In this way, seeing o constitutes the subject's reason for judging that o is F. This, I contend, explains the contribution of perceptual experience to perceptual knowledge: experience acquaints us with the grounds for empirical truth.

In developing this central idea to begin with, I focus on the most basic case of perception from a relatively canonical point of view and in relatively standard circumstances. Illusory judgement and other kinds of perceptual error and epistemic failing are deviations from this basic case that are in my view to be handled separately and derivatively, as I indicate briefly below.

The fact that o thinly looks F as I explain above makes the predication of 'F' *appropriate* given what 'F' means. For o is presented in experience and has visually relevant similarities with various paradigm exemplars of F. The fact that o thickly looks F involves precisely the subject's conceptual registration of these relevant similarities, regardless of whether or not the

---

[5] See Johnston (2006) for a somewhat different development of a similar core claim. As he puts it, 'What is distinctive about non-hallucinatory and non-illusory sensory experience is that it presents the truthmakers for the propositions that we immediately judge true on the basis of sensory experience' (pp. 278–9). There are very important differences between our views, though. To begin with, his conception of the relevant truthmakers is significantly broader than mine of the direct objects of perceptual acquaintance. In particular, his involves metaphysical correlates of the determinate predications that I regard as the product of our noticing certain similarities between presented mind-independent physical objects and paradigms of various kinds of such things. In the veridical case, therefore, we are acquainted not only with the object perceived but also with certain of its specific properties. In illusion, we are again acquainted with a particular mind-independent object; but here this is conjoined with acquaintance with an *uninstantiated complex of properties* corresponding with the ways that the object illusorily appears. An immediate difficulty for the resultant position in my view is the consequent disanalogy in the ways in which it is supposed to be the presented object itself that appears thus and so in both veridical perception and illusion. In the former case, this is due to the fact that the properties presented are actually instantiated by that very object. This is precisely not so in the latter case of illusion. The situation here is in certain respects structurally similar to that of (CV) in connection with veridical v. illusory experiences as discussed in ch. 4 above and I contend that Johnson faces somewhat similar problems as a result in accounting for the limits upon the nature and extent of error that is compatible with genuine perceptual presentation.

concept 'F' is actually applied in judgement. If it is, then this application of 'F' is evidently warranted by o itself. If it is not, for whatever reason, then the subject at least appreciates that o looks F. In a slogan: acquaintance in perception provides the evident ground for concept application in judgement. Thus, in appropriate circumstances, perceptual judgement amounts to empirical knowledge.

To elaborate this account I clarify both what perceptual acquaintance *contributes* to the acquisition of empirical knowledge; and what more must be conjoined with it for this to succeed.

First, when S is presented in perception with a mind-independent object, o, that is F, from a relatively canonical point of view and in relatively standard circumstances, then the fundamental nature of her experience is conscious visual acquaintance, say, with that very object, o, which itself constitutes the ground for an application of the concept 'F' in judgement. O itself is the reason that 'o is F' is true given what 'F' means; and her experience is a matter of being visually conscious of that very thing, o, from a given point of view and in certain circumstances. In noticing, recognizing, or *registering*, its visually relevant similarities with paradigm exemplars of F, in the absence of countervailing evidence, application of 'F' therefore strikes her as correct in the light of those paradigms' involvement in her acquisition and understanding of that concept. Given her grasp of the concept in question, acquaintance with o makes its application to that very object evidently correct. It is the ground for her registration of precisely the similarities that constitute the truth of the application in question. The reason for the correctness of her judgement of F-ness is o itself, along with the paradigms that give this concept its content; and this reason, o, is precisely what enters into the fundamental nature of the subject's perceptual experience. For her experience just is conscious visual acquaintance, from a given point of view and in certain circumstances, with that very thing. Hence the fundamental contribution of perceptual experience itself to the acquisition of empirical knowledge is the presentation to the subject of the reasons for the correct application of her empirical concepts: the particular mind-independent physical objects themselves to which those concepts correctly apply.

Second, as I insisted above, perceptual knowledge that o is F itself depends upon far more than mere visual acquaintance with o. For S has to *register* o's visually relevant similarities with paradigm exemplars of F conceptually; and she may be acquainted with o and yet it fail thickly to look *F* in this way for a variety of reasons.[6] Furthermore, she must actually make the judgement that *o* is *F* rather than merely noting *o*'s thick look, as it were, and withholding judgement for some reason. Hence perceptual acquaintance is significantly more basic than any empirical knowledge itself; and, indeed, *S* may be acquainted with *o* without even actively entertaining any content concerning *o* at all. Acquaintance itself is therefore not a matter of being somehow guaranteed certain factual information about its mind-independent physical objects, or indeed of getting something right about those things at all. Rather, it provides a fundamental ground for getting anything right or wrong about the worldly constituents thereby presented in perception. Thick, conceptually registered, looks are the *product* of such acquaintance, from a given point of view and in certain circumstances, along with recognition or categorization of its objects as of various kinds. As I put it earlier, the ways things *look* are the ways perceptually presented *things* look. And perceptual knowledge additionally involves actually endorsing thick looks in judgement. Thus, acquaintance has to be combined with conceptual registration and endorsement for the acquisition of knowledge.

A great deal of the weight of this account clearly falls on the notion of the *conceptual registration* of visually relevant similarities with various paradigms. In particular, it is pressing once again to say something to distinguish this from perceptual representation as this figures definitively in the (CV) characterization of the nature of perceptual experience. I do not think that this can be done by giving some kind of alternative reductive analysis of registration as it figures in the (OV) notion of thick looks. Conceptual registration is in my view an irreducibly primitive notion that I attempt to convey throughout by appeal to such familiar commonsense activities as noticing, recognizing, and seeing as. Still, two points in my opinion serve to establish the required distinction between (OV) registration and (CV) representation. First, acquaintance itself does not presuppose conceptual registration. Hence registration is not in this sense part of the fundamental nature of our basic perceptual relation with the mind-independent physical world. Second, registration is something that subjects themselves *do*, although they may be relatively automatically induced to do so in certain circumstances. Hence, again, this is not a

---

[6] See §6.3 below for more detailed discussion of these possibilities.

feature of the most basic deliverances of our perceptual systems in our conscious experience of the world around us. Finally by way of clarification of conceptual registration as this figures in the (OV) epistemological account under development, it is worth pointing out explicitly again that this is absolutely not a matter of actually making any specific judgements about the mind-independent physical objects presented in perception, but rather of coming to appreciate the evident or apparent appropriateness of such judgements on the basis of conscious acquaintance with those very objects and understanding of the empirical concepts concerned.

I mentioned above that mistaken perceptual judgement and other epistemic failings of various kinds have to be handled separately and derivatively. These of course raise a number of epistemological issues; and I cannot possibly address all or even any of them fully here. I confine myself to brief comments outlining the (OV) treatment that I would propose of three kinds of case.

First, as I have been using the category throughout my discussion, an illusion is an experience in which a physical object, o, looks F, although o is not actually F.[7] According to (OV), this comes about when a person is visually acquainted with that very object, o, from a point of view and in circumstances in which it has visually relevant similarities with paradigm exemplars of F although it is not itself an instance of that kind. Let us suppose that o is G instead, where G is an alternative determinate, incompatible with F, of a shared determinable. If the subject registers o's visually relevant similarities with paradigm exemplars of F conceptually, then, although she is in fact acquainted with an object that constitutes a reason to apply the concept G, she understandably but mistakenly takes this to be a reason to apply the concept F instead. If she actually does apply 'F' in judgement, then this will of course not be a case of knowledge, since her resultant belief is false. She may take herself to be presented with a reason for that false judgement. In fact she is not. For o is in fact no genuine reason to apply F at all: 'o is F' is simply false; and o is instead a reason to apply G. Still, given the misleading point of view and/or circumstances involved, her error is perfectly understandable.

---

[7] As will become clear below, this characterization is not necessary for an illusion. There are complex cases in which complementary illusory factors 'cancel out' and an object looks F and is F, yet the experience is still illusory. See Johnston (2006). See ch. 1 n. 8 for possible counterexamples also to its sufficiency.

Second, in hallucination, according to (OV), the subject is in a condition that cannot be distinguished by introspection alone from one of being perceptually presented with mind-independent physical objects of such and such kinds arranged thus and so before her.[8] She may thereby take herself to be acquainted with good reasons to make all sorts of judgements about the world around her. Again, though, none of these will be cases of knowledge, even if some of them turn out accidentally to be true. For she is not in fact acquainted with any such reasons at all.

Third, there may also be cases in which a person *is* visually acquainted with a mind-independent physical object, *o*, that is *F*, and in which *o* thickly looks *F*. Furthermore, she may endorse this thick look in judgement but still fail to acquire knowledge, as a result of the presence in her immediate environment of suitable 'ringers' for *F*s: objects that are not *F*s but that she might in the circumstances sufficiently easily have likewise taken to be *F*s as to undermine the epistemic standing of her actual true belief. I am not myself convinced that the mere presence of ringers always undermines the status of her simple perceptual demonstrative judgement that *o* is *F* as knowledge. But in any such cases in which it does, I cannot see how the account I propose is less well placed than any other to accommodate this fact.

I cannot possibly resolve all the various familiar epistemological problems that come up in connection with each of these three kinds of obstacle to knowledge. I do hope to have said enough, though, at least to demonstrate that the present development of (OV) has a natural way to accommodate and characterize them, and is no less well equipped than any other available alternative to deal adequately with them.

All this does raise a pressing question, though:[9] what are the respective epistemological contributions of (*a*) the direct object of perception itself and (*b*) the point of view and circumstances from which its visually relevant similarities with various paradigms come to light? I answer thus: (*a*) It is a necessary condition upon a perceiver's having an experientially based reason of the kind that I am elucidating here to apply the concept '*F*' in judgement that she should be consciously acquainted with what is in fact a reason for such application, namely, a direct object of perception, *o*,

---

[8] See §5.2 for discussion of the (OV) approach to hallucination.
[9] A question urged on me recently in very fruitful discussion with Anil Gupta.

that is in fact F.[10] That object o itself is a reason in the relevant sense to make the concept application in question in judgement. (*b*) It is a further necessary condition on that very reason coming to light in her experience that she be acquainted with o from a point of view and in circumstances that enable her registration of the appropriate visually relevant similarities that it has from that point of view and in those circumstances with the paradigms that are involved in her grasp of the concept 'F'. Satisfaction of the former but not the latter results in a case of acquaintance with what is in fact a reason to apply the concept 'F' in judgement that may nevertheless not be evident to the subject. Satisfaction of the latter but not the former, in an illusory experience of an object that is actually G and not F, say, from a point of view and in circumstances relative to which it has visually relevant similarities with paradigm exemplars of F, results in a case in which perception is misleading in a way that may issue in understandable error in judgement.

These two necessary conditions are not jointly sufficient, though. For there may be cases of compensating compound illusion of the kind remarked by Mark Johnston (2006). In such cases a perceiver is acquainted with a direct object, o, that is in fact F, from a point of view and in circumstances relative to which it has visually relevant similarities with paradigm exemplars of F *due to the mutually compensating presence of two or more misleading factors normally individually responsible for illusion.* For example, she may be looking at twins of the same height. One is wearing horizontal stripes making him look shorter than he is; but they are in an Ames room in which the gradual reduction of height towards one corner induces the illusion of people being increasingly taller than they are as they approach. If the striped twin is closer to the compressed corner than his brother by just the right amount, then they look the same height. Still this is a complex illusion in which two compensating illusory effects are offset. In such cases the subject does not have an experientially based reason of the kind that I am elucidating here to apply the concept 'F' in judgement. In the case I describe, the perceiver does not have a perceptual reason to judge that the twins are the same height, even though she is acquainted

---

[10] It is of course possible to come to know that o is F on the basis of perception without actually seeing o at all, say, as when I know that my neighbour is at home by seeing her car in the drive; and this may be non-inferential knowledge. Still such cases are in my opinion more complex and less basic than those I have in mind here.

with the twins who are the same height from a point of view and in circumstances in which they look the same height. I do not know how to add to the two necessary conditions given above in order to achieve sufficiency in the face of such possibilities. I am certainly not attempting an *analysis*, though; and I doubt very much that any such thing could be provided. The point is rather simply to illustrate the necessity of both (*a*) and (*b*) to the (OV) account of experience-based reasons outlined above. As we saw earlier with the potentially undermining effect of easily accessible ringers, and is evident here again with Johnston's veridical illusions, these two important necessary conditions fall short of sufficiency on their own for the subject's perceptual knowledge that *o* is *F*.[11]

6.3 Epistemic priority

I return now to the positive epistemological account of the basic case of successful perceptual knowledge acquisition offered above on behalf of (OV). Sellars' initial concern about theorists' appeal to a 'given' in perception has the following general form. There is a philosophical problem concerning how to explain the status of perceptual experience as a source of factual empirical knowledge. It cannot possibly be an adequate solution to this problem to identify a feature of perception that is purportedly not subject to the same problems—namely that perceptual experience is simply *conscious*, 'as a person who has been hit on the head is not conscious whereas a new born babe, alive and kicking, is conscious' (Sellars, 1997: 20)—and at the same time to insist that such experience is *therefore* already an instance of the initially problematic category of factual empirical *knowledge*. The proposed feature of perceptual experience cannot without serious explanation meet the following two conditions simultaneously. First, it is sufficiently undemanding not to be subject to the philosophical

---

[11] Johnston (2006) himself uses these cases of 'veridical illusion' in an argument against what he calls the 'Fact-Directed Attitude View' of sensing. For, although the subject's experience is clearly defective in such cases, there is plausibly no *false* proposition suited to bring out the specific defect in question. My hostility to (CV) clearly makes me sympathetic to Johnston's opposition here. According to (OV), on the other hand, the subject is consciously acquainted with the mind–independent physical objects in question all right; and these may strongly look certain of the ways that they actually are; but the corroboration of various misleading features that lead to this result bar her possession of experience-based reasons for the relevant judgements that correlatively fail to attain the status of knowledge.

difficulties attending perceptual knowledge. Second it is sufficiently rich as itself to constitute a case of perceptual knowledge. I have explained how (OV) as I understand it avoids Sellars' own initial formulation of the inconsistency here. I consider now a recent formulation of a similarly structured challenge to any adequate theory of perceptual knowledge that emerges from Quassim Cassam's (2009) discussion of Barry Stroud's work in this area (esp. Stroud, 2000a, 2000b).

Although Stroud (2009) himself questions this, Cassam regards Stroud as imposing the following *Epistemic Priority Requirement* (EPR) upon any adequate *philosophical* explanation of knowledge of a certain kind, K: that we should explain how knowledge of kind K could come to be out of something that does not imply or presuppose knowledge of kind K (Cassam, 2009: 571 and esp. 577ff.). There are certainly many moves in the history of epistemology that appear to be motivated by *some* such requirement. In particular, perfectly adequate everyday answers to questions about how a person knows what she does about the mind-independent physical world are universally rejected as satisfactory solutions to *philosophical* problems in the area apparently on the basis of failings along these lines. Still there is an important question of what the principled *motivation* is for the requirement itself; and this immediately raises a number of important questions about its formulation, not least, how *kinds* such as K are to be individuated and what is involved in an *explanation* of how knowledge of a given such kind could come to be out of something else. What I propose is to suggest provisional answers to these two questions at least in the course of explaining how (OV) as I have been developing it may therefore be in a position to meet an appropriately formulated version of (EPR).

Let us suppose again that the target phenomenon is S's visually based knowledge that o is F for an appropriate mind-independent physical object, o, placed before him in relatively standard viewing conditions. According to the (OV) epistemological account sketched above, S is visually acquainted with o, which thickly looks F to him; and on this basis he judges that o is F. There are two points in this account where (EPR) threatens to bite. First, in the conditions upon its being determinately the case that the direct object of S's perception *is* the persisting mind-independent physical object o itself, rather than a mere surface, time-slice, or something even less substantial like the visual appearance of o from the relevant spatiotemporal point of view and in the relevant circumstances. Second, in the conditions upon *S*'s conceptual registration of *o*'s visually relevant similarities with the paradigms involved in his grasp of the concept *F* and his actual application of that concept to *o* in the judgement that *o* is *F*. I consider these briefly in turn.

The first point to make in connection with conscious acquaintance with particular mind-independent physical objects is that it is part of the point of (OV) that this is more basic than knowledge of empirical facts about those objects in at least the following sense. For any predicate '*Φ*' that applies to *o S* may see *o* and not *register* its visually relevant similarities with paradigm *Φ*s, either because he has no conception of what a *Φ* is, and so has himself no relevant paradigms associated with that predicate, or because he pays no attention to *o*'s similarities with any paradigm *Φ*s that he does associate with it—he is simply paying attention to other things. Furthermore, *S* may see *o* and register its visually relevant similarities with such paradigm *Φ*s and still fail to judge that o is *Φ* because he has a reason to take the situation to be misleading in some way. So simply seeing *o*, being visually acquainted with that very thing in perception, neither implies nor presupposes any perceptual knowledge about *o* or indeed, it seems, about anything else.

The situation is not quite so straightforward, though, even here in connection with the first point of application for (EPR) as distinguished above. For in ch. 7 below I consider the question of how the fact that the direct objects of perception according to (OV) *are* persisting mind-independent physical objects comes to light from the perceiver's own perspective in perception. Two features of my account are relevant here, although I can only state them without defence at this stage. First, the fact that we are acquainted with mind-independent physical objects themselves in perception shows up from our own perceptual perspective in our patterns of commonsense explanation: in the fact that we explain the actual and counterfactual order and nature of our perceptual experience of physical objects in general on the basis of the perceptible natures of those very objects that we perceive. For example, we explain the variation in the visual appearance of a coin viewed from head on and then increasingly from an angle on the basis of its constant circularity and the variation in viewing position; or we explain the fact that a jumper looks mauve by appeal to its red colour and the misleading paucity of the artificial lighting conditions. Second, given the theoretical role of the notion of a direct object of perception in elucidating the fundamental nature of the perceptual experience in question, in characterizing what it is to be in that very conscious condition, it is a necessary condition on its *being* a correct characterization of perception as acquaintance with *mind-independent physical objects* that this fact does indeed show up in this way from the perceptual perspective.[12]

Thus, conscious acquaintance determinately with mind-independent object *o* involves *S* in patterns of commonsense-physical explanation of the actual and counterfactual order and nature of his perceptual experience of physical objects in general on the basis of the perceptible natures of the very objects that he perceives. This certainly involves *S* in an evolving *world-view*, of what is out there, how it comes to light in his experience, and his own place in it. Much of this may in fact be *knowledge* about the physical world and about himself; and it may be difficult in practice to describe a situation in which none of it has this status; but its role in securing determinate acquaintance with the mind-independent physical object *o* does not depend upon or presuppose this fact. The de facto *truth* of his explanatory world-view would suffice for this purpose. So the conditions on perceptual acquaintance with mind-independent *o* itself are so far as I can see no obstacle to (OV) meeting (EPR).

I now turn to the conditions upon *S*'s conceptual registration of *o*'s visually relevant similarities with the paradigms involved in his grasp of the concept *F* and upon his actual application of that concept to *o* in the judgement that *o* is *F*. According to the (OV) account outlined above, perceptual knowledge consists in suitable circumstances in the endorsement in judgement of the way that mind-independent physical objects thickly look in perception. Such thick looks in the case in question involve *S*'s conceptual registration of *o*'s visually relevant similarities relative to his point of view and circumstances with certain paradigm exemplars of *F* that are central to his grasp of that very concept that he then goes on to apply in the judgement that *o* is *F* whose status as perceptual knowledge is in question. The general task before us is to assess the extent to which the outline epistemology I offer on behalf of (OV) is consistent with (EPR), the requirement that, for any relevant kind of knowledge, K, we should be able to explain how knowledge of kind K could come to be out of something that does not imply or presuppose knowledge of kind K.

---

[12] See ch. 7 for extended discussion and defence of these ideas.

In particular, the current question is whether the conceptual registration and application in judgement that are involved may be in tension with this requirement. Prima facie this may appear to be so. For conceptual registration apparently implies or presupposes perceptual knowledge at least concerning other Fs in his environment that they are F. How else does he ever come to associate appropriate paradigms with the predicate 'F' in a way that genuinely contributes to his *understanding* of the relevant concept? Concept possession is an *epistemic* skill, at the very least a capacity to know an F when one encounters one in perception in the present case. So registering o's visually relevant similarities with paradigm exemplars of F as this absolutely crucially figures in the epistemic proposal that I have been advancing implies or presupposes perceptual knowledge that a, b, and c are F for various other objects in the world around him. This is surely inconsistent with the intended interpretation of (EPR).[13]

One strategy to reinstate (EPR) at this stage would be to remark that, although the proposed account of perceptual knowledge that o is F does indeed imply or presuppose knowledge that a, b, and c are F for various *other* objects in the world for the reasons given, it does not imply or presuppose prior knowledge that o is F, or indeed any other knowledge about o. Thus, severely restricting the range of 'K' in the initial formulation that we should explain how knowledge of kind K could come to be out of something that does *not* imply or presuppose knowledge of kind K preserves (EPR) intact. The claim would be that an account may still be given of how perceptual knowledge that o is F comes to be out of something that does not imply or presuppose any prior knowledge about o. My own assessment is that this is quite unsatisfactory, or at the very least not the best that we should aim for here. Stroud (2000a, 2000b, 2009) himself presents a number of powerful considerations in support of the idea that the properly philosophical epistemological project involves understanding the possibility of knowledge in a more *general* way than this interpretation of (EPR) requires; and I believe that we can hold out for something significantly more general than this approach yields.

---

[13] It is perhaps worth pointing out that, even in the face of his distaste for any explicit formulation of (EPR), this is precisely Stroud's (2009) objection to the role of simple seeing in any adequate philosophical explanation of perceptual knowledge. See Dretske (1969) for the original introduction of simple seeing.

The strategy is correct in my opinion, though, in focusing attention upon the individuation of *kinds* of knowledge as these figure in (EPR). But the crucial distinction is not between knowledge about *o*, in particular knowledge that *o* is *F*, on the one hand, and knowledge about *a*, *b*, and *c*, in particular that *they* are *F*, on the other. It is rather the distinction between *perceptual* knowledge and *testimonial* knowledge about the various objects that we see in the world around us, in particular to the effect that they are *F*. I grant that *S*'s registration of *o*'s visually relevant similarities with the paradigm exemplars of *F* that play a central role in his understanding of that concept involves an *epistemic association* of such paradigms with the predicate '*F*' in a way that does imply or presuppose, at least in the most basic cases in which the concept possession in question is simple and non-descriptive, some knowledge that certain objects in the world around him are indeed *F*. But I would claim that this knowledge is in the first instance testimonial in kind. Crudely: *S* simply sees various objects around him and is told that they are *F*.[14] A great deal more needs to be said about the transition; but I claim that this enables him to go on and know for himself, as it were, on the basis of perception alone, that certain of the objects he simply sees in the world around him are also instances of the predicate '*F*', just as I explain above. In this way he acquires the capacity for perceptual knowledge that *o* is *F* on the basis of an epistemic-predicational skill that does not imply or presuppose *perceptual* knowledge.

It is worth remarking explicitly here on the dependence of perceptual knowledge upon testimonial knowledge that is embedded in this account of predication in perceptual knowledge. The epistemological order as I present it runs from the simple seeing of particular mind-independent physical objects in the world around us, through testimonial knowledge of their instantiation of various observational predicates, to our autonomous perceptual knowledge of the instantiation of those and suitably related predicates by the physical objects that we encounter in experience. This clearly raises many large issues and no doubt objections. All I would say for now here is that I take perceptual knowledge of empirical facts to be linguistically articulated propositional knowledge that depends upon our *understanding* of the terms used in its linguistic expression. The role of the crucial testimonial knowledge upon which such perceptual knowledge in

---

[14] Perhaps a fuller story might even start more minimally with the idea initially at least of being told simply *of that perceptually presented object—o*—that '*F*' applies.

my view depends is I take it precisely in the service of our acquiring understanding of the various predicational categories in terms of which our resultant perceptual knowledge is to be framed.[15]

In any case, according to the epistemological account that I offer on behalf of (OV), perceptual knowledge that o is F comes to be—in the language of (EPR)—out of two components. First, experiential acquaintance with o in perception: simply seeing that particular object in our case. Second, registering its visually relevant similarities with the paradigm exemplars of F that play a central role in understanding the predicate 'F', and judging that o is F on that basis. I claim that neither of these components implies or essentially presupposes perceptual knowledge. So the account is in good standing with respect to (EPR) at this stage.

The kind of *explanation* in demand in connection with (EPR) and putatively on offer above is also a delicate matter. For reasons that we have already seen, this is bound to be less than analytic entailment. That is to say, there may be cases of endorsement in judgement of a true thick perceptual look in just the way outlined above that nevertheless fall short of knowledge due to the easily accessible presence of ringers in the vicinity or to any of the other obstacles to knowledge that are prominent in the literature of counterexamples to various purported analyses of knowledge in general or perceptual knowledge in particular. I am myself persuaded by Williamson's (2000) thesis that no such *analysis* is possible. So no such analytically entailing explanation is possible. Still, the explanation offered above is in my view an illuminating theoretical elaboration of the commonsense explanation in answer to the question of how one knows on any given occasion that o is F that one can see o and knows an F when one sees one. For it illustrates in a way that is easily generalizable how this particular piece of knowledge about a particular mind-independent physical object comes to be, in de facto cooperating circumstances at least, out

---

[15] This idea of an epistemologically fundamental role for testimony or something like it may also be of value in filling out my account of the consistency of (EPR) with the importance I insist upon of our facility with certain commonsense explanations of our perceptual experience in validating the identification of the direct objects of such experience with mind-independent physical objects themselves. Some such explanations may well have an epistemic standing derived from testimony rather than perception itself in such a way as to preserve (EPR) under the current individuation of kinds of knowledge 'K'. See Eilan et al. (2005) for an excellent survey of issues and options here for understanding the crucial role in the development of cognition of joint attention and engagement with the physical world that we share with others in perception and action.

of more basic perceptual acquaintance with that very thing along with conceptual registration of its visually relevant similarities with the paradigm exemplars of F that are involved in possession of that very concept. Neither of these components implies or presupposes *perceptual knowledge* about that object, that kind, or indeed anything else—although the latter predication, and perhaps even the visual acquaintance itself, may well depend upon testimonial knowledge or something like it concerning various mind-independent objects in the world around the subject and also presented in perception. Of course this doesn't solve all possible epistemological questions concerning perception; but it does give a genuine explication of a particular piece of perceptual knowledge on the basis of conscious and cognitive capacities that do not presuppose it.

6.4 Perception and reason

It will be immediately apparent to anyone at all familiar with my previous book *Perception and Reason* (1999) that my views on the rational basis for empirical knowledge have changed. In certain respects the changes are very significant. In other respects much remains the same. I certainly do not wish to get overly preoccupied with my own philosophical autobiography; but it may help in clarifying the present position to highlight a single key development in my views that has crucial application in connection with a prominent argument of that book. The key difference with the earlier work is that I now recognize that perceptual experience consists most fundamentally in conscious acquaintance, from a given point of view, in a particular sensory modality, and in specific circumstances of perception, with mind-independent physical objects themselves. These very objects constitute the reasons for the correctness of the application of certain empirical concepts in judgement. Thus, when a person is visually presented with a given mind-independent physical object, o, that is F, from a relatively standard point of view and in relatively standard conditions, she is consciously acquainted with the very reason for applying the concept 'F'; and, given her registration of its visually relevant similarities with the paradigms involved in her grasp of that concept, she recognizes o as just such a reason. Thus, o is the evident reason for her application of 'F' in judgement given her perceptual acquaintance with o and grasp of the concept 'F'.

This key difference has crucial application in connection with a prominent argument of my previous book. In ch. 5 of *Perception and Reason* I argue that the reasons that perceptual experiences must provide for empirical beliefs require a conceptualist version of (CV). That argument has two stages. The first stage makes explicit a connection between reasons and inference, and hence between giving reasons and identifying contents of a form which enables them to serve as the premisses and conclusions of inferences. The second establishes a constraint upon genuine reasons—reasons *for the subject*—imposed by the way in which his own conceptual resources are available for the configuration of his mental states. Given the definition of conceptual mental states, as those with a representational content which is characterizable only in terms of concepts which the subject himself possesses and which is of a form which enables it to serve as a premiss or the conclusion of a deductive argument or of an inference of some other kind, this yields the required conclusion, that having reasons in general consists in being in a conceptual mental state, and hence, in particular, that perceptual experiences provide reasons for empirical beliefs only if they have conceptual contents.

(OV) provides a radical alternative to the first stage of this argument. My previous idea was that making something intelligible from the point of view of rationality in the way essential to giving reasons necessarily involves identifying a valid deductive argument, or inference of some other kind, that articulates the source of the rational obligation (or permission) in question. The question then is how these crucial warranting inferences relate to the reason-giving states in question; and the second stage of the argument from *Perception and Reason* attempts to establish that such reason-giving states must themselves *have* contents of precisely the kinds that figure as the premisses of the relevant inferences. Hence conceptualism follows. I now believe that my previously single-minded focus on the rationality of *inference* obscured the more fundamental normativity of *concept application* that plays the central grounding role in the epistemology of perceptual knowledge according to my development of (OV) here.

(OV) denies that the fundamental rational role of perceptual experience in connection with empirical belief is to be articulated by reference to any warranting inference. The core phenomenon is rather that of rationally subsuming a particular object under a general concept given conscious experiential acquaintance with the former and grasp in understanding of the latter. Perceptual presentation of particular mind-independent physical objects in this way provides conscious acquaintance with those very things that constitute reasons for the correctness of the application of certain empirical concepts in judgement. In registering the visually relevant similarities that a perceptually presented object o has with the paradigms involved in our grasp of the empirical concept F, we recognize o's status as a reason *for us* applying that very concept in judgement, provided that we are interested in the question of what o is like in respect of F-ness of course. In this way, perceptual experience provides us with genuinely recognizable reasons for empirical beliefs without any commitment to (CV) at all, never mind a specifically conceptualist such commitment. Of course, endorsing the thick looks of mind-independent physical objects in judgement in this way does provide conceptual contents that in turn offer inferential reasons for further empirical beliefs. The omission in my previous account was of the absolutely essential fundamental ground for this whole enterprise of empirical knowledge acquisition in the evidently rational subsumption of perceived particulars under the general concepts available in understanding.

Finally, recall the argument that I mentioned in ch. 4 from the transparency of perceptual experience to (CV).[16] The premiss, very roughly, is that in attempting introspectively to scrutinize the nature of our perceptual experience we seem to alight directly upon the mind-independent physical world—at least as it appears to be—rather than any evident constituents or qualities of the experience itself. Hence it is supposed to follow that the nature of perceptual experience is to be given by how things appear in that experience to be in the mind-independent physical world, that is, by its representational content.

As I remarked then, proponents of (CV) who appeal explicitly to the transparency claim in this way do so effectively in order to motivate their position over some form of indirect realist theory along the lines discussed in ch. 3, or perhaps over versions of (CV) that appeal to nonrepresentational *qualia* as well as worldly representational contents in accounting for the nature of perceptual experience.[17] They may or may not assume that their position is the only possible alternative to such views. In any case, we are now in a position to see more clearly how (OV) is at least as well placed as (CV) to endorse transparency. For it is quite right to

---

[16]   Strictly speaking this is an argument against certain alternatives to (CV).

[17]   For examples of the latter target see Peacocke (1983) and Block (1996, 1998, and 2003).

insist that the result of our introspective scrutiny of visual experience, say, is simply the way that things in the mind-independent physical world look. The whole point of (OV), though, is that the way things look in perception, which is the target of such introspective scrutiny, just *is* the way the *things* look that are the direct objects of conscious visual acquaintance and whose such looks are explained precisely on this basis above. So transparency is a direct result of the view and therefore certainly fails to favour (CV) in the current context.

This concludes my elucidation, motivation, and defence of the core of my own positive account (OV) of the nature of perceptual experience. I claim that this is the most promising context for a full and satisfying defence of empirical realism as the simple conjunction of (I) and (II), along with the rejection of (III), from my opening Inconsistent Triad.

(I) Physical objects are mind-independent.
(II) Physical objects are the direct objects of perception.
(III) The direct objects of perception are mind-dependent.

(OV) offers an entirely adequate explanation of illusion and hallucination that is integrated with a suitably nuanced account of the way things look in visual perception quite generally; and it provides a fully compelling explication of the role of perceptual experience in the provision of empirical knowledge. The central claim is that perceptual experience consists most fundamentally in a relation of conscious acquaintance, from a spatiotemporal point of view, in a sense modality and in certain circumstances of perception, with particular mind-independent physical objects in the world around the perceiver. The question that I pursue in ch. 7 is how the *mind-independence* of these direct objects of perception shows up from the subject's own perceptual perspective, how this aspect in particular of the nature of the proposed objects of conscious perceptual acquaintance is evident *to the subject*.

7

Realism and Explanation

According to (OV), perceptual experience is most fundamentally a matter of a person standing in a relation of conscious acquaintance, from a given spatiotemporal point of view, in a particular sense modality, and in certain specific circumstances of perception, with various mind-independent physical objects in the world around him that therefore constitute the *direct objects* of his experience in the early modern sense that I have been working with throughout. Thus, the truth of *empirical realism* consists in the conjunction of (I) and (II) along with a simple rejection of (III) from the Inconsistent Triad that I began with in ch. 1.

(I) Physical objects are mind-independent.

(II) Physical objects are the direct objects of perception.

(III) The direct objects of perception are mind-dependent.

In short, the direct objects of perception are mind-independent physical objects.

The question to be addressed here in my final chapter is this: in what way, if at all, does the *mind-independence* of the direct objects of perception show up from the subject's point of view? It is one thing for us as philosophical theorists to advance an account, of the fundamental nature of our perceptual relation with the physical world in such a way as to vindicate our most basic pre-theoretic commitments about perception and its objects, to give arguments for this account, and to defend it from various objections. The proposed account is that perceptual experience is acquaintance with mind-independent physical objects. It is quite another thing to explain the extent to which the correctness of that very account is *evident* in our own experience *as perceivers of the physical world around us.*[1]

---

[1] The philosophical account must of course be *consistent* with the facts about how things seem from the subject's point of view; but it is a substantive philosophical question in its own

My particular question here is how the *mind-independence* of the proposed direct objects of perception comes to light from the perceiver's point of view; and the focus will be upon how best to solve a problem that arises for a familiar and attractive approach to answering this question.

It is important to begin with to clarify the question a little further and to distinguish it from other related questions. My question is not how perceivers *know* that the objects that are presented to them in perception are mind-independent, although the answer to my own question provides a start on answering this one. That is to say, I am not concerned right away with the epistemological project of explicating the status as knowledge of any reflective belief that perceivers may have that the physical objects that they perceive are mind-independent. Nor is my question best put directly in terms of perceivers' explicit *beliefs* that physical objects are mind-independent or the process by which they acquire them. Such beliefs, which do in my view often amount to knowledge, are based upon the perceptual presentation itself of mind-independent such things that I claim provides perceivers with a provisional conception at least of what physical objects *are*. Having perceptual experience as I conceive of it is a matter of the subject's conscious acquaintance with mind-independent physical objects themselves. This already constitutes a determinate implicit commitment to a realm of such things. My question here is how this determinate *experiential* commitment, which grounds any explicit belief or knowledge that perceivers may attain on its basis, is itself manifest in perceivers' own engagement with their perceptual experience and the world around them that is presented in it. Perception itself consists in a relation of conscious acquaintance, from a given spatiotemporal point of view, in a particular sense modality, and in certain specific circumstances of perception, with various mind-independent physical objects in the world around us. My question here is how the mind-independence of those direct objects of perception manifests itself in this way to us *as perceivers*, so as to constitute such a determinate experiential commitment on our part.

---

right what further constraint, if any, the subject's perspective places on the correct philosophical account of perception, and how exactly this should be taken into account in the development and defence of the philosophical theory. I hope to make some kind of progress with these issues in explaining in particular how I think that the truth of (OV) shows up in our own perception of the physical world (see esp. §7.3); but any engagement with the issues in general is beyond the scope of the present work. For helpful recent discussions see Martin (forthcoming: esp. ch. 1) and Spener (in preparation (a)).

I insisted in ch. 3 that it is a necessary condition upon any satisfactory account of the *presentation* of physical objects to us in perception that this provides us with an initial conception at least of what such physical objects are. I call this basic idea that physical objects are the very things that are presented to us in perception in such a way as to provide us with a rough and provisional conception at least of what such physical objects are, *empiricism*. The (OV) contention that mind-independent physical objects are the *direct objects* of perception is ideally suited to comply with *empiricism* in the most straightforward way. For, as I explained in ch. 5, it is precisely the nature of those very physical objects themselves that provides, along with the subject's spatiotemporal point of view, the sense modality in question, and the other relevant circumstances of perception, the most fundamental account of how things look to the subject in perception on this view.

The specific question that I focus on here, though, is how the *mind-independence* of such physical direct objects is supposed to come to light from our own perspective as perceivers of the physical world around us according to (OV). How is empiricism compatible with *realism* concerning the physical objects that we perceive?[2] That is, how is the idea that our provisional conception of what physical objects are is provided by their presentation to us in perceptual experience compatible with the fact that what physical objects are is *mind-independent* things? A natural and familiar answer appeals to the centrality to our thought about the physical world and our experience of it of our *explanations* of the actual and counterfactual order and nature of our perceptual experience of physical objects by appeal to the prior and independent nature of those very physical objects themselves that we perceive. Thinking of physical objects as the entities whose nature explains our own experience in this way, I claim, plays a crucial role in grounding our conception of them as genuinely mind-independent. On its most familiar interpretation and development, though, this answer, that we explain the order and nature of our perceptual experience of physical objects by appeal to the nature of the physical objects themselves, raises a serious problem. For it threatens the basic empiricist idea that we are genuinely *presented* with those mind-independent physical objects themselves in perceptual experience, that it is *through our experience of*

[2] Throughout this chapter I use 'realism' to denote physical realism: the thesis that physical objects are mind-independent in nature.

them that we acquire a rough and provisional conception at least of what the mind-independent physical objects in question actually are.

I argue that this threat may be avoided by resisting the orthodox development of the explanatory proposal. The idea that we explain the actual and counterfactual order and nature of our perceptual experience of physical objects by appeal to the prior and independent nature of the physical objects themselves that we perceive succeeds in securing realism in our conception of the physical world around us without threatening empiricism, provided that we respect the autonomous standing of our everyday commonsense explanations of experience. These are in no need of any fundamental scientific revision in such a way as to undermine empiricism.

The chapter has three parts. First (§7.1), I elaborate the explanatory proposal, explain in detail its role in securing our grasp as perceivers of the *mind-independence* of the physical objects that we perceive, and outline the threat that the orthodox development of this proposal poses to the presentation of those very objects to us in experience. Second (§7.2), I suggest how this threat should be avoided. I argue that there is a perfectly adequate implementation of the explanatory proposal that secures the realist status of physical objects as mind-independent from our perspective as perceivers without in any way threatening the empiricist idea that these are the very things that are presented to us in perception. Third (§7.3), I end with my conclusions.

7.1 Explanation, realism, and scientific-physics

We normally cite the properties of physical objects in explanation of the actual and counterfactual order and nature of our perceptual experience of those very things. In vision, for example, we regularly give explanations along the following lines.

(E1) The coin looks circular to Janet because it is circular and she is viewing it from head on.

(E2) The coin looks elliptical to John because it is circular and he is viewing it from an angle.

(E3) The coin would look elliptical to Janet if she were to change her point of view because it is circular and she would then be viewing it from an angle.

(E4)   The jumper looks red outdoors because it is red and lighting conditions are normal outdoors.

(E5)   It looks mauve in the store because it is red and the lighting conditions are artificially dingy in the store.

(E6)   It would look red if the lights in the store were improved because it is red and it would then look its actual colour.

I contend that our offering and accepting such explanations constitutes a commitment to realism about the physical objects that they cite. For, first, as we have seen, realism consists in a certain priority of the natures of physical objects themselves over the perceptual appearances to which they may give rise; and, second, the explanatory standing of such explanations depends upon our appreciation of this very priority. I elaborate both of these points in turn.

First, recall the *standard account* of the distinction between primary and secondary qualities that I gave in ch. 3.[3]

According to the standard account, the most basic distinctions concerning secondary qualities are between, say, red-type and green-type *appearances*, and the rest, conceived quite independently of the question of what their worldly correlates, if any, may be. The characterization of such appearances is prior to, and independent of, any characterization of the worldly properties that may in some way be presented or indicated by them. Having given such a characterization, of red-type appearances, say, we may then define a property—*redness*—which applies to mind-independent objects, as that of being disposed to produce those kinds of appearances—red-type ones— or, alternatively, as the property of having whatever underlying physical constitution happens in the actual world to ground that disposition.

In contrast, according to the standard account, the most basic distinctions concerning the primary qualities are those between, say, squareness and circularity, and the rest, *as properties of mind-independent things themselves*, conceived quite independently of the question of what appearances, if any, they might produce. Having first identified which property squareness is,

---

[3]   Recall also that I do not myself endorse the standard account. See Campbell (1993) for an alternative that I prefer. This will become relevant later with my inclusion of the colour explanations (E4)–(E6) alongside shape explanations (E1)–(E3) throughout. I appeal to the standard account rather as a relatively well-known framework in which to bring out the issues that are my focus here.

we can then identify square-type appearances as those that present something as having *that property*—squareness. So, the relevant appearances are to be characterized only by appeal to a prior, and independent, characterization of the worldly properties that they may present.

Generalizing this basic idea, I claim that the mind-independence of the objects that we perceive consists in the individuative priority of their nature over the various appearances that show up in our perception of them. As I explain and illustrate in what follows, the resultant individuation of appearances by appeal to the prior nature of their objects proceeds in specific instances on the basis of particular determinate modifications of the general nature of the mind-independent physical objects that we perceive. Skipping ahead to the version of the position that I myself favour, the picture is something like this. Mind-independent physical objects are persisting, unified, extended space occupants. A specific modification of this general nature would be that of being circularly extended, for example; and the corresponding visual appearance is to be individuated precisely as the look of a circular physical object presented from head on in normal lighting conditions, say. In any case, the key point at this stage is that realism shows up from our perspective as perceivers if and only if we have from that perspective some means of appreciating the fact that the nature of the physical objects themselves that we perceive is in this way individuatively basic in relation to the various appearances that such objects may present to us in perception.

It is natural to object to this whole approach right away that priority of individuative *characterization* is one thing, *metaphysical status* quite another. The first is a matter of how *we* identify the phenomena in question; the second is a matter of the nature of *those phenomena themselves*. Indeed, the standard account of secondary qualities outlined above surely serves to make just this point. Suppose that we do first of all characterize the red-type appearances, as specific conscious experiential phenomena, conceived quite independently of the question of what their worldly correlates, if any, may be; and suppose that we do then go on derivatively to characterize the redness of physical objects as their possession of whatever underlying physical constitution happens in the actual world to ground the disposition to produce such red-type appearances in normal subjects under normal circumstances. Then an object's possession of *that underlying physical property*, whichever it may be, is a perfectly mind-independent matter. It is entirely independent of the way in which it does or might appear to anyone. Thus, although the redness of physical objects is *characterized* only on the basis of a prior characterization of the experiential appearances to which it gives rise, the property itself is perfectly mind-independent.

In reply I admit entirely that there is *a* mind-independent property here: whichever underlying physical property it is that turns out actually to ground objects' disposition to produce red-type appearances in normal subjects under normal circumstances. The crucial point, though, is that, by the explicit lights of the account under consideration, this is absolutely not the property that such objects are subjectively *presented* as having in our perceptual experience of their colour. It is not, as it is sometimes said, redness-as-it-appears-to-us. For we have no idea whatsoever which property this underlying physical property is on the basis of our perception of it on the standard account of secondary qualities in question. The property presented is rather that of appearances being a *red-type*, which is in itself quite neutral on what the worldly correlate, if any, of such appearances may be. Thus, the property, if any, that physical objects are presented as having in our colour experience, *on this view*, is *not* mind-independent at all, but rather a mind-dependent one.[4] Suppose that colour appearances were conceived quite differently. Suppose, that is to say, that they were correctly characterized *as* presentations of specific properties of things not themselves individuated by any reference to their appearances, as appearances of squareness are characterized according to the standard account of primary qualities above as presentations of a specific geometric shape. This is in my view the correct account of colour appearances, although it is of course quite contrary to the standard account currently under consideration here by way of illustration of the notion of mind-dependence in play. In *that* case the colour properties presented in perception would indeed be mind-independent. (Contrast with the above the fact that the squareness of physical objects themselves *is* squareness-as-it-appears-to-us according to the standard account.) This is precisely what is not the case on the standard account of the secondary qualities.

I conclude therefore that this standard account of the distinction between primary and secondary qualities in fact serves strongly to confirm

---

[4] I take this to be the substance of Descartes's (1986) contention—and indeed his argument for it—that the ascription of secondary qualities *as we perceive them* to mind-independent physical objects is not just contingently false but entirely confused and incoherent, presupposing as it does that such objects effectively have sensations.

my criterion of mind-independence. The point here is absolutely not that the standard account is a correct account of the distinction between the shapes and colours of physical objects that entails my criterion of mind-independence. It is rather that the standard account would, if it *were* correct, characterize a respect in which the shapes of things that we are presented with are mind-independent and in which the colours that we are presented with are not. It marks a genuine distinction between mind-independence and mind-dependence. I do not myself agree that perceived colours are mind-dependent in this sense, although I give no argument for that view here. That is why I reject the standard account *as* an account of distinction between the familiar primary and secondary qualities themselves. Still, I do adopt the genuine distinction that that account marks in characterizing what it is for the direct objects of our perception to *be* mind-independence. Thus, the mind-independence of the objects that are presented in perception consists in the individuative priority of their nature over the various appearances that show up in our perception of them.[5]

Second, the explanatory standing of our explanations of the order and nature of perceptual experience on the basis of the nature of the physical objects themselves that we perceive depends upon our appreciation of precisely this individuative priority of objects over appearances. For suppose that we conceived the individuative priority in reverse, as in the standard account of secondary qualities given above. In that case, purportedly explanatory ascriptions of properties of physical objects are in reality ascriptions of properties essentially characterized in terms of the disposition to produce such and such appearances in normal subjects under normal circumstances. Thus, the resultant explanations of those very appearances are either unsatisfying or evidently mere placeholders for genuine explanations in quite different terms that re-establish the individuative priority with properties of objects independent and prior to any question of their appearances. Simply being told that something appears a certain way because it is disposed to do so gives us no substantive understanding as to *why* it appears as it does without some indication of what grounds the relevant disposition. Articulating this ground, along with the general law that things that are so constituted normally appear thus and so, does

---

[5] The key claims involved in this illustration from the standard account of the primary/secondary quality distinction, and especially the crucial role of empiricism as defined above, return at the heart of the main argument of §7.2.

provide an explanation; but only by citing a grounding constitution that is characterized prior to and independently of any question as to what appearances, if any, things so constituted may produce. Thus, the genuine explanatory standing of explanations of perceptual appearances depends upon our appreciation of the individuative priority of the explanatory properties of physical objects over the appearances to be explained.

It is sometimes said that the relation between certain perceptible properties of physical objects and the appearances that these present in perception is one of no straightforward priority either way (McDowell, 1985b). I find it difficult to articulate the proposal fully; but the essential outline is as follows. On the basis of certain experiences that we have, we are able directly to sort various objects into groups, without, as it were, paying any heed to the nature of the experiences that provide our cues to do so. We may call the relevant groups of objects 'red', 'green', and so on. Reflecting on this capacity for object categorization, we may go on to sort our experiential cues into groups also, characterizing these in turn as appearances of red, appearances of green, and so on. Thus there is an epistemological priority, on the subject's part at least, from the colour properties of objects to their colour appearances. Still, there is nothing 'in reality' that unifies all the red objects other than their disposition normally to produce appearances of red in us. These appearances are unified *metaphysically* as a single kind in virtue of their intrinsic subjective type, entirely independently of the question of what their worldly correlates, if any, may be; and this in turn, and derivatively, imposes a metaphysical unity on the red physical objects, as those disposed to produce such appearances in normal subjects under normal circumstances. Thus, there is a metaphysical priority from colour appearances to the colour properties of objects. There is no straightforward single priority either way.

If this really were a view on which there is no individuative priority *of the relevant kind* either way between the perceptible properties of physical objects and the various appearances that show up in our perception of them, then my argument above would fail. For I conclude that the explanatory standing of our explanations of perceptual appearances by their objects depends upon our appreciation of the individuative priority from objects to appearances from the fact that they are incompatible with the assumption of an individuative priority from appearances to objects. I ignore the possibility of any genuinely no-priority view. Fortunately for my argument, the position outlined above is categorically not a no-priority view of this threatening kind. For the primary unification is at the level of appearances, in the characterization of which subjective condition is that of something 'looking red', say, only on the basis of which is it then possible to characterize the corresponding property of physical objects themselves: being red. So, regardless of the epistemological claims about our capacity for sorting coloured objects in advance of sorting their colour appearances, there is a clear *individuative* priority of the relevant kind from appearances to objects. The point is confirmed by the fact that any genuinely mind-independent unity that there may be to the objects sorted as red, say, on this view, is not the unity that those things are subjectively presented as having. For we have no idea whatsoever what this may be on the basis of our perception of them. So this position is definitively an instance of the order of individuative priority characteristic of the standard account of *secondary* qualities given above.

Indeed it is difficult to see how there possibly could be a genuinely no-priority view of the kind required to block my argument. For what it is to be appearances of F-ness must in general have something to do with what it is to be F. I offer two possibilities: being F is characterized in terms of appearing F (as in the case of the standard account of secondary qualities); or appearing F is characterized in terms of being F (as in the case of the standard account of primary qualities). A no-priority view must presumably either endorse neither of these claims or endorse both of them. If it endorses neither, then the worry is that appearing F and being F fail to be related to each other in any way that is adequate to sustain the prima facie impression that 'F' is being used without equivocation between them. If it endorses both, then the danger is that the resultant circularity will obstruct any attempt to distinguish the two pairs being F and appearing F, on the one hand, and being G and appearing G, on the other, for any F and G of the same general type—e.g. colours. For example, suppose that what it is to *be* red is defined in terms of what it is to *appear* red—R = Δ(A-R), for some function Δ taking experiences to the disposition to produce them, say—and what it is to *appear* red is defined in terms of what it is to *be* red—A-R = $\prod$(R), for some function $\prod$ taking properties of objects to the perceptual appearance of them, say. Suppose also that the same goes for the relations between what it is to be blue and what it is to appear blue: B = Δ(A-B) and A-B = $\prod$(B). Suppose finally that these are both genuinely no-priority views. That is to say, there is no more fundamental characterization of what it is to appear red, v. to appear blue, in terms of which the property of being red, v. being blue, may be defined by the equation $R = \Delta(A\text{-}R)$; and there is no more fundamental characterization of what it is to be red, v. to be blue, in terms of which the corresponding appearance of red, v. appearance of blue, may be defined by the equation $A\text{-}R = \prod(R)$. It follows that there is no obvious basis on which to distinguish between the two supposedly quite distinct pairs R and A-R, on the one hand, and B and A-B, on the other. These are merely notational variants. So far as I can see, then, breaking the symmetry requires an assignment of definitional priority. Either the appearance of red is identified, and distinguished from the appearance of blue, as *that specific kind of appearance*, in which case the property of being red may be defined in its terms. Or the property of being red is identified, and distinguished from the property of being blue, as *that specific property of physical objects*, in which case the appearance of red may be defined in its terms. Thus, in the absence of any clearly articulated candidate for a defensible genuinely no-priority view, I contend that my argument goes through.

To reiterate my second key point then about explanations of perceptual appearances by appeal to the physical objects that we perceive, their explanatory standing depends upon our appreciation of the individuative priority of the natures of the physical objects themselves over the perceptual appearances to be explained.

Putting this together with the constitutive account of mind-independence in terms of precisely such individuative priority, it follows that the explanatory standing of our explanations of the order and nature of our perceptual experience of physical objects on the basis of the nature of the physical objects themselves that we perceive delivers a clear positive verdict on the status of physical objects *as* mind-independent from our own perspective as perceivers. Offering and accepting such explanations constitutes a commitment from our perspective to realism about the physical objects that we perceive: it constitutes our recognition of the mind-independence of the direct objects of perception. Call this the *Explanatory Proposal* (EP) as to how realism comes to light from our perceptual perspective upon the physical world. The key claim is that the mind-independence of the physical objects that we perceive shows up from our own perspective as perceivers in our appeal to such objects as the explanatory grounds of our various perceptual experiences of those very things from different points of view and in different circumstances of perception.

To be absolutely clear, (EP) is the proposal that the mind-independence of the objects that we perceive is evident from our perspective as perceivers in virtue of our explanation of the actual and counterfactual order and nature of our perceptual experience on the basis of the prior and independent nature of those objects themselves, that is to say, in virtue of our recognition of the physical objects that we perceive as the explanatory grounds of our perceptual experience of them. In this way we appreciate the status of the physical objects that we perceive as providing the *mind-independent* unifying explanations of the various actual and possible experiences that we may have of those very things from different points of view, in different sense modalities, and in different circumstances of perception.

(EP) raises a serious problem, though. For it is prima facie plausible for us implicitly at least to accept the best scientific-physical theories as providing essential substantive revisions to our initial commonsense explanations (E1)–(E6) of our perceptual experience by appeal to the physical objects that we perceive. Thus, we may be inclined to defer ultimately to fundamental scientific-physics for the complete and *correct* articulation of such explanations. Call this the *scientific* implementation of (EP).

On this way of thinking, the correct and genuinely explanatory explanations of the actual and counterfactual order and nature of our perceptual experience of physical objects are to be given only in the language of fundamental scientific-physics. This in turn determines the natures of the objects whose mind-independence is thereby secured by (EP). For these are the entities whose natures are explanatorily relevant in such fundamental scientific-physical explanations. Thus, in so far as (EP) provides a correct account of how their mind-independence shows up from the perceptual perspective, physical objects themselves must be conceived as mereological sums, over regions of space and time, or perhaps some other kind of composition, of whatever turn out to be the most basic elements of the correct fundamental scientific-physical theory.

The theoretical conception that most of us have of what such things are actually like is obviously extremely primitive. Indeed, as we saw in ch. 2, Lewis (2009) presents a powerful argument for the claim that we are irremediably ignorant of the intrinsic natures of their fundamental scientific-physical components.[6] In any case, it is quite clear that these are not the very things that

---

[6] See §7.3 for my own response to this important argument.

we are *presented* with in perception. For, as I recalled from ch. 3 at the outset, perceptual presentation provides us with at least a rough and provisional conception of what the objects *are* with which we are presented; and we have no conception whatsoever of what the most fundamental scientific-physical primitives are simply on the basis of perception. So we have no conception whatsoever of what any simple mereological sum or composition of such things might be either. The objects whose mind-independence is ultimately secured by the current scientific implementation of (EP) are therefore not *presented* to us in perception. Thus, the scientific implementation of (EP) is incompatible with *empiricism* as defined above.

This approach to explaining the way in which the mind-independence of the physical objects that we perceive shows up from our own perspective as perceivers apparently compels us to accept that those mind-independent objects are not the very things that are *presented* to us in perception after all, at least not in the demanding sense in which this provides us with at least a rough and provisional conception of what the objects *are* with which we are so presented. This rejection of empiricism is really not a viable option though. For empiricism plays an absolutely fundamental role in setting the domain for the whole debate. The question that we are interested in as perceivers of the physical world of stones, tables, trees, and animals around us, and, indeed, as philosophical theorists who are also perceivers of such things, is what is the metaphysical status of *those very things*? Arriving at the conclusion that some quite different domain of entities somehow related to our perception is truly mind-independent is of little or no significance to us.

At this point, then, there appear to be three options. First, we may try to live with some form of anti-realism concerning the physical world of such things as stones, tables, trees, and animals, perhaps attempting to soften the blow by going along with Berkeley's (1975a, 1975b) strategy of insisting nevertheless that a great deal that we take to be *indicative* of realism may nevertheless be maintained. Second, we may reject the whole (EP) approach and attempt to explain how the mind-independence of the physical objects that are genuinely presented to us in perception shows up from our own perceptual perspective in some quite different way. Third, we may retain (EP) and yet insist upon an alternative to its *scientific* implementation. This third option is my own preferred response; and I develop and defend an alternative *commonsense* implementation of (EP) in §7.2 that follows.

7.2 Explanation, realism, and commonsense physics

(EP) is absolutely the right strategy for securing realism from our own perspective as perceivers in my view, for the reasons set out in §7.1. The unacceptable consequence of undermining empiricism that follows from its scientific implementation may however be avoided. It is correct to explain how the mind-independence of the physical objects that we perceive shows up from the perceptual perspective on the basis of our conception of those very objects as the explanatory grounds of the actual and counterfactual order and nature of our perceptual experience of them from various different points of view, in different sense modalities, and in different circumstances of perception. It is a mistake, though, to accept that fundamental scientific-physical explanation is required to provide and characterize what are therefore phenomenologically mysterious targets of this identification. The key lies, instead, in our initial commonsense-physical explanations themselves, which I claim are in excellent standing absolutely as they are, in no need of any scientific-physical revision.

Thus, the scientific-physical option outlined above, which is incompatible with empiricism, is not the only possible implementation of (EP). An alternative *commonsense* implementation is available that preserves empiricism and is also in my view a perfectly stable and adequate explication of how realism shows up from our own perspective as perceivers of the physical world. The explanatory standing of our initial commonsense-physical explanations of perceptual appearances *as they stand* is sufficient to secure the mind-independence of the physical objects that are presented to us in perception. Furthermore these commonsense-physical explanations are in absolutely no need of any substantive revision and correction by anything from scientific-physics. For they have features that any purported scientific-physical explanations of perceptual appearances lack that are crucially relevant to precisely this project of securing empirical realism from our own perceptual perspective. These features simultaneously establish the autonomous explanatory standing of commonsense-physical explanations and avoid the unacceptable anti-empiricist consequences that come with the move to scientific-physics in elucidation of realism.[7]

To begin with, then, recall that the explanatory standing of common-sense-physical explanations of the actual and counterfactual order and nature of our perceptual experience of physical objects by appeal to the familiar perceptible natures of those very things, along with our point of view and other relevant circumstances of perception, depends upon our appreciation of the individuative priority of the natures of the physical objects presented in perception themselves relative to their various appearances. For the latter appearances are explicitly individuated *in terms of* the prior natures of the physical objects that they present. Thus, in my toy examples, the explananda visual appearances are individuated explicitly in terms of the shape and colour properties that they (apparently) present: as the coin's looking *circular* or *elliptical*, and the jumper's looking *red* or *mauve*. As we saw above in connection with the standard account of secondary qualities, if the order of individuative priority were the reverse, then in so far as the proposed explanations offer anything genuinely explanatory this would inevitably point towards imperceptible grounding properties of the physical objects in question. The definitive feature of *commonsense*-physical explanations, that these appeal precisely to the familiar *perceptible* natures of physical objects in explaining their perceptual appearances, would be lost entirely.

Most importantly at this stage of the argument, commonsense-physical explanations of the order and nature of perceptual experience by appeal to the perceptible properties of the physical objects that we perceive have two distinctive features that make them far superior for the purpose of elucidating empirical realism to anything available at the level of scientific-physical explanation. First, what I call their explanatory *robustness* avoids the purported *need* for any scientific-physical revision of commonsense-physical explanations in connection with securing *realism* from the perceptual perspective on the basis of (EP). Second, the particular realization of the priority relation between the natures of the physical objects that

---

[7] Note that it is entirely compatible with this fundamental role for commonsense-physical explanations that these may be elaborated and refined to some extent on the basis of research in the psychology of vision, say. This holds no threat along the lines of that elaborated above in connection with the scientific-physical implementation of (EP). For the commonsense nature of the world of mind-independent physical objects that we perceive is simply taken for granted in advancing and testing the relevant explanatory hypotheses.

constitute the explanantia of such explanations and the appearances that are their explananda ensure in contrast with the scientific implementation of (EP) considered in §7.1 that *empiricism* is preserved. I take these two points in turn.

First, in comparison with any candidate scientific-physical explanations of perceptual appearances, commonsense-physical explanations are *robust*. That is to say, they maximize modal correlation with the perceptual appearances that they explain in the following sense. All other things being equal, objects with quite different scientific-physical properties that share the same commonsense-physical properties will appear in the same way; and what unifies the various respects in which their scientific-physical properties might differ in such a way as to alter these appearances is precisely that these are precisely those scientific-physical variations that significantly alter the commonsense explanatory properties in question.

By way of illustration from a related area independent of perceptual appearances, compare Putnam's (1978) famous observation that the best explanation of the fact that a given one-inch square peg passes through a one-inch square hole and not through a one-inch round hole is provided by citing its size and shape. All other things being equal, it is precisely this property—one-inch squareness—whose presence facilitates, and absence obstructs, its passage. Any proposed move in the direction of scientific-physical explanation by appeal to lattices of elementary particles and the like reduces this robust modal generality. For one-inch square pegs of quite different materials equally pass through a one-inch square hole and not through a one-inch round hole, regardless of the fact that the scientific-physical properties involved in explanation of their motion and interaction are quite different; and whatever their scientific-physical differences may be—within reason[8]—appropriately sized pegs that are not square will not pass through a one-inch square hole, and square pegs greater than one inch in size will not do so either. Thus, all other things being equal, the scientific-physical differences between pegs that do, and pegs that do not, pass through a one-inch square hole but not through a one-inch round hole, are explanatorily unified as those in which the peg is one inch square versus those in which it is not. This is what I mean by the explanatory virtue of robustness.

---

[8] Excluding, for example, pegs made of material that dissolves the sides of the hole and so on.

In just this way, in connection with the explanations of our perceptual experience of physical objects that are central to (EP), commonsense-physical explanations are robust in comparison with scientific-physical explanations. The most robust explanation of why a coin looks circular to Janet viewing it head on and elliptical to John viewing it from a specific angle is given by citing its stable circular shape and their different points of view, not by appeal to the way in which its fundamental scientific-physical properties affect their respective perceptual systems. For, other things being equal, similarly circular objects of quite different materials look equally circular and elliptical respectively, to them and to other observers, from these same points of view, regardless of the fact that what is going on in scientific-physical terms may be quite different; and the scientific-physical changes to such objects that would alter these appearances are precisely those that significantly affect the commonsense-physical explanatory shape. This, rather than anything specific at the scientific-physical level, is what unifies the objects that look circular and elliptical from these respective points of view as against those that do not. Thus, commonsense-physical explanations of such appearances have the explanatory virtue of robustness.

Again, I contend, the most robust explanation of why a jumper looks red outdoors and mauve in the store is given by citing its red colour and the relevant variation between normal and artificially dingy lighting conditions, not by appeal to the way in which its fundamental scientific-physical properties affect viewers' perceptual systems in the two conditions. For, other things being equal, similarly red objects of quite different materials look equally red and mauve respectively in these same lighting conditions, regardless of the fact that what is going on in scientific-physical terms may be quite different; and the scientific-physical changes to such objects that would alter these appearances are precisely those that significantly affect the commonsense-physical explanatory colour. This, rather than anything specific at the scientific-physical level, is what unifies the objects that look red and mauve in these respective lighting conditions as against those that do not. Thus, commonsense-physical explanations of such appearances again have the explanatory virtue of robustness.[9]

---

[9] Notice that in extending the commonsense-physical explanatory picture in this way to secondary quality appearances, such as those of an object's colour, I am explicitly rejecting the standard model of the primary v. secondary quality distinction set out above. See, again, Campbell (1993) for discussion and defence of this idea. Note, though, that this extension is not essential to the main argument of the current work.

Having said all this, there is no obvious conflict, so far as I can see, between the robustness of commonsense-physical explanations of perceptual appearances of the kind involved in (EP), on the one hand, and the equal robustness of fundamental scientific-physical explanations of closely related *but distinct* phenomena, on the other. For example, it may well be that certain highly specific retinal or neural phenomena that are involved in and indeed enable our perception of some red objects in some circumstances are most robustly explained by appeal to the very specific scientific-physical properties of the light arriving at the eye reflected from the surfaces of such objects. That is to say, I see no good reason in what has been said here to deny that commonsense-physics and scientific-physics are two perfectly compatible but quite distinct explanatory projects running in parallel and in no real competition with each other.[10] In any case, the key point from this discussion is that commonsense-physical explanations have the virtue of robustness over candidate scientific-physical explanations in connection with the perceptual appearances that figure in (EP).

This provides an illustration of how and why any blanket explanatory *reductionism* is to be rejected, where this is the crude idea that the best explanation of anything going on in the physical world is ultimately to be given in terms of fundamental scientific-physics. It certainly blocks directly any suggestion, however prima facie plausible, that the commonsense physical explanations of perceptual appearances that we began with in setting out (EP) are *essentially* subject to substantive revision by scientific-physics, in a way that then threatens empiricism as I understand it here. There *is* no such general obligation; and thus, so far at least, such commonsense-physical explanations are in perfectly good explanatory standing absolutely as they are.

There may be another worry about their explanatory status, though. For the properties of physical objects that are involved sound very much like the perceptual appearances that they are invoked to explain. How can the fact that something *is* red, or round, say, be a genuine explanation of the fact that it looks red, or round? It is far from obvious what the general necessary condition on satisfactory explanation is supposed to be that is

---

[10] See McDowell (1985a), Campbell (1993), Burge (1994), Rudder Baker (1994), Hornsby (1986, 1994, 1995), and Brewer (1998) for examples of this idea in connection with the relation between commonsense and scientific explanations of human behaviour.

failed by such explanations. Furthermore, I explain below how the close individuative relation between the natures of objects and appearances involved here is crucial to the preservation of empiricism. So this actually constitutes a benefit to the position rather than any kind of cost in my view. Still, it is worth emphasizing two points about commonsense-physical explanations that should in any case silence this general line of objection.

First, an object may clearly be F (red, or round, for example) without looking F, because it is not seen at all; because although it is seen the subject is attending exclusively to certain other features, and so only has eyes for them, as it were; or because it is seen in misleading perceptual conditions and so looks G instead.[11] Second, an object may look F and yet not be F, again due to any number of variously misleading perceptual circumstances. So in so far as the general worry is that there is insufficient modal independence between explanans and explanandum for common-sense-physical explanations to get any genuine explanatory purchase, then this seems to me to be simply false.

I conclude therefore that the commonsense implementation of (EP) suffices as it stands to secure *realism* as defined at the outset from our own perspective as perceivers of the mind-independent physical world as articulated by (OV). Physical objects are the mind-independent direct objects of our perceptual experience; their nature is entirely independent of their appearance, and not in any way a matter of how they do or might appear to anyone; and their mind-independence is evident from our own perceptual perspective in virtue of our commonsense-physical explanation of the order and nature of our experience on the basis of the prior and independent perceptible nature of those very objects.

Furthermore, in avoiding the need for any substantive revision of commonsense-physical explanations by scientific-physics, this version of (EP) avoids the loss of empiricism that I argued above comes with any such move. I end this section by explaining in a little more detail how exactly this commonsense implementation also positively secures empiricism. This is the second point that I distinguished above: the particular realization of

---

[11] Note that the latter two circumstances yield cases in which *o* does not *thickly* look *F*, although it may thinly do so. In the nature of the case, though, it is bound to be thick looks that are subject to explanation of the kind in question. For acknowledgement of the explanandum essentially involves the conceptual registration of visually relevant similarities characteristic of thick looks. So the crucial point holds that these are all possibilities in which the explanans obtains although the explanandum does not.

the priority relation between the natures of the physical objects that constitute the explanantia of such explanations and the appearances that are their explananda *ensures* in contrast with the scientific implementation of (EP) considered earlier that empiricism is preserved.

The standard account of primary qualities outlined earlier lies at the heart of the commonsense implementation of (EP). According to the current approach, this model applies to all the properties of physical objects and their appearances that figure in commonsense explanations of our perceptual experience.[12] That is to say, the natures of the perceptual appearances to be explained are characterized precisely *as* the subjective presentation of certain specific and independently individuated properties of physical objects in the world around the perceiver. Even in illusory cases, in which something that is *F* looks *G*, say, the appearance in question transparently presents the object as being a specific way that such things may be, although this one is in fact not. In the normal veridical case, something's looking *F* makes absolutely evident which way that very thing out there is. The explanatory ground of that very appearance in its mind-independent object's *F*-ness itself is entirely transparent to the subject in that very experience. Hence physical objects really are the very things that we are presented with in experience—our perception of them provides us with at least a rough provisional conception of what such physical objects are. Thus, the commonsense implementation of (EP) also preserves empiricism as defined above.[13]

So the *mind-independent* physical word *is* the world of the *familiar* macroscopic objects that we all know and love; and the physical objects whose mind-independence shows up from our own perspective as perceivers on the basis of the commonsense implementation of (EP) are

---

[12] Note again that my inclusion of secondary quality explanations of perceptual experience such as (E4)–(E6) above, alongside primary quality explanations such as (E1)–(E3), marks a significant departure from orthodoxy by embracing the secondary qualities under the familiar primary quality model. See Campbell (1993) for defence of this 'Simple View'.

[13] My point is not that the application of the primary quality model here *rules out* the innatist claim that natural selection, for example, leaves us with an innate propensity to think of physical objects as persisting, unified, extended space occupants. It is rather that its vindication of the empiricist idea that perception itself is a genuine source of such a conception of what mind-independent physical objects are reduces very significantly the theoretical *need* for any appeal along these lines to innate endowment. See ch. 3 n. 7 above; and see Ayers (1993: i) for development of this kind of argument in Locke against the need for innate concepts and knowledge.

precisely those objects with which we are genuinely presented in perception. Commonsense (EP) secures and elucidates empirical realism.

7.3 Conclusions

In this final section I tie up some loose ends, clarify my overall conclusions, and offer a number of short additional considerations concerning related topics.

Recall my conclusion from ch. 2 above, that a crucial necessary condition for sustaining empirical realism is the identification of the explanatory grounds of the actual and counterfactual nature of human perceptual experiences of physical objects with the direct objects of those very experiences. We are now in a position to see that this is precisely what is achieved by the development of (OV) that I have offered. Accordingly, the direct objects of perception are the mind–independent physical objects themselves that are the commonsense explanatory grounds of the nature of the various experiences that we actually do or counterfactually might have of those very things from various points of view, in various sense modalities, and in various conditions of perception.

Certain of the perceptible properties of these mind–independent physical objects accordingly constitute a counterexample to a crucial premiss of Lewis's argument for (HT). Recall his assumption from the outset that none of the intrinsic properties that play an active role in the actual working of the physical world are named in O-language, 'except as occupants of roles' (Lewis, 2009: 206). Hence our only epistemic route onto the identities of such properties is supposed to be their identification *as* the properties that play such and such specific theoretical roles in relation to our observations. Given combinatorialism and quidditism, although there is a true proposition as to which intrinsic property actually plays each such specific theoretical role, there are distinct alternative possibilities that no evidence can ever rule out. So we cannot even in principle know which property actually plays which role. We are therefore irremediably ignorant of the nature of the intrinsic properties that play an active role in the working of the physical world. According to (OV) as developed here, though, in being presented with mind–independent physical objects themselves as the direct objects of our perception, we are perfectly adequately placed to name their active intrinsic properties in our O-language, without the need for any theoretical-descriptive inter-mediary. For the nature of these objects themselves determines in the way that I explained in ch. 5 above how the physical world looks to us in perception from various points of view and in various circumstances of perception. In normal circumstances, and viewed from the right angle, for example, a one-inch square peg before me looks square; and its being that very shape is precisely what provides the most basic explanation, both of why it looks the way it does, and also of why it behaves the way it does in relation to other physical objects of various kinds, e.g. why it passes through a one-inch square hole and not through a one-inch round hole. Thus, Lewis's argument for (HT) is blocked before it even gets started, at least in connection with the relatively intrinsic properties that play an active role in certain of the workings of the mind-independent physical world that we perceive.

Of course Lewis himself assumes that the intrinsic properties that play an active role in the actual working of the physical world are all properties involved in fundamental scientific-physical explanations; and I agree with him that none of these are named in O-language except as occupants of roles. Part of my point in the present chapter has been to resist the reductionist assumption, though, that *all* the workings of the physical world are to be explained in such scientific-physical terms. Thus, I claim that we are in a position to know some at least of the relatively intrinsic properties that play an active role in the working of the physical world directly on the basis of perception.

It is worth making a brief comment here also about a closely related argument that is owed to Rae Langton (1998). Drawing on ideas from Kant (1929), Langton also argues that we are irremediably ignorant of the intrinsic nature of mind-independent physical objects, along the follow-ing lines. Physical objects are the very objects that we perceive. Percep-tion is *receptive* in a way that involves a causal relation between such objects and our experiences of them that is incompatible with any kind of a priori relation between the physical object cause and the perceptual experience effect. Yet knowledge of the intrinsic nature of physical objects on the basis of perception depends upon such an a priori relation. For this is required to *derive* their intrinsic nature from their experiential effects upon us. No such knowledge is therefore possible. All that is available instead is relational knowledge of the mind-independent physical objects that we perceive as those objects that produce such and such experiences in us in such and such circumstances, whatever their intrinsic nature may be.

The simple reply on behalf of (OV) is that the receptivity involved in our perceptual relation with mind-independent physical objects is perfectly compatible with all that is required for our knowledge of the intrinsic nature of physical objects on the basis of our perception of them. In a way, this is the whole point of the position: to elucidate and vindicate empirical realism. (OV) is designed precisely to achieve this result. The receptivity of perception consists in the fact that mind-independent physical objects are the *explanatory grounds* of our various actual and counterfactual perceptual experiences of them from different spatiotemporal points of view, in different sense modalities and in different circumstances of perception. This is certainly compatible with the possibility that a mind-independent physical object, o, may be F and not look F—because it is not seen at all or not appropriately attended to, or because it is seen from a misleading point of view or in misleading circumstances.[14] It is also compatible with the possibility of illusion in which o looks F although it is not actually F. Still, the intrinsic nature of such mind-independent physical objects is the evident source of the way things look and otherwise perceptually appear to us in the way that I explained in §5.3 above; and our perceptual experience is most fundamentally a matter of our direct conscious acquaintance with those very things. Thus, in normal circumstances, in which o looks F because it is F, our perceptual experience makes absolutely evident which way that very thing out there is. The explanatory ground of the appearance in o's F-ness itself is entirely transparent to the subject in that very experience. So knowledge of the nature of mind-independent physical objects is perfectly possible in our perception of them. No dubious *derivation* from anything else is required.[15]

This leaves at least the following two options open in diagnosing the precise error in Langton's Kantian argument. I myself am inclined to accept that the explanatory grounding relation constitutive of the receptivity of perception is causal at least in the sense that explanations such as (E1)–(E6) above are genuinely *causal* explanations. It absolutely does not follow, though, that the phenomenon of a particular circular coin's

---

[14] See again n. 11 above for clarification here.

[15] Note again that this is knowledge in the first instance of specific determinations of the general nature of the objects in question as persisting, unified, extended space occupants.

looking circular to me when viewed from head on, say, is something from which I could only possibly arrive at a conception of the coin's intrinsic shape by some kind of *derivation* on the basis of an a priori relation between the two that is ruled out by the causal explanation in question. My perceptual condition is rather one of direct visual acquaintance with that very coin, which de facto has visually relevant similarities, from the point of view and in the circumstances in question, with various paradigm exemplars of circularity, along perhaps with my conceptual registration of those very similarities in categorizing it *as* circular. Even though it looks circular (causally-explanatorily) *because* it is circular, then, its circular look is perfectly transparent to its intrinsic circular shape: its look is my registration in perception of that very shape.

Alternatively, it may be said that the explanatory grounding relation in which mind-independent physical objects stand to our various actual and counterfactual perceptual experiences of them is non-causal. After all, each such experience is most fundamentally a matter of the subject standing in a relation of conscious acquaintance, from a given spatiotemporal point of view, in a particular sense modality, and in certain specific circumstances of perception, with particular such objects themselves. Still, the way that they actually do and counterfactually might look in perception is to be explained by their intrinsic nature along with the relevant point of view and circumstances in such a manner as to acknowledge the receptivity of perception in a way that is compatible with the (OV) account of how our perceptual experience presents us with the mind-independent physical objects around us in such a way in turn as to make our knowledge of their intrinsic nature perfectly intelligible.[16]

It is far from obvious to me at least that there is even a single unequivocal issue here—perhaps explanatory grounding according to (OV) is causal in some admissible senses and not in others. In any case, either way, Langton's Kantian argument fails.

I began my discussion in ch. 1 with the Inconsistent Triad of claims about the nature of perceptual experience and its objects:

(I) Physical objects are mind-independent.
(II) Physical objects are the direct objects of perception.
(III) The direct objects of perception are mind-dependent.

---

[16] See ch. 6 above for more on epistemological issues.

Reflection in ch. 2 on the options offered by Berkeley's (1975a, 1975b) rejection of (I) and also on three structurally similar more modern metaphysical options driven by Lewis's argument for (HT) suggested a necessary condition upon any fully adequate defence of empirical realism. This is the condition discussed above that the explanatory grounds of our perceptual experience should be the direct objects of those very experiences. Chapter 3 brought out the deep tension between any indirect realist rejection of (II) along the lines articulated by Locke (1975) and the pretheoretic intuition that we are *presented* with mind-independent physical objects in perception in such a way as to provide us with at least a rough and provisional conception of what such objects are.[17] Unsurprisingly, therefore, the key to resolving the inconsistency is to reject (III).

The orthodox rejection of (III) effectively denies that there are any direct objects of perception in the early modern sense that is my defining context for this key notion throughout. I argued in ch. 4 that the resultant position, (CV), faces its own difficulties in accounting for illusion and hallucination that in turn derive from its fundamental failure satisfactorily to reconfigure the phenomenon of the perceptual experiential presentation of particular mind-independent physical objects outside this early modern context.

Thus, I advanced my own (OV) in ch. 5. This insists upon a simple rejection of (III). Perceptual experience is most fundamentally a matter of a person standing in a relation of conscious acquaintance, from a given spatiotemporal point of view, in a particular sense modality, and in certain specific circumstances of perception, with various mind-independent physical objects in the world around him that therefore constitute the *direct objects* of his experience in the early modern sense. The direct objects of perception are mind-independent physical objects themselves and the truth of empirical realism consists in the natural pre-theoretically compelling conjunction of (I) and (II). (OV) offers what I claim is a fully

---

[17] I should perhaps say a little more cautiously that this is a pre-theoretic intuition at least amongst the very broadly empiricist-minded. I have tried to demonstrate over the course of the book that my own preferred (OV) account of the nature of perceptual experience succeeds in sustaining such empiricist presumptions. I claim that this neutralizes any argument to the effect that some form of innatist alternative is required to fill what would otherwise be a damaging explanatory gap. See again ch. 3 n. 8; and see Ayers (1993: i) for development of this kind of argument in Locke against the need for innate concepts and knowledge.

satisfactory explanation of both illusion and hallucination, along with a rich and appropriately nuanced account of the various ways that mind-independent physical objects look in perception. Furthermore, as I outlined in ch. 6, (OV) provides an excellent setting for a fully satisfying positive epistemological account of the role of perceptual experience as a source of empirical knowledge.

In the main body of the present chapter I completed the development of the (OV)'s account of empirical realism by explaining how the mind-independence of the physical objects that we perceive shows up from our own perspective as perceivers in a way that is also perfectly compatible with the empiricist idea that we are genuinely presented with these very things in perceptual experience. The key is our commitment to common-sense-physical explanations of the actual and counterfactual order and nature of our perceptual experience on the basis of the perceptible natures of the very mind-independent physical objects that we perceive.

In this way I conclude that (OV) provides the only fully adequate setting for a complete elucidation and defence of empirical realism.

I end with some thoughts concerning the interaction between offering and evaluating a philosophical theory of the nature of perceptual experience, on the one hand, and articulating the subject's own perspective upon the physical world in perception, on the other. The former was my core concern in chs. 1–6; the latter came to the fore in the current ch. 7.

(OV) is in the first instance a philosophical theory concerning the nature of our perceptual relation with the physical world. Its central proposal is that perceptual experience is most fundamentally a matter of a person standing in a relation of conscious acquaintance, from a given spatiotemporal point of view, in a particular sense modality, and in certain specific circumstances of perception, with various mind-independent physical objects in the world around him. The basic idea is that mind-independent physical objects themselves are in this way the direct objects of perception in what I have been calling the early modern sense. That is to say, any given perceptual experience is most fundamentally to be characterized, *as the specific conscious condition that it is*, as a case of conscious acquaintance, from a point of view, in a particular sense modality, and in certain circumstances, with particular mind-independent physical objects. The nature of the experience itself is to be elucidated by reference to those very things that are presented in perception. We can now see that this idea has a number of interrelated components.

First, the mind-independent physical direct objects of perception are the very objects that are *perceptually presented* and are the source of the way that things look to the subject in experience: o thinly looks F iff o is the direct object of a visual experience from a point of view and in circumstances relative to which o has visually relevant similarities with paradigm exemplars of F; o thickly looks F iff o thinly looks F and the subject recognizes it *as an* F, or registers its visually relevant similarities with paradigm exemplars of F in an active application of that very concept.

Second, this account of the way in which the direct objects of perception determine how things look in perceptual experience depends upon the individuative priority of their nature over the various looks and other appearances that show up in our experience of them that is constitutive according to (OV) of their mind-independence. For the way that things look just *is* a matter of the way *those things are* in visually relevant respects from the point of view and in the circumstances in question.

Furthermore, and third, as well as the various ways that things look in perception, as thus determined, this individuative priority *itself* shows up from the perceiver's own perspective in the way in which his experience is integrated with the commonsense-physical explanations that are correctly given of how mind-independent physical objects do and might look from various points of view and in various circumstances on the basis of their prior and independent, although perfectly perceptible, nature itself. Thus, the mind-independence of the physical direct objects of perception that is central to the philosophical theory (OV) is evident from the perceiver's perspective according to my development of (OV) in his understanding of the way in which such objects determine the way that things look as elucidated by (OV) itself.

I began this final phase of my discussion by raising the issue of the appropriate interaction between offering and evaluating a philosophical theory of the nature of perceptual experience, on the one hand, and articulating the subject's own perspective upon the world in perception, on the other. I do not remotely presume to have given any general recipe for such interaction. All I offer is some further clarification as to how the interaction is supposed to work in the context of (OV) as developed and defended here. Thus, philosophical theory and subjective characterization are not simply consistent, but mutually supporting in what I take to be an illuminating way. The philosophical theory (OV) offers and explains an accurate characterization of our own subjective perspective upon the mind-independent physical world in perception that in turn confirms and secures key features of the philosophical theory itself. In particular, I insist that the mind-independence of the physical objects that we perceive, and that are the direct objects of perception according to (OV), has to show up in the way that I explain from the subject's own perspective in perception itself if this is not to be a gratuitous addition to the theory that effectively imposes upon it without justification our pre-theoretic commitment to realism. A fully satisfying *defence* of realism depends upon its adequate grounding in the nature of perceptual experience from the perceiver's own perspective as an experiential perspective upon an evidently mind-independent physical world of the stones, tables, trees, and animals that we all know and love. I contend that (OV) succeeds in providing just such an integrated elucidation and defence of empirical realism from the theoretical and perceptual perspectives.

Bibliography

Alston, W. P. 1993. *The Reliability of Sense Perception*. Ithaca, NY: Cornell University Press.

Anscombe, G. E. M., 1962. 'The Intentionality of Sensation: A Grammatical Feature'. In R. Butler (ed.), *Analytic Philosophy*, 2nd ser. Oxford: Blackwell.

Armstrong, D. M. 1968. *A Materialist Theory of the Mind*. London: Routledge.

——1973. *Belief, Truth and Knowledge*. Cambridge: Cambridge University Press.

——1991. 'Intentionality, Perception and Causality: Reflections on John Searle's *Intentionality*'. In E. LePore and R. Van Gulick (eds.), *John Searle and His Critics*. Oxford: Blackwell.

Ayer, A. J. 1956. *The Problem of Knowledge*. London: Macmillan.

——1963. *The Foundations of Empirical Knowledge*. London: Macmillan.

Ayers, M. 1993. *Locke*, 2 vols. London: Routledge.

——1997. *Locke: Ideas and Things*. London: Phoenix.

Baldwin, T. 1992. 'A Projective Theory of Sensory Content'. In T. Crane (ed.), *The Contents of Experience*. Cambridge: Cambridge University Press.

Berkeley, G. 1975a. *Three Dialogues Between Hylas and Philonous*. In M. Ayers (ed.), *George Berkeley: Philosophical Works*. London: Everyman.

——1975b. *A Treatise Concerning the Principles of Human Knowledge*. In M. Ayers (ed.), *George Berkeley: Philosophical Works*. London: Everyman.

Block, N. 1996. 'Mental Pain and Mental Latex'. *Philosophical Issues*, 7, 19–49.

——1998. 'Is Experiencing Just Representing?'. *Philosophy and Phenomenological Research*, 58, 663–70.

——2003. 'Mental Paint'. In M. Hahn and B. Ramberg (eds.), *Reflections and Replies: Essays on the Philosophy of Tyler Burge*. Cambridge, Mass.: MIT.

Breitmayer, B. G., and Ogmen, H. 2006. *Visual Masking: time slices through conscious and unconscious vision*, 2nd edn. Oxford: Oxford University Press.

Brewer, B. 1995. 'Mental Causation: Compulsion by Reason'. *Proceedings of the Aristotelian Society*, suppl. vol., 69, 237–53.

——1998. 'Levels of Explanation and the Individuation of Events: A Difficulty for the Token Identity Theory'. *Acta Analytica*, 20, 7–24.

——1999. *Perception and Reason*. Oxford: Oxford University Press.

——2005. 'Perceptual Experience has Conceptual Content'. In E. Sosa and M. Steup (eds.), *Contemporary Debates in Epistemology*. Oxford: Blackwell.

Broad, C. D. 1925. *The Mind and its Place in Nature*. London: Routledge & Kegan Paul.

Burge, T. 1986. 'Cartesian Error and the Objectivity of Perception'. In P. Pettit and J. McDowell (eds.), *Subject, Thought and Context*. Oxford: Oxford University Press.

——1991. 'Vision and Intentional Content'. In E. LePore and R. Van Gulick (eds.), *John Searle and His Critics*. Oxford: Blackwell.

——1994. 'Mind–Body Causation and Explanatory Practice'. In J. Heil and A. Mele (eds.), *Mental Causation*. Oxford: Oxford University Press.

Byrne, A. 2001. 'Intentionalism Defended'. *Philosophical Review*, 110, 199–240.

——2005. 'Perception and Conceptual Content'. In E. Sosa and M. Steup (eds.), *Contemporary Debates in Epistemology*. Oxford: Blackwell.

——2009. 'Experience and Content'. *Philosophical Quarterly*, 59, 429–51.

Campbell, J. 1993. 'A Simple View of Colour'. In J. Haldane and C. Wright (eds.), *Reality, Representation, and Projection*. Oxford: Oxford University Press.

——2002a. 'Berkeley's Puzzle'. In T. Szabo Gendler and J. Hawthorne (eds.), *Conceivability and Possibility*. Oxford: Oxford University Press.

——2002b. *Reference and Consciousness*. Oxford: Oxford University Press.

——2009. 'Consciousness and Reference'. In B. McLaughlin and A. Beckermann (eds.), *Oxford Handbook of Philosophy of Mind*. Oxford: Oxford University Press.

Cassam, Q. 2007. *The Possibility of Knowledge*. Oxford: Oxford University Press.

——2009. 'Knowing and Seeing: Responding to Stroud's Dilemma'. *European Journal of Philosophy*, 17, 571–89.

Chalmers, D., Manley, D., and Wasserman, R. 2009. *Metametaphysics*. Oxford: Oxford University Press.

Charles, D. 2000. *Aristotle on Meaning and Essence*. Oxford: Oxford University Press.

Child, W. 1994. *Causality, Interpretation, and the Mind*. Oxford: Oxford University Press.

Conee, E., and Feldman, R. 1998. 'The Generality Problem for Reliabilism'. *Philosophical Studies*, 89, 1–29.

Crane, T. 1988. 'The Waterfall Illusion'. *Analysis*, 48, 142–7.

——1992. 'The Non-Conceptual Content of Experience'. In T. Crane (ed.), *The Contents of Experience*. Cambridge: Cambridge University Press.

Cussins, A. 1990. 'The Connectionist Construction of Concepts'. In M. Boden (ed.), *The Philosophy of Artificial Intelligence*. Oxford: Oxford University Press.

Davies, M. 1992. 'Perceptual Content and Local Supervenience'. *Proceedings of the Aristotelian Society*, 92, 21–45.

——1997. 'Externalism and Experience'. In N. Block, O. Flanagan, and G. Guzeldere (eds.), *The Nature of Consciousness*. Cambridge, Mass.: MIT.

Demopoulos, W., and Friedman, M. 1985. 'Russell's Analysis of Matter: Its Historical Context and Contemporary Interest'. *Philosophy of Science*, 52, 621–39.

Descartes, R. 1986. *Meditations on First Philosophy*, trans. J. Cottingham. Cambridge: Cambridge University Press.

Dretske, F. 1969. *Seeing and Knowing*. Chicago: University of Chicago Press.

——1981. *Knowledge and the Flow of Information*. Oxford: Blackwell.

Eilan, N., Hoerl, C., McCormack, T., and Roessler, J. 2005. *Joint Attention: Communication and Other Minds*. Oxford: Oxford University Press.

Evans, G. 1980. 'Things Without the Mind'. In Z. Van Straaten (ed.), *Philosophical Subjects*. Oxford: Oxford University Press.

——1982. *The Varieties of Reference*. Oxford: Oxford University Press.

Fine, K. 1994. 'Essence and Modality'. *Philosophical Perspectives*, 8, 1–16.

Fodor, J. 1987. *Psychosemantics: The Problem of Meaning in the Philosophy of Mind*. Cambridge, Mass.: MIT.

——1998. *Concepts: Where Cognitive Science Went Wrong*. Oxford: Oxford University Press.

Foley, R. 1985. 'What's Wrong with Reliabilism?'. *Monist*, 68, 188–202.

Forster, K. I., and Davis, C. 1984. 'Repetition Priming and Frequency Attenuation in Lexical Access'. *Journal of Experimental Psychology: Learning, Memory and Cognition*, 10, 680–98.

Foster, J. 1985. 'Berkeley on the Physical World'. In J. Foster and H. Robinson, (eds.), *Essays on Berkeley*. Oxford: Oxford University Press.

——2000. *The Nature of Perception*. Oxford: Oxford University Press.

Frege, G. 1993. 'On Sense and Reference'. In A. Moore (ed.), *Meaning and Reference*. Oxford: Oxford University Press.

Gendler, T. S., and Hawthorne, J. 2002. *Conceivability and Possibility*. Oxford: Oxford University Press.

Goldman, A. 1967. 'A Causal Theory of Knowing'. *Journal of Philosophy*, 64, 357–72.

——and Olsson, E. 2008. 'Reliabilism and the Value of Knowledge'. In D. Prichard, A. Millar, and A. Haddock (eds.), *Epistemic Value*. Oxford: Oxford University Press.

Grice, H. P. 1962. 'The Causal Theory of Perception'. *Proceedings of the Aristotelian Society*, suppl. vol., 35, 121–68.

——1989a. 'Logic and Conversation'. *Studies in the Way of Words*. Cambridge, Mass.: Harvard University Press.

——1989b. 'Further Notes on Logic and Conversation'. *Studies in the Way of Words*. Cambridge, Mass.: Harvard University Press.

Gupta, A. 2006a. *Empiricism and Experience*. Oxford: Oxford University Press.

——2006b. 'Experience and Knowledge'. In T. Szabo Gendler and J. Hawthorne (eds.), *Perceptual Experience*. Oxford: Oxford University Press.

——Forthcoming. *An Account of Conscious Experience*.

Harman, G. 1990. 'The Intrinsic Quality of Experience'. In J. Tomberlin (ed.), *Philosophical Perspectives*, 4. Atascadero: Ridgeview.

Hawthorne, J. 2001. 'Intrinsic Properties and Natural Relations'. *Philosophy and Phenomenological Research*, **63**, 399–403.

Heck, R. G. 2000. 'Non-Conceptual Content and the "Space of Reasons"'. *Philosophical Review*, **109**, 483–523.

Hofstadter, D. 1979. *Gödel, Escher, Bach: An Eternal Golden Braid*. New York: Basic Books.

Hornsby, J. 1985. 'Physicalism, Events and Part-Whole Relations'. In E. LePore and B. McLaughlin (eds.), *Actions and Events*. Oxford: Blackwell.

——1986. 'Physicalist Thinking and Conceptions of Behaviour'. In P. Pettit and J. McDowell (eds.), *Subject, Thought, and Context*. Oxford: Oxford University Press.

——1994. 'Agency and Causal Explanation'. In J. Heil and A. Mele (eds.), *Mental Causation*. Oxford: Oxford University Press.

Huemer, M. 2001. *Scepticism and the Veil of Perception*. Lanham, Md.: Rowman & Littlefield.

Hume, D. 1978. *A Treatise of Human Nature*, ed. L. A. Selby-Bigge, rev. P. H. Nidditch. Oxford: Oxford University Press.

Jackson, F. 1977. *Perception: A Representative Theory*. Cambridge: Cambridge University Press.

Jastrow, J. 1900. *Fact and Fable in Psychology*. New York: Houghton Mifflin.

Johnston, M. 2004. 'The Obscure Object of Hallucination'. *Philosophical Studies*, **120**, 113–83.

——2006. 'Better than Mere Knowledge? The Function of Sensory Awareness'. In T. Szabo Gendler and J. Hawthorne (eds.), *Perceptual Experience*. Oxford: Oxford University Press.

Kant, I. 1929. *Critique of Pure Reason*, trans. N. Kemp Smith. London: Macmillan.

Kaplan, D. 1989. 'Demonstratives: An Essay on the Semantics, Logic, Metaphysics, and Epistemology of Demonstratives and Other Indexicals'. In J. Almog, J. Perry, and H. Wettstein (eds.), *Themes From Kaplan*. Oxford: Oxford University Press.

Kelly, S. D. 2001. 'Demonstrative Concepts and Experience'. *Philosophical Review*, **110**, 397–420.

Kennedy, M. 2010. 'Explanations in Good and Bad Experiential Cases'. In F. Macpherson and D. Platchias (eds.), *Hallucination*. Cambridge, Mass.: MIT.

Kripke, S. 1980. *Naming and Necessity*. Oxford: Blackwell.

——1982. *Wittgenstein on Rules and Private Language*. Oxford: Blackwell.

Kvanvig, J. L. 2003. *The Value of Knowledge and the Pursuit of Understanding*. Cambridge: Cambridge University Press.

Langton, R. 1998. *Kantian Humility*. Oxford: Oxford University Press.

——and Lewis, D. 1998. 'Defining "Intrinsic"'. *Philosophy and Phenomenological Research*, **58**, 333–45.

Langton, R. 2001. 'Marshall and Parsons on "Intrinsic"'. *Philosophy and Phenomenological Research*, **63**, 353–5.

Lewis, D. 1980. 'Veridical Hallucination and Prosthetic Vision'. *Australasian Journal of Philosophy*, **58**, 239–49.

——1983a. 'Extrinsic Properties'. *Philosophical Studies*, **44**, 197–200.

——1983b. 'New Work for a Theory of Universals'. *Australasian Journal of Philosophy*, **61**, 343–77.

——1998. 'The Problem of Temporary Intrinsics: An Excerpt from *On the Plurality of Worlds*'. In P. Van Inwagen and D. W. Zimmerman (eds.), *Metaphysics: The Big Questions*. Oxford: Blackwell.

——2009. 'Ramseyan Humility'. In D. Braddon-Mitchell and R. Nola (eds.), *Conceptual Analysis and Philosophical Naturalism*. Cambridge, Mass.: MIT.

Locke, J. 1975. *An Essay Concerning Human Understanding*, ed. P. H. Nidditch. Oxford: Oxford University Press.

MacBride, F. 2005. 'The Particular-Universal Distinction: A Dogma of Metaphysics?' *Mind*, **114**, 565–614.

McCauley, R. N., and Henrich, J. 2006. 'Susceptibility to the Müller-Lyer Illusion, Theory-Neutral Observation, and the Diachronic Penetrability of the Visual Input System'. *Philosophical Psychology*, **19**, 79–101.

McDowell, J. 1982. 'Criteria, Defeasibility and Knowledge'. *Proceedings of the British Academy*, **68**, 455–79.

——1985a. 'Functionalism and Anomalous Monism'. In E. LePore and B. McLaughlin (eds.), *Actions and Events*. Oxford: Blackwell.

——1985b. 'Values and Secondary Qualities'. In T. Honderich (ed.), *Morality and Objectivity*. London: Routledge.

——1986. 'Singular Thought and the Extent of Inner Space'. In P. Pettit and J. McDowell (eds.), *Subject, Thought, and Context*. Oxford: Oxford University Press.

——1991. 'Intentionality De Re'. In E. LePore and R. Van Gulick (eds.), *John Searle and His Critics*. Oxford: Blackwell.

——1994. *Mind and World*. Cambridge, Mass.: Harvard University Press.

——2008a. 'Responses'. In J. Lindgaard (ed.), *McDowell: Experience, Norm and Nature*. Oxford: Blackwell.

——2008b. 'The Disjunctive Conception of Experience as Material for a Transcendental Argument'. In A. Haddock and F. Macpherson (eds.), *Disjunctivism: Perception, Action, Knowledge*. Oxford: Oxford University Press.

Magidor, O. 2009. 'The Last Dogma of Type Confusions'. *Proceedings of the Aristotelian Society*, **109**, 1–29.

Marshall, D., and Parsons, J. 2001. 'Langton and Lewis on "Intrinsic"'. *Philosophy and Phenomenological Research*, **63**, 347–51.

Martin, M. G. F. 2002. 'The Transparency of Experience'. *Mind and Language*, 17, 376–425.

——2004. 'The Limits of Self-Awareness'. *Philosophical Studies*, 120, 37–89.

——2006. 'On Being Alienated'. In T. Szabo Gendler and J. Hawthorne (eds.), *Perceptual Experience*. Oxford: Oxford University Press.

——2010. 'What's in a Look?'. In B. Nanay (ed.), *Perceiving the World*. Oxford: Oxford University Press.

——Forthcoming. *Uncovering Appearances*. Oxford: Oxford University Press.

Mather, G., Verstraten, F., and Anstis, S. (1998). *The Motion Aftereffect: A Modern Perspective*. Cambridge, Mass.: MIT.

Mill, J. S. 1867. *A System of Logic*. London: Longmans.

Moore, G. E. 1953. *Some Main Problems of Philosophy*. London: George, Allen & Unwin.

Newman, M. H. A. 1928. 'Mr. Russell's Causal Theory of Perception'. *Mind*, 37, 137–48.

Nozick, R. 1981. *Philosophical Explanations*. Oxford: Oxford University Press.

O'Brien, L. 2007. *Self-Knowing Agents*. Oxford: Oxford University Press.

——2009. 'Mental Actions and the No-Content Problem'. In L. O'Brien and M. Soteriou (eds.), *Mental Actions*. Oxford: Oxford University Press.

O'Shaughnessy, B. 2003. 'Sense Data'. In B. Smith (ed.), *John Searle*. Cambridge: Cambridge University Press.

Owens, D. 1992. *Causes and Coincidences*. Cambridge: Cambridge University Press.

Pautz, A. 2009. 'What are the Contents of Experiences?'. *Philosophical Quarterly*, 59, 483–507.

——2010. 'Why Explain Visual Experience in Terms of Content?'. In B. Nanay (ed.), *Perceiving the World: New Essays on Perception*. Oxford: Oxford University Press.

Peacocke, C. 1983. *Sense and Content*. Oxford: Oxford University Press.

——1989. 'Perceptual Content'. In J. Almog, J. Perry, and H. Wettstein (eds.), *Themes from Kaplan*. New York: Oxford University Press.

——1992. *A Study of Concepts*. Cambridge, Mass.: MIT.

——2001. 'Does Perception have a Nonconceptual Content?'. *Journal of Philosophy*, 98, 239–64.

——2006. 'Mental Action and Self-Awareness (I)'. In J. Cohen and B. McLaughlin (eds.), *Contemporary Debates in the Philosophy of Mind*. Oxford: Blackwell.

——2009. 'Mental Action and Self-Awareness (II): Epistemology'. In L. O'Brien and M. Soteriou (eds.), *Mental Actions*. Oxford: Oxford University Press.

Pettit, P., and McDowell, J. 1986. 'Introduction'. In P. Pettit and J. McDowell (eds.), *Subject, Thought and Context*. Oxford: Oxford University Press.

Phillips, I. 2005. 'Experience and Intentional Content', B.Phil thesis, University of Oxford <http://users.ox.ac.uk/~magd1129/BPhil%20Thesis.pdf>, accessed 16 November 2010.

Plantinga, A. 1993. *Warrant: The Current Debate*. Oxford: Oxford University Press.

Price, H. H. 1950. *Perception*, 2nd edn. London: Methuen.

Putnam, H. 1978. *Meaning and the Moral Sciences*. London: Routledge.

Ramsey, F. P. 1990a. 'Knowledge'. *Philosophical Papers*, ed. D. H. Mellor. Cambridge: Cambridge University Press.

——1990b. 'Universals'. *Philosophical Papers*, ed. D. H. Mellor. Cambridge: Cambridge University Press.

Robinson, H. 1994. *Perception*. London: Routledge.

Rodriguez-Pereyra, G. 2002. *Resemblance Nominalism: A Solution to the Problem of Universals*. Oxford: Oxford University Press.

——2008. 'Nominalism in Metaphysics'. In E. N. Zalta (ed.), *The Stanford Encyclopedia of Philosophy*. <http://plato.stanford.edu/archives/fall2008/entries/nominalism-metaphysics/>, accessed Nov. 2010.

Rudder Baker, L. 1994. 'Metaphysics and Mental Causation'. In J. Heil and A. Mele (eds.), *Mental Causation*. Oxford: Oxford University Press.

Russell, B. 1917. 'Knowledge by Acquaintance and Knowledge by Description'. *Mysticism and Logic*. London: George, Allen & Unwin.

——1927. *The Analysis of Matter*. London: Routledge.

——2001. *The Problems of Philosophy*. Oxford: Oxford University Press.

Salmon, N. 1986. *Frege's Puzzle*. Cambridge, Mass.: MIT.

Schellenberg, S. Forthcoming. 'Perceptual Content Defended'. *Nous*.

Searle, J. 1983. *Intentionality*. Cambridge: Cambridge University Press.

——1991. 'Response: Reference and Intentionality'. In E. LePore and R. Van Gulick (eds.), *John Searle and His Critics*. Oxford: Blackwell.

Sellars, W. 1997. *Empiricism and the Philosophy of Mind*. Cambridge, Mass.: Harvard University Press.

Sider, T. 1993. 'Intrinsic Properties'. *Philosophical Studies*, 83, 1–27.

——2001. 'Maximality and Intrinsic Properties'. *Philosophy and Phenomenological Research*, 63, 357–64.

Siegel, S. 2004. 'Indiscriminability and the Phenomenal'. *Philosophical Studies*, 120, 91–112.

——2006. 'Direct Realism and Perceptual Consciousness'. *Philosophy and Phenomenological Research*, 73, 378–410.

——2008. 'The Epistemic Conception of Hallucination'. In A. Haddock and F. Macpherson (eds.), *Disjunctivism: Perception, Action, and Knowledge*. Oxford: Oxford University Press.

——2010. 'Do Visual Experiences Have Contents?'. In B. Nanay (ed.), *Perceiving the World*. Oxford: Oxford University Press.

Smith, A. D. 2001. 'Perception and Belief'. *Philosophy and Phenomenological Research*, 62, 283–309.

——2002. *The Problem of Perception*. Cambridge, Mass.: Harvard University Press.

Snowdon, P. 1992. 'How to Interpret "Direct Perception"'. In T. Crane (ed.), *The Contents of Experience*. Cambridge: Cambridge University Press.

Sosa, E. 1991. 'Reliabilism and Intellectual Virtue'. *Knowledge in Perspective*. Cambridge: Cambridge University Press.

——2007. *A Virtue Epistemology*. Oxford: Oxford University Press.

Soteriou, M. 2000. 'The Particularity of Visual Perception'. *European Journal of Philosophy*, 8, 173–89.

——2009. 'Mental Agency, Conscious Thinking, and Phenomenal Character'. In L. O'Brien and M. Soteriou (eds.), *Mental Actions*. Oxford: Oxford University Press.

Spener, M. In preparation (*a*). 'Phenomenal Adequacy and Introspective Evidence'.

——. In preparation (*b*). 'The Two Claims of Transparency'.

Steward, H. 1997. *The Ontology of Mind: Events, Processes and States*. Oxford: Oxford University Press.

Stoneham, T. 2002. *Berkeley's World*. Oxford: Oxford University Press.

Strawson, P. F. 1959. *Individuals*. London: Methuen.

——1980. 'Reply to Evans'. In Z. Van Straaten (ed.), *Philosophical Subjects*. Oxford: Oxford University Press.

Stroud, B. 2000*a*. 'Scepticism and the Possibility of Knowledge'. *Understanding Human Knowledge*. Oxford: Oxford University Press.

——2000*b*. 'Understanding Human Knowledge in General'. *Understanding Human Knowledge*. Oxford: Oxford University Press.

——2001. 'Sense-Experience and the Grounding of Thought'. In N. Smith (ed.), *Reading McDowell on Mind and World*. London: Routledge.

——2009. 'Explaining Perceptual Knowledge: Reply to Quassim Cassam'. *European Journal of Philosophy*, 17, 590–6.

Travis, C. 2004. 'The Silence of the Senses'. *Mind*, 113, 59–94.

Tye, M. 1992. 'Visual Qualia and Visual Content'. In T. Crane (ed.), *The Contents of Experience*. Cambridge: Cambridge University Press.

——1995. *Ten Problems of Consciousness*. Cambridge, Mass.: MIT.

——2000. *Consciousness, Colour and Content*. Cambridge, Mass.: MIT.

——2002. 'Representationalism and the Transparency of Experience'. *Nous*, 36, 137–51.

Vogel, J. 2000. 'Reliabilism Leveled'. *Journal of Philosophy*, 97, 602–23.

Weatherson, B. 2001. 'Intrinsic Properties and Combinatorial Principles'. *Philosophy and Phenomenological Research*, **63**, 365–80.

Wiggins, D. 1995. 'Substance'. In A. C. Grayling (ed.), *Philosophy: A Guide Through the Subject*. Oxford: Oxford University Press.

——2001. *Sameness and Substance Renewed*. Cambridge: Cambridge University Press.

Williams, B. 1978. *Descartes: The Project of Pure Enquiry*. London: Penguin.

Williamson, T. 1996. 'Cognitive Homelessness'. *Journal of Philosophy*, **93**, 554–7.

——1998. 'The Broadness of the Mental: Some Logical Considerations'. *Philosophical Perspectives*, **12**, 389–410.

——2000. *Knowledge and its Limits*. Oxford: Oxford University Press.

——2006. 'Can Cognition be Factorized into Internal and External Components?'. In R. Stainton (ed.), *Contemporary Debates in Cognitive Science*. Oxford: Blackwell.

Wittgenstein, L. 1958. *Philosophical Investigations*. Oxford: Blackwell.

——1974. *Tractatus Logico-Philosophicus*. London: Routledge.

Wright, C. 1981. 'Rule-Following, Objectivity and the Theory of Meaning'. In S. Hotzman and C. Leich (eds.), *Wittgenstein: To Follow a Rule*. London: Routledge.

——2008. 'Comment on John McDowell's "The Disjunctive Conception of Experience as Material for a Transcendental Argument"'. In A. Haddock and F. Macpherson (eds.), *Disjunctivism: Perception, Action, Knowledge*. Oxford: Oxford University Press.

Yablo, S. 1999. 'Intrinsicness'. *Philosophical Topics*, **26**, 479–505.

Zöllner, F. 1860. 'Ueber eine neue Art von Pseudoskopie und ihre Beziehungen zu den von Plateau und Oppel beschrieben Bewegungs Phaenomenen'. *Annalen der Physik*, **186**, 500–25.

Index

Lightning Source UK Ltd.
Milton Keynes UK
UKOW030435210213

206583UK00002B/2/P